# The Ultimate Book of

# FOOTBALL

# GRUDGES

CHRISTIAN SMYTH

Chrysalis
Impact

First published in 2002 by Chrysalis Impact,
An imprint of Chrysalis Books plc
64, Brewery Road,
London N7 9NT
United Kingdom

A member of **Chrysalis** Books plc
© 2002 Chrysalis Books plc

ISBN 1 84411 001 X

Text © Christian Smyth 2002
Volume © Chrysalis Books plc 2002

Credits
Commissioning editors: Will Steeds, Chris Stone
Designed by Grade Design Consultants, London
Illustrations by Russ Carvell
Printed and bound by Creative Print and Design (Wales), Ebbw Vale

# The Ultimate Book of

# FOOTBALL GRUDGES

# Contents

| | |
|---|---|
| Introduction | 6 |
| Personal Grudges | 8 |
| Team Grudges | 78 |
| Fan Grudges | 152 |
| Player Grudges | 200 |
| World Cup Grudges | 246 |
| International Grudges | 294 |

# Introduction

From the moment you collect the ball at your feet, dip the shoulder one way and nudge the ball past your opponent you've established a grudge. This is a scenario that could be played out anywhere in the world – in the street, in the park or the school playground. The point of difference has been made. You are playing on separate teams. You are no longer football 'mates'.

When you take the first steps towards establishing your football credentials you are immediately setting yourself up for a fall. As a fan, it is relatively simple to see which side of the fence you're on.

But what of the players? Say you're Rio Ferdinand. Peckham's finest export since Rodney Trotter. If you ask one set of supporters across the Pennines what they think about their adopted son honing his talent in the Manchester United finishing school they'll say the lad should be motivated by more than just his earning potential. They'll tell you what really makes a Del Boy 'wide'. They'll mention words like 'Judas' and 'scab'. But Ferdinand is a modern pro, a commodity to be shifted about the market like any piece of stock. Giving value, making profit in return.

Still, say supporters… Let's blame it on Rio.

The footballers of today are harder to associate with a single club. But what of the people behind the scenes? Club chairman enter the football arena as saviours and can be hounded out as traitors. Managers can promise gold and end up running a fool's errand. Broadcasters offer the world and fall down to earth.

And there will always be a place for the football villain.

In the past a bad tackle, missed chance in front of goal or howling error of judgement inside the box was enough to place you at the top of a supporter's list of grudges. There

Football is a dirty business but grudges are the grits that stick in your teeth, slip inside your shoe and rub up the inside of your shorts.

were the personal attacks on the field, the moments of madness when two players decided to settle old scores with their fists instead of their feat. Achievement was measured by the allocation of red cards and disciplinary points. These were the players you watched out for on the field, the men who's boots you'd struggle to avoid.

In this, *The Ultimate Book of Football Grudges*, we examine what made Billy Bremner and Kevin Keegan throw punches, why Argentina's most bitter local derby, Boca Juniors vs River Plate, is madness personified, how managers and chairman have started best of friends and ended up in court, and why national jingoism can lead to more than just the traditional tabloid forage through an autumn vegetable patch.

From City's to United's, Cloughie at Leeds, Schumacher knocking out Battiston with a forearm smash to the day Christian Gross arrived at Spurs with a manifesto written on the back of a London Underground ticket. Every kind of football rivalry and festering resentment is here, for whoever you'd would most like to have a one to one with...

Football is a dirty business but grudges are the grits that stick in your teeth, slip inside your shoe and rub up the inside of your shorts. They are the meat and drink of our national sporting digest. Enjoy.

# Chapter 1

# Personal

# grudges

'One thing I will say is that Alex Ferguson doesn't disturb my nights at all.' **Arsene Wenger**

# Spurs and Boots

## Venables and Sugar

Together with Terry Venables, Alan Sugar took control of Tottenham Hotspur a month after they lifted the FA Cup for a then record eighth time in June 1991. Spurs were in deep financial trouble and were threatened with closure by the Midland Bank. At the time, there were rumours that Captain Bob Maxwell was interested in the club but the fans were happier with the Venables-Sugar partnership. Venables was the most exciting coach in the game and Sugar was one of the richest men in the country. The team had won the Cup and although Gazza was on his way to Italy, what could go wrong? Sugar became the largest shareholder of the PLC, with Venables risking everything he had to become the second largest shareholder.

Having won the battle for the club, Spurs put together a decent run in the Cup Winners Cup under the day-to-day direction of Peter Shreeves. It was always intended that Venables would be able to keep his eye on *other things*. Quite what they were was never made clear. Spurs reached the semi-final of the League Cup before a home defeat to Forest and a mid-season slump in league form meant the rest of the season was spent scratching around for points to avoid relegation.

### Not-so-steady Eddie

Having begun work as Chief Executive, Venables saw himself as the J.R. Ewing of the football world. To avoid getting bogged down in paperwork, Venables appointed a crony of his called Eddie Ashby. Ashby had a long list of failed businesses behind him (46 in all) but Venables brushed aside concerns about him. Sugar was getting increasingly anxious about Venables' own business dealings and the limelight the manager enjoyed. When

# The world fell apart when Sugar sacked Venables on the eve of the FA Cup final.

Sugar discovered Ashby's history, he gave Venables an ultimatum – sack Ashby or be sacked himself. Venables refused.

## Bitter-sweet

The world fell apart when Sugar sacked Venables (and Ashby) on the eve of the FA Cup final. Venables used the courts to get himself reinstated, but it was clear the partnership was over and a battle for the club had developed. A legal fight ensued over the summer, which despite large numbers of Spurs fans turning up at the High Court to show their support for Venables, Sugar won. In an unlikely turnaround in 2000, the by-now Sir Alan Sugar added his backing to the increasing support for Terry Venables to be the England coach again. The entrepreneur singled out Venables as the best man for the job. He said: *'As a football coach I am told that Terry Venables is one of the best around and from what I have seen I don't disagree.'*

# Out of Order

## Christian Gross and Spurs' players

Alan Sugar has always had something of a love-hate relationship with the fans. He saved Spurs from bankruptcy, bought them the occasional star player, yet at the same time he was never seen as having Spurs in his heart. But, while Sugar admits the fans were *'the most important element of the club'*, he believed that their extraordinary demands to *'not only win, but win in a certain style'* led to the demise of Gerry Francis. *'It was a case of Gerry changing his principles to try and pacify them,'* he once said.

So imagine the surprise of Spurs fans when Sugar announced the name of the manager he'd brought in to replace Francis. It was Christian Gross, a bald-headed man with a patchy record at Swiss side, Grasshoppers. A man who arrived at his first press conference clutching a return ticket from Heathrow to White Hart Lane and a barely tangible grasp of the English language. This was the man Alan Sugar had decided could bring out the best in Klinsmann, Ferdinand and the rest of the team. This was the man he could trust to spend his millions wisely. Unbelievable! Behind the PR sound bites and white teeth smiles of Tottenham luminaries it seemed that storm clouds were gathering right from the start. The signs were there that Sugar seemed less than confident that Gross could turn things around when he said, *'Could Franz Beckenbauer put it right? Is it a matter of tactics? Is it physical or is it mental?'*

### Revolting players

It wasn't long before the inevitable happened. Sugar sacked Christian Gross after less than a year in charge and just three games into the new season. Gross, who joined the club in November 1997, left immediately.

# Behind the PR sound bites and white teeth smiles of Tottenham luminaries it seemed that storm clouds were gathering.

Spurs acted in the face of growing fan dissatisfaction with Gross, who had only just managed to keep the club in the top flight the previous season. The Tottenham Action Group, representing the fans, demanded his removal following a 3-0 home defeat by Sheffield Wednesday.

Tottenham defender John Scales admitted a players' revolt had also hastened the end of the Swiss coach's reign at White Hart Lane. Gross had always struggled to impose his authority after disputes with former German star and Tottenham favourite, Jurgen Klinsmann, and England striker Les Ferdinand, who accused Gross of making him train while injured.

### Gross insult

When Gary Mabbutt, the Spurs captain, retired he recalled the Gross era. *'The trouble with Christian Gross is that no one had heard of him. The communication was not brilliant and I decided, as captain, to explain to him how things worked and what the players liked and were used to. I do not believe he listened to a word I said.'*

# Wright On

## Ian Wright and self-discipline

*'I would love to take someone like David Elleray out for a meal and get the players' point of view across in the hope that it would open his eyes. David and I don't see eye-to-eye at the best of times. He's a school master and treats players as if they're in the playground or have forgotten their homework.'*

Ian Wright was born in Woolwich Military Hospital, London, on 3 November 1963. He moved around south east London when he was young, which partly explains why he couldn't settle down and didn't start his professional career until he was 22.

In his autobiography Wright wrote, *'My mum seemed to just deal with it and take it all in her stride, except when I would come home with my best shoes smashed to bits through playing football. My trainers would last about two minutes before being busted up from kicking about in the street or school playground, so I would wear my best shoes, and my mum would just go mad that they were ruined.*

*'My first organized game was when I was eight and at Gordon Brock Junior. I can still remember it because the teacher, Mr King, had to lend me a pair of boots and they were too big.*

*'It was also the start of my disciplinary problems. Even at that age I would go mental if we were losing or things weren't going right for me.'*

## Pitching in

Fans would either love or hate the cheeky young Londoner. At the end of a Leicester-Arsenal game, Wright raced onto the pitch and started arguing with the ref and opposing players. He shouldn't have been on the pitch, and he certainly shouldn't have been shoving people around.

Wright raced onto the pitch and started arguing with the ref and opposing players. He shouldn't have been on the pitch, and he certainly shouldn't have been shoving people around.

Wright said to the media: *'The reaction [of the media] made me feel like I was back at school.'*

Arsene Wenger told the media that his centre forward's catalogue of disciplinary problems should not be taken into consideration by the FA. This included Wright's hefty tackle on Peter Schmeichel at Highbury that resulted in the FA Disciplinary Committee saying if he ever came before them again he'd face a lengthy ban. Wright later claimed that Schmeichel taunted him with racial abuse... but nothing was ever proved and the pair went on to trade smiles rather than blows as part of BBC TV's 2002 World Cup panel.

**Rage Counsellor**

Wright continued to play into his thirties and sought the help of a rage counsellor. After seeing Eileen Drewery, the faith-healer Glenn Hoddle had introduced to the game, Wright said: *'Why can't I deal with anger the way someone like Dennis Bergkamp can? Maybe it is in his nature, but anyone should be able to do it. This lady has shown I can channel my aggression in a good way and still smile.'*

# Aussie Rules

## Kevin Muscat and the football world

When controversial Rangers signing Kevin Muscat arrived in Glasgow he was seeking a clean slate and some silverware. Dubbed the 'Angry Australian' after picking up more bookings than Thomas Cook during six stormy years in England, Muscat was relishing what he called the biggest challenge of his career after a bitter split with Wolves.

Muscat had a reputation for take-no-prisoners tackling and for winding up opponents but he told reporters he wouldn't be changing his ways, despite picking up 57 yellow cards and four reds in 250-odd games at Crystal Palace and then Wolves.

He said: *'I just want to come to Ibrox with a clean slate and go from there. I've never been more hungry and I just want to get on with it. I don't want to talk about the past. I don't see myself as a hard man. I call it competitive and committed. I love to win but I certainly don't go out to deliberately hurt people – no professional worth his salt would do that. There are players with worse records than mine out there.'*

Two seasons before the move Muscat was heavily criticised by Birmingham City defender Martin Grainger, who accused him of stamping. Then there was a famous spat with former Arsenal star Ian Wright who described Muscat as *'a nobody and a lowlife'*. That was followed by a dubious tackle on France's Christophe Dugarry in a 'friendly' against Australia.

## Crying wolf

Muscat denied his Wolves exit was hastened by boss Dave Jones' dissatisfaction with his discipline. But his departure from Wolves was acrimonious.

Muscat was accused by Molineux Chief Executive Jez Moxey of being lured by Rangers

# He had a reputation for take-no-prisoners tackling and for winding up opponents but he told reporters he wouldn't be changing his ways.

into signing an illegal pre-contract something Muscat denied saying: *'I'd grown stale and a bit complacent after five good years with Wolves and I needed a fresh challenge. That's why I left*

*'Rangers first came in for me at the beginning of last season but nothing happened. I'm glad it has now. It was an offer too good to refuse. The club didn't need any selling and I'm grateful for the opportunity.*

*'The only thing I've won in football was promotion from the English First Division with Crystal Palace and I'm hungry for a lot more than that before I retire.'*

He added: *'I'm looking forward to playing alongside my old mate Craig Moore. We've appeared numerous times together for our country and have been friends for 10 years. There's a special chemistry between us.'*

## Spot of bother

Muscat, 28, arrived as a free agent and signed a four-year deal, which, it was hoped, would help ease the disappointment of Australia missing out on the World Cup after losing a play-off with Uruguay.

During Australia's World Cup campaign, they thrashed Tonga 22-0. Muscat scored four goals, but branded the match a 'joke' and argued that his country shouldn't be forced to play such weak sides. He said, *'I don't want to sound arrogant but we should not be playing these sides – it's unfair on us as much as them. Hopefully, results like we had last season will prove to FIFA they should change our qualification structure.'*

# Clock Watchers

## David Elleray and Fergie

It's easy to see how the two most famous clock watchers in football could come to dislike each other. When one of them is standing on the sideline, stopwatch in hand noting every mistake made on the pitch and making sure that each and every minute of playable time is used up in the noble pursuit of total football while the other struts around the park with the pompous distain for these foul-mouthed hooligans who wouldn't last five minutes if they behaved like that in his playground… well you can see why Alex Ferguson and David Elleray don't exactly get along.

But the Manchester United manager Sir Alex Ferguson was not expecting to come under fire from none other than David Elleray's grandmother.

Dorothy Elleray took him to task in a programme broadcast on Channel 4 called *Man In Black – Confessions of a Whistle Blower*, which focused on the her grandson.

One game in question was United's draw with Liverpool in May 1999. The official, a master at Harrow school, received death threats in the wake of his controversial decision to send off Denis Irwin. Ferguson said after the game: *'The referee handed it to them. We would have won but for him.'*

Chairman Martin Edwards made an equally scathing condemnation of Elleray's display but it was Ferguson's behaviour which really infuriated Mrs Elleray.

*'I can't stand Alex Ferguson. I saw a newspaper which showed my grandson and Alex Ferguson saying: "If I lose the league, it will be because of David Elleray". I thought: "How could anybody be that cruel?"'*

The official, a master at Harrow school, received death threats in the wake of his controversial decision to send off Denis Irwin.

## Devil of a job

Elleray had alarms fitted in his home after the storm which followed the game. In the TV documentary he explained: *'I can now press a button and have every police car within 10 miles of my house here instantly.'* Elleray talked candidly about the abuse he had received in his career, recalling the occasion when a Chelsea fan described him as *'Satan'*, and added: *'On one occasion, when I was a linesman at Millwall, one guy walked up and down behind me saying: "Look at me, linesman. I want you to recognize my face because the next time you see it will be the moment you're going to die."'*

# Chin Wags

## Jimmy Hill and the Scots

*'An England win would mean having to listen to Jimmy Hill and company for another 24 years – the best way of guaranteeing Scotland gets independence.'*
Chris McLean, SNP spokesman, before England's appearance in the 1990 World Cup.

Scotland are being beaten by Belgium on a night when dreams of qualifying for the World Cup 2002 fizzle out and the thoughts of 12,000 or so despairing Scotsmen turn to topics of convivial scorn-making, subject matter that will raise the spirits and ensure that in the matter of singing, the Scots will never be outclassed. Easily outdoing the home support and even managing to compete with a public address system that could be heard in neighbouring Holland, young and old folk, men and women, Scots from every part of the country and members of the Caledonian diaspora all gather to get behind their favourites – and make one hell of a racket.

Among the traditional Scottish paraphernalia of kilts, orange wigs and other Bay City Roller regalia one group has gone to the trouble of translating a favourite anthem about the sexual practices of Jimmy Hill on a banner in French. It's amazing what a few ill-chosen words about the Scottish football team can do for a television pundit.

## Fans forum

In 1997, Jimmy Hill and the Scots came together over a series of 'articles' on a website called the *Tartan Army*. These stories posted information about the Scottish football team, and was sponsored by the brewers, Scottish Courage. The site contained a forum where fans could directly post their views about 'the beautiful game'. Unfortunately one of the main topics of discussion was our old friend Jimmy Hill and various obscene, rude

WE HATE JIMMY HILL
HE'S A POOF! HE'S A POOF!

It's amazing what a few ill-chosen words about the Scottish football team can do for a television pundit.

and defamatory comments and jokes were posted about him in a variety of languages. The most interesting point about the case, perhaps, is that Mr Hill chose not to sue the website owners themselves, nor their ISP, but instead Scottish Courage, the sponsor. This set a worrying precedent for other sponsors and advertisers on the web, who have next to no control over what is displayed in proximity to their name. The case might have serious implications for commercial exploitation of the web.

### Book cheque

However, a book called *Over the Top with the Tartan Army* (Luath Press) has a chapter entitled 'Jimmy Hill is William Wallace isnae'. Given the content of the chapter, and the potential relationship between Jimmy Hill and the Scotland fans, Jimmy Hill received an advance copy of the book to read. The author received a letter from Mr Hill. It thanked him for the book and said he had enjoyed reading it, but 'not to call round for tea when his wife was in!' He also enclosed a cheque for £100 made out to the Children's Hospice Association Scotland, which is receiving all the royalties from the sales of the book.

# The Origins of the Game

- The Chinese started it. Five thousand years before gangs of youths in south east Asia saw the attraction of painting their faces, banging a drum and cheering on a bunch of lads with too much energy to burn, Chinese ball jugglers were thinking of what to do with the balls they juggled, using their feet. The answer came when some bright spark saw the possibility of a team game and organized the early risers who had come to their usual entertainment spots into sets of teams.

- The net was in the centre of the field and the players had to keep the ball off the ground using only their feet. At this stage the idea of installing a goalkeeper hadn't been conceived so the most gymnastic juggler was commissioned to stand in goal and do his best to leap in the air and block an attempt on goal. This happy pastime continued over the ensuing dynasties and it is possible to see evidence of their prowess in Ming Dynasty engravings.

- Ancient Egyptians broke up the tedium of pyramid building with a relaxing kick about under those giant slabs of stone the workers were entrusted with shifting. Like modern-day football, teams often picked themselves, as most stone shifters were too weak or incapable of playing. Greek archaeologists have unearthed marble carvings from five centuries before the birth of Christ showing a man participating in an early form of keepy-uppy.

- Britain first got a taste of the game it was later to claim as its own when the Roman soldiers booted a ball about under the cross where Christ was crucified. Julius Caesar was said to be a gifted winger but Emperor Nero had trouble scoring unless intimidation was applied to the goalkeeper.

# At this stage the idea of installing a goalkeeper hadn't been conceived, so the most gymnastic juggler was commissioned to stand in goal.

- Even more amazing is how the game spread in the following centuries. Football never codified itself, rustled up any rules or embraced a following of kindred spirits. But, like all developing ideas, it splintered and mutated into a variety of forms without ever having a clue what it was doing or where it was going. What is undeniable is that everyone was playing it. If a gathering of people came across a ball, be it in a field, park or street, they would drop their belongings and conjure up a game. In those days, the games were almost always violent, physical contests that appalled the authorities. Puritans damned it as a *'bloody and murdering pastime rather than a fellowly sport'*, and proclaimed that *football playing and other devilish pastimes on the Sabbath'* were the beginning of the end of civilized society.

- In 1314, Edward II decreed that the game people had picked up in the Roman days was a disgraceful act liable to cause a riot. *'There is a great noise in the city caused by hustling over large balls, from which many evils arise, which God forbids,'* he boomed. Football had just witnessed its first incarnation of a modern-day FIFA ruling.

- By the turn of the 19th Century, England was on the threshold of the modern game. But, like so much in life, while the working classes did all the hard work and dragged the game up from the humble beginnings of British civilization, it was the upper classes who fine-tuned the process and gave us something closer to what is known today as the beautiful game.

# Blue Chips

## Thatcher's plans for membership cards and fans

The events of the spring of 1985 proved to be a watershed for government responses to football violence. At Bradford, 56 people were killed in a horrific fire in the ground. Serious disorder occurred at Birmingham City, Chelsea and Luton Town and, most significantly, Liverpool fans were seriously implicated in the deaths of 39 Italian fans in the Heysel stadium in Brussels. Prime minister Maggie Thatcher was asked by Alan Hardaker, then secretary of the Football League, when she was going to *get her hooligans out of our football grounds?'* Her response came in the form of the 1989 Football Spectators Act.

The report into the Bradford fire raised awareness of the vital issue of spectator safety at football grounds and, in particular, re-introduced the issue of identity cards for football fans.

### Shocking idea

The main proposals of the Act concerned the introduction of compulsory identity cards for spectators at every league, cup and international match played in England and Wales. Throughout the sixties and seventies, various clubs had experimented with their own membership schemes in an attempt to prevent *'unwanted'* fans from entering their grounds.

The government and, in particular, Thatcher, strenuously backed the use of identity cards and reciprocal membership schemes as the most effective way of enforcing exclusion orders at football grounds.

Indeed, even before the Football Spectators Act (1989) had been finalized, the Football League had agreed with the government to introduce membership schemes at all clubs,

# The obvious response of ticket touts in London, Manchester and Liverpool was to buy Luton Town season tickets.

though the clubs themselves were very slow to implement the recommendations. Only 13 (out of a total of 92) actually satisfied government requirements to meet the initial deadline of August 1987. A survey of police views on membership schemes revealed that 40 percent did not favour them.

### Identity crisis

The proposal to introduce ID cards and membership schemes united football more than any national competition could possibly achieve. When the Luton Town chairman suggested identity cards the scheme never got further than Luton, although most clubs introduced some form of membership. Luton also attempted to ban away fans by offering no tickets to the visiting club. The obvious response of ticket touts in London, Manchester and Liverpool was to buy Luton Town season tickets. The opposition of supporters to the last significant crusade against hooliganism was vocal and apparent. In the event, legislation imposing compulsory identity cards was shelved in the aftermath of the Hillsborough disaster, when Justice Taylor condemned such schemes.

# Hunting Wolves

## Mark McGhee and Leicester

No one should be surprised that Mark McGhee did to Leicester what he did to Reading. In one season between 1994 and 1995, he promised his future to one club before promptly upping sticks and moving on to another before the supporters could muster a petition, strike up a *'don't go'* banner or at least have the opportunity to slag the bloke off at his last home game. Football fans are the last people to know what's going on at their club and in a period of a few years Mark McGhee had managed to hop, skip and jump from Reading to Leicester to Wolves and still not get out of the First Division!

When McGhee left Reading for Filbert Street the locals instigated a ban on Leicester-based Walker's crisps. Other fans handled it differently. One spent many a happy hour ringing up the Leicester City switchboard, shouting, ***'Leave our manager alone you bastards'*** before slamming the phone down. When he quit Leicester for Wolves the response was equally vehement. Leicester supporters were reminded that if you live by the sword and poach other people's managers you've got to be prepared to die by the same sword. Fans had trusted the Scotsman and were dismayed that he could do the same thing twice.

### Tricky business

Much later in his career, and following a successful season at Millwall, the respected journalist Ian Ridley wrote in *The Guardian*, ***'Manager Mark McGhee is rehabilitating himself with a promising, promoted young side after an ill-advised walkabout from Reading to Leicester City to Wolves, where he lost the plot.'*** The fact that McGhee was a given another chance by a club chairman says a lot about the blind optimism that

# When McGhee left Reading for Filbert Street the locals instigated a ban on Leicester-based Walker's crisps.

drives football. Not since the days when Clive Allen moved from QPR to Arsenal and then to Crystal Palace without actually kicking a ball had we seen such nimble footwork and dexterity among lawyers eager to clock up billing time for all those tricky contract negotiations.

### Taylor-made

In preparing for the 2002-03 season back in the First Division, Leicester fans have bemoaned the departure of one former manager from a club they will be facing (Peter Taylor, having quit Brighton) but can look forward to a reunion with Mark McGhee when Leicester take on Millwall. Should be quite an afternoon.

One fan said: *'The icing on the cake would be if Peter Taylor took on another managerial role at a First Division club. We had the hatred, the bile and the banners ready and it was a really cruel blow when we learned he had done the dirty on Brighton. Mind you, Brighton have had a lucky escape and we still have the prospect of venting our spleen when Mark McGhee returns!'*

# ManStock 2000

### Stockport County chairman and big name change

The 2000-01 season was not shaping up to be a good one. First there were accusations of foul play directed against County by way of BBC Five Live during the pre-season build-up. Apparently someone named Mr Bean, from the FA's compliance department, was investigating allegations of fraud against members of the club. Then lifelong servant and terrace hero James Gannon was allowed to leave by means of that most awful of agreements, *'mutual consent'*, so mutual in fact that he took the club to court for unfair dismissal (a case he lost).

The chairman, Brendan Elwood was becoming one of the least popular people in Stockport, heaving his weight about and coming up with increasingly absurd ways of expanding the club. He dug a deeper hole for himself by publicly opposing his manager on several player sales: Ian Moore, Tony Dinning, Kevin Cooper and Carlo Nash, all of whom the gaffer, Andy Kilner, was keen to hold on to.

### Taking stock

In December, the chairman voiced the first of several *'thinking forums'* on the situation regarding the club's ground at Edgeley Park. He admitted that the ground needed a fair bit of work to bring it up to the standard of a top notch stadium and the first sound bites about a possible move to Maine Road were heard. Now every team and its dog has suggested taking up residence at the theatre of shattered dreams since the incumbent's move to the Commonwealth Stadium in Moss Side but few would have come up with the brilliant idea to completely change the name of the team too. County, a team with an average home gate of under 7,000, could do worse than to scatter this hardcore support inside the relative vacuum at Maine Road with its 30,000 seats, but not much worse. However just as those in the region were beginning to feel that this was some kind of

# The chairman, Brendan Elwood was becoming one of the least popular people in Stockport, heaving his weight about and coming up with increasingly absurd ways of expanding the club.

wind-up, Elwood announced that should such a move take place then Stockport County could do worse than to change their name to ManStock County. No, really.

### Plumbing the depths

Two seasons on, Stockport County found themselves at the bottom of Division One. No wins in nine games, no goals in six, a 6-0 defeat one Saturday, no manager, a striker about to depart and a chairman still trying to live down the fact that he was actually serious about renaming the team. Chairman Elwood finally decided he needed to fill the manager's position created by Andy Kilner's departure, having decided that caretaker boss Craig Madden wasn't his thing. Given that Madden had begged the chairman for a quick appointment (*'I'm finding it difficult to be positive,'* said Madden), you could appreciate the despair being felt round the club.

Unbeknown to supporters, great things were being discussed behind the scenes. Chairman Elwood announced that two-thirds of a thrilling new team was in place, this on the same day he asked fans to continue visiting the club's official site as the hits provide the club with much needed sponsorship money. The suggestion that a high profile appointment was imminent could be taken with the proverbial pinch of salt. But fans had not reckoned with Elwood's incredible nerve and tactical acumen. This, remember, was a man who had decided that Gary Megson wasn't up to the job of leading Stockport County through the divisions and into the Premiership.

# Safe Crackers

## George Reynolds and his players

When an angry and frankly disbelieving Darlington chairman George Reynolds condemned his players as greedy, he lifted the lid on the club's wage bill but more importantly, heralded the move by club chairmen to take stock of their financial position and begin the painful process of fiscal realignment.

The former safe-cracker, a colourful character at the best of times, released details to *The Northern Echo* newspaper about how much Quakers players had earned in one season. This step was taken after his players had walked out of a meeting where he suggested making cuts in their bonuses.

The figures for the 1999-2000 season revealed that Darlington's highest wage earner, understood to be Neil Heaney, was paid a basic salary of £72,708. But with match appearances and other bonuses, this figure was boosted to £139,251.

Even a player on an apparently *'low'* salary of £23,399, and who played only 19 games a season, was paid £35,575 when bonuses were taken into consideration. The average salary for a third division player is £37,000.

The total wage bill for the season came to just under £1.4m and Reynolds maintained that this was too high.

His plan was to scrap the existing bonus structure and replace it with a system which was more in line with the bank balance of a Third Division club. Unsurprisingly, he met with stiff resistance from the players.

### Greed

In a statement to the press at the time he said: *'All we are asking is to take away the greed so the fans can benefit for a change... We have never baulked at paying*

# The fans were appalled at what they had just heard and George and Susan Reynolds were booed out of the room.

*wages for high-calibre players, but the bonuses which are being paid are too high.'*
Reynolds wanted to pay his players a £500 win bonus if the club finished in the top three that season and £250 if they were placed fourth to seventh. They would also get £150 for a draw.

## Clearout

In February 2002, at the Ambassador Suite, Darlington, around 30 fans, staff and squad attended a fans' forum after a dismal display against Torquay. The forum was hosted by George Reynolds and his wife Susan. It was supposed to be a clear-the-air session where George would explain where the club was going in the future and explain where they thought things were going wrong.

That is, until Susan got up to deliver a lengthy list of rights and wrongs to do with life at Darlington FC and accused the players of throwing games. At this point the players had heard enough – they got up and walked out. Susan was jeered by the fans, who were appalled at what they had just heard. George and Susan Reynolds were eventually booed out of the room.

By contrast, the players were applauded as they left. Darlington manager, Tommy Taylor, said: *'Ladies and gentleman. I am a bit upset at what the Chairman's wife has had to say. I don't think any professional player goes out on the field to have a bad game. All the players were asked to turn up tonight. I, and they, didn't know what was going to be said. My players will not give in on any game whatsoever, they will give you 100 percent.'*

# Tiger Roars

## Hull City and Terry Dolan

They say that Terry Dolan didn't believe in magic. He believed in six at the back, the long ball game, and force-feeding penalty area opportunists like Andy Mason and Paul Hunter with full fat burgers in the expectation this would turn the lads into beefy centre forwards. The modern game was all well and good but you could stick your broccoli-based diet regimes. What the lads up front needed was slap-up tucker. You can see where the fans and the management begged to differ. If results had gone their way perhaps the Hull City faithful would have had more patience. The 1995-96 season proved to be arguably the worst in the club's history as the side were relegated to the basement for the second time. Only 36 goals were scored in accumulating a meagre 31 points.

A ten-match unbeaten league run at the beginning of the 1996-97 season saw City remain in the top six until the beginning of October, but the side drifted towards a mid-table placing by Christmas. The Tigers progressed through to the second round of the FA Cup following an extraordinary first round replay against Whitby Town. Duane Darby scored a double hat-trick in City's 8-4 victory.

Their league form was less impressive, and City finished in sixteenth place – their lowest-ever position. The campaign was played out amid growing unrest from the dwindling support. The vitriol generated against Dolan and Chairman Martin Fish led Christopher Needler – son of the former chairman – to sell his major shareholding.

### Net results

Not many keepers can have scored two goals from open play in a single season, and Alan Fettis' goalscoring feats were one of the few genuinely memorable moments in the dismal reign of Terry Dolan. The first goal was scored after coming on as a substitute, pouncing on a left-wing cross from Craig Lawford, not known for his ability to cross a ball, and blasting it over the line. As the ball hit the back of the net, his goalkeeping instincts came to the fore so instead of turning to celebrate he headed straight into the goal to pick the ball out. Fettis' second outing as a forward, on the last day of the 1994-95 season, was a full game. Inevitably, some of the mystique was lost, as it became obvious that the lad would never be a striker. He was ungainly, slow to read the play, and could barely control the ball but he still managed to score an injury time winner. Needless to say, delirium followed.

The modern game was all well and good but you could stick your broccoli-based diet regimes. What the lads up front needed was slap-up tucker.

# Green Envy

## Plymouth and Joe Kinnear

In writing about Plymouth Argyle's 2001-02 season, a fan said he could fill four pages with *'Are you watching Joe Kinnear?'* repeated over and over again. Why? Apparently Joe, or *'Big Fat Joe'* as the scribe decided to call him, had spent the best part of a season telling Plymouth and their followers that Luton Town would be the winners of the division and that some of the Plymouth players weren't fit to wear the shirt.

Plymouth went on an excellent unbeaten run of 19 matches at the start of the season that ended at Scunthorpe with a 2-1 defeat just before Christmas. This included a sterling performance against the league leaders, Luton, on 29 September. The Home Park crowd saw Plymouth's Mickey Evans get sent off but Luton still lost to 10 men. Kinnear called their stalwart defender Russell Coughlan *'an average Joe Soap centre-half'*. Plymouth manager Paul Sturrock insisted the 2-1 win testified to the quality in Division Three. He said: *'I think the standard in the Third Division is improving more and more. This match bears that out. I thought it was a great game and on clear-cut chances we matched them.'*

In the return leg fixture at Kenilworth Road the police had riot shields and helicopters. Kinnear had the hump. Evidently some people in Luton thought that this was a needle match. Unfortunately for the couple of thousand fans who had made the long trip from south Devon, no one seemed to have told the Plymouth players.

Faced with a hard-running Luton prepared to push any number of players forward, the team that had threatened to run away with the title could do little more than hold on.

### Rack and ruin

*'We massacred them 2-0'*, Kinnear said after the game. *'We had more will to win. We had the better opportunities. We slaughtered them down the sides.*

# In the return leg fixture at Kenilworth Road the police had riot shields and helicopters. Kinnear had the hump.

*'There were no shocks as to how they came and played,'* he said, suggesting that they set out merely to spoil. *'I started with four up front and put them on the rack. I just don't think they could cope. I thought they might shit themselves.'*

Paul Sturrock had claimed that Luton had stopped his team playing their passing game. When Kinnear was told this, he summoned up more scorn than anyone who has managed Wimbledon legitimately can. *'What passing?'* he said. *'I only saw them lump the ball back to front. I didn't see them doing anything else.'*

## They're not worthy

At the end of the season, and with both teams promoted, Kinnear protested that it wasn't fair that the team that scored most goals didn't win the championship. He also mocked the fact that it took the club four years to win promotion while he had achieved it in just one. But the 18,517 crammed into a new Home Park to salute Sturrock's side weren't too concerned.

Kinnear called Plymouth one-season wonders and vowed to beat them home and away in the forthcoming season. *'I don't know about worthy champions the fact is they are. It's taken them five years to get out of this division whereas it's taken us one season. But I'm delighted they've come up because that's another six points for us next season.'*

# United Stand

## Sir Alex Ferguson and Alan Green

When Ferguson became manager of Manchester United in 1986, these two actually became friends – Green would invite him to the BBC to watch live feeds of Scottish teams in action. It didn't last though. According to Green, one of Radio Five Live's leading commentators, Fergie's success at United made him much less tolerant of his opinionated ways. Green claimed in his recent book that Ferguson had become a *'foul-mouthed, arrogant, aggressive control freak'* and a *'shocking bully'*. Fergie hasn't spoken to Green since 1993 and has not gone public on the feud – although he did once remind the abrasive Irishman: *'You don't pick my f*****g teams.'*

### Angelic upstart

Fans might recall Ole Gunnar Solskjaer's challenge at Liverpool – a 50-50 challenge but one which saw Sami Hypia come off worse as his toes connected with Ole's studs. A completely malice-free clash, just one of those innocuous incidents that occurs every weekend at all levels, up and down the country. Commentating on the incident, Green saw the tackle completely differently from most people. He was apoplectic, launching into a verbal on-air assault on the poor, cherubic Solskjaer. According to Green, the Norwegian's challenge was reckless, over-the-top and deserving of at least a red card. Hypia's career, he suggested, was seriously threatened as a consequence of such a horrific lunge. In reality the only thing over-the-top was the Ulsterman's hysterical reaction.

Green claimed in his recent book that Ferguson had become a *'foul-mouthed, arrogant, aggressive control freak'* and a *'shocking bully'*.

### Voicing his opinion

The consensus among the Old Trafford faithful is that Green is a dyed-in-the-wool Koppite. For those unfamiliar with his commentaries, the man from Five Live prides himself on telling it like it is. If a particular game is dismal he will say so. His style is abrasive, enthusiastic and judgmental, and this has made his voice the most distinctive, some would say irritating, on Radio Five. There is a feeling though, that his enthusiasm for Liverpool borders on the partisan, something he's at pains to deny. And that's even though Fergie accused him of being a Liverpool fan – which caused the row in the first place.

# Football Violence

**Football has been associated with violence since its early beginnings in 13th-century England. The original *'folk'* form of the game, most often played on Shrove Tuesdays and other holy days, involved quasi-structured battles between the youth of neighbouring villages and towns. The presence of a ball, in the form of a leather-bound inflated pig's bladder, was almost incidental to this semi-legitimized opportunity for settling old scores, land disputes and engaging in manly, tribal aggression. Parallels existed in other European countries, such as the German *knappen* and the Florentine *calcio* in costume, but the modern game is firmly rooted in these ancient English traditions.**

Such rituals, often accompanied by extended bouts of drinking, quite regularly resulted in serious injuries and even death to the participants. To a large extent, however, they constituted what Elias and Dunning have described as *'an equilibrating type of leisure activity deeply woven into the warp and woof of society'*. While the sporadic outbursts of violence at contemporary football matches in Europe give rise to almost hysterical sanction, our ancestors found nothing particularly strange or sinister in these far bloodier origins of the modern game.

- Tolerance of football violence was not, however, universal, but only because ordinary citizens were being driven away from the market towns on match days, which was bad for business. When the game spread to London, it was banned in 1314, though no-one really paid any attention to the new law:

# At the turn of the 17th century, Scottish football was characterized by *'its association with border raids and forays with violence generally.'*

*'And whereas there is a great uproar in the City through certain tumults arising from the striking of great footballs in the field of the public – from which many evils perchance may arise... we do command and do forbid... upon pain of imprisonment, that such games shall not be practised henceforth within this City.'*

- The Scots were no less passionate about this warring game. At the turn of the 17th century, Scottish football was characterized by *'its association with border raids and forays with violence generally.'*

- By the 18th century, the game took on a more overt political significance. A match in Kettering, for example, consisting of 500 men on each side, was a scarcely disguised food riot in which the object was to loot a local grain store.

- The game became a modern sport largely as a result of urbanization, which corralled the game into small arenas. The disorder of the game itself then provoked outrage. In 1829, a Frenchman who saw a football match asked: *'If this is what they call football, what do they call fighting?'* Similar questions are still being asked.

# Getting Shirty

## Keegan and Bremner

*'Bremner seemed intent on making Kevin Keegan's afternoon an absolute misery. He kicked him just about everywhere – up the arse, in the balls – until it became only a matter of time before a confrontation exploded. There is only so much any man can take. Eventually, inevitably, Keegan snapped – and they were both sent off, Keegan whipping off his shirt and flinging it to the ground as he went. It was a stupid gesture, but you could understand the man's anger and frustration. It was the action of a player who felt he had been wronged, not only by an opponent but by a referee who had failed to stamp out intimidation before it reached the stage of retaliation. Keegan will have regretted his touchline tantrum immediately. A Liverpool shirt was not something to be thrown away.'* So said Brian Clough in a diary note on the FA Charity Shield match between Leeds and Liverpool in 1974.

*'Keegan was a victim, not a culprit, that day at Wembley. The double dismissal was all down to Bremner. Keegan was an innocent party who had been pushed beyond the limit by an opponent who appeared determined to eliminate him from the match, one way or another. I told Bremner afterwards that he had been responsible for the confrontation. He should have been made to pay compensation for the lengthy period Keegan was suspended.'*

## Billy's boots

The two players had clashed in the Leeds penalty area and then they started brawling. They had to be pulled apart and separated by players and officials and were then sent from the field. *The Times* was typical in its condemnation: *'That, in itself, would have*

# 'Never before had Wembley witnessed such a disgrace as two British players were dismissed from the stadium for the first time.'

*been enough to disgust.'* But both men compounded the felony as they began the long walk to the dressing rooms by shamelessly stripping off the shirts they should have been proud to wear. Bremner, indeed, petulantly threw his to the ground, where it lay crumpled like a shot seagull until cleared away by a linesman. It was a disgusting scene, the volcanic climax of three earlier affrays that had seen Smith and Giles booked.

Sadly, Keegan could have been the man of the match. Leeds patently realized this by half-time and seemed intent on eliminating him by fair means or foul. They chose the unfair method, finally goading the little Liverpool man into hot headed retaliation with all the dire consequences for those who consider themselves above the law.

*'Never before had Wembley witnessed such a disgrace as two British players were dismissed from the stadium for the first time. It made child's play of the Rattin affair in the World Cup of 1966.'*

## Sign of the Times

One spectator tried to have the red-headed Bremner and feather cut-flaunting Keegan charged with a breach of the peace, but a magistrate refused to issue a summons. Instead the FA banned Keegan and Bremner for 11 matches in all and fined them £500 apiece, but no further action was taken.

It was the first Charity Shield match ever to be shown on television, and the chairman of the disciplinary committee, Vernon Stokes, admitted that the punishment might not have been quite so severe if the match had not been played at Wembley and shown to millions.

# Sausage Factory

## Burnley and Frank Teasdale

May 1987 and the famous Clarets are 92nd in the football league. Frank Teasdale called for the *'Dunkirk/Rochdale spirit'* from the fans as the Clarets prepared for their home game against Southend United, an away game at Crewe on the Bank Holiday Monday and the final match of the season when Orient were to visit Turf Moor. He said, *'It is now up to the lads on the field to save us, but I appeal to everyone who has the club at heart to back them in these next three games with the sort of Dunkirk spirit which so many of our fans produced when the team responded by winning 2-0 at Rochdale on Easter Monday.'*

The final match of the season against Orient was crucial. Journalists travelled up from London to see if the Clarets would go down while the bank looked on, wondering if their investment was about to go bust. If the club had lost and dropped out of the old fourth division and into the Vauxhall Conference, even the TSB would have been taking an extraordinary gamble to tell Burnley to carry on.

The relief that greeted the Clarets' eventual survival produced never-to-be-forgotten scenes. People laughed and cried together with unashamed relief; one Burnley director flung his arms round an embarrassed policeman in the directors' box at the end and hugged him.

The following season the re-appointed Frank Casper came dangerously close to fulfilling his promise to get Burnley out of Division Four at the first attempt as the Clarets were beaten home and away to a backdrop of '*Vauxhall Conference here we come, doo dah, doo dah, Vauxhall Conference here we come doo dah doo dah dey*', echoing from the terraces. Several hundred disgruntled Lancastrians massed each match in the car park to noisily demand the resignation of both Casper and chairman Frank Teasdale.

Several hundred disgruntled
Lancastrians massed each
match in the car park
to noisily demand
the resignation
of both Casper
and chairman
Frank Teasdale.

### Scratch the surface

Teasdale had come to Burnley as one of those *'saviour chairman'* in 1985 but the fans
saw how he'd taken a club that was £800,000 in debt and left it 14 years later five times
worse off and with a team driving downhill to the basement division. With 5,000
signatures on a *'Teasdale Out!'* petition Teasdale announced he was off. Then came the
promise of money from incoming board member and scratch card winner, Barry Kilby. He
promised a share issue to the tune of £4m. Auditors discovered that the outgoing
chairman had run up huge debts and was losing £80,000 a month. Twelve months later,
Teasdale was re-elected onto the board.

# Eagles Landing

## Mark Goldberg and Crystal Palace

Football fans generally greet news of a tycoon wanting to take over their club ecstatically, in the expectation that money will be spent on players who will bring success on the pitch. These must have been the thoughts of most Crystal Palace fans when news emerged that Mark Goldberg, who had made £23m from his recruitment business, had bought Ron Noades' majority shareholding in the club in August 1998. But 18 months later Palace were on the verge of liquidation and the once proclaimed saviour of the club was bankrupt. How did it all go so terribly wrong?

Goldberg made three critical mistakes: he over-stretched himself financially, he failed to heed the caution of his business advisers, and he let down his best friend who had assisted him in achieving his goal. During 1998, Peter Browne had agreed to assist Goldberg in his twin objectives of purchasing a majority stake in Palace and completing the purchase of potentially lucrative development land in Kent. Browne invested £1.5m of his personal fortune in these projects and, later, when Goldberg started to run into financial difficulties, agreed to pledge shares worth £800,000 as security. He also transferred the development land into Goldberg's name to allow it to be charged to Palace's bankers. When Goldberg desperately needed money to fund the administration of the club (to avoid its otherwise inevitable liquidation), he sold the development land without informing Browne. In an interview, Goldberg explained his strategy. *'Everybody told me not to buy Crystal Palace. But I bought it for £22.6m and still had over a million shares in MSB, which at that time was valued at £10 a share, so I believed there to be a £10m cushion. If the share price had held at £10 instead of falling to £2 within six months of my buying the club, and if Terry Venables had been able to achieve Premiership status, then I would have doubled my money in two years.'*

### Lack of funds

Terry Venables had been lured back to Crystal Palace in June 1998 by Goldberg. He was reputedly on a huge wage at Selhurst Park, and after a less than successful seven-month spell he left the south London club. It had become clear that Goldberg didn't have the funds to run a football club, and Venables' contract had allegedly crippled the club.

### Heavy going

*'I must have been the biggest mug in the world to pay £23m for this club. I thought too big, too quickly,'* said Mark Goldberg after Crystal Palace went into administration in 1999. Three fans were allowed into a room to present a petition to Goldberg demanding he leave the club. One of the fans was dressed up as the Grim Reaper wielding a plastic scythe and Goldberg, protected by several hired heavies including the menacing features of celebrity gangster Dave Courtney was told by the police not to go outside *'for his own safety'*.

# But 18 months later Palace were on the verge of liquidation and the once proclaimed saviour of the club was bankrupt. How did it all go so wrong?

# Homeless

## David Lloyd and Hull City

Hull City were facing a winding-up order over an unpaid tax bill that was believed to be as high as £500,000. The club had debts of up to £1.5 million and a high court hearing was looming. Could things get any worse?

Well yes, they could. It was reminiscent of the dramas that had unfolded at Brighton. The fans could see that if you replaced the Brighton chairman, Bill Archer with their own nemesis, the former tennis player, David Lloyd, you had a potential disaster in the making. While the FA took belated action in Brighton's case, they were standing by and doing nothing as Hull sank into the mire.

Matters came to a head when Lloyd, no longer club chairman but still the owner of the club's crumbling Boothferry Park stadium, decided he would lock the ground's gates. It emerged that the incumbent chairman Nick Buchanan had failed to come up with £103,000 in rent, and Lloyd – whose tenure at Hull wasn't exactly popular – had changed the locks on the basis that if you don't pay, you can't play. Hull City were suddenly homeless and theoretically could have been thrown out of the league on that basis.

The matter was resolved temporarily, but then in February 2001, Lloyd did it again. City still owed him thousands of pounds in rent. Notices were pinned up saying no one would be allowed into the ground until all debts were settled. *'We have to stand firm,'* Lloyd told Radio 5 Live. He defended his action, adding: *'It's the only way to bring the parties to the table. I want the parties involved – the owners, the council and the Inland Revenue – to come to a deal.'*

### Dark Ages

During the course of several agitated interviews, the former tennis player and entrepreneur ranted, *'They're living in the dark ages. They want to have showers that don't work, courts that have holes in the nets. That's what they want and that's what*

# At a televised game the fans bought hundreds of tennis balls and wrote '*No*' on them, which were thrown onto the pitch.

*they'll get! I'm out! I'm going! I'm not going to stay!'* Lloyd wanted to take the club to a ground share with Hull's rugby league side. The fans told him were he could stick it. At a televised game the fans bought hundreds of tennis balls and wrote '*NO*' on them, which were thrown onto the pitch just prior to kick-off.

## Fill

A two-week adjournment was granted in order for Administrators to find a potential buyer for the club and their first job was to negotiate with Lloyd in order to re-open Boothferry Park. (Lloyd had sent in the bailiffs just days before the Tigers were due to entertain Leyton Orient and the club was placed into Administration just hours before the High Court hearing.) They succeeded in that task and the highest gate of the season pitched up for an emotional afternoon on 10 February, when the Tigers played their part by gaining a 1-0 victory. They went on to run up a sequence of consecutive league wins – five – that had not been achieved for nearly 16 years. They say that Lloyd wanted to wind up the Tigers up for no other reason than he had '*Had my fill of people around here'* but fortunately that didn't happen once the club got another backer and new chairman, Adam Pearson. The former commercial director of Leeds was brought in and promised a revolution, a club run by fans for fans. Stuff that was familiar to any club with a bleeding heart.

# Rovers Returns

## Roy Hodgson, Brian Kidd and Blackburn's relegation

In the 1998-99 season, the venerable Blackburn fanzine *4,000 Holes* proclaimed: *'If you want a guarantee, buy a toaster.'* While the fanzine credited Clint Eastwood with the etymology the point was simple: Jack Walker had somehow allowed two managers to spend £24m in the same season and still their team had been relegated. This compared with an expenditure of £2m the year they'd won the Premiership title. Chief culprit (among many) was seen as Roy Hodgson, who spent £7.5m on Kevin Davies, £5m on Christian Dailly and £4.5m on Nathan Blake. Hodgson had come from Inter Milan where he hadn't done badly but hadn't won anything either. Before that he'd been the national Swiss coach and taken the country all the way to the World Cup finals in the USA in 1994. Although he never set the world on fire with his personality he was seen as a sound manager and a decent man. Just hours before he parted with Blackburn he wrote: *'The way a manager behaves in times of crisis can often be the decisive factor in determining whether a team pulls through or slides deeper into trouble.'*

### Rock bottom

Another fan, writing an opinion piece on the web said: *'"Roy of the Rovers" they called him, and although he showed a lot of great managerial qualities, guiding Rovers to a healthy top seven position in his first full season, he then lost it, Blackburn were dreadful during the second season with Roy in charge, they couldn't lift themselves from off the bottom. Roy Hodgson was sensationally, unsurprisingly in my view, sacked by the Blackburn board of officials.'*

The hunt for a new manager, to try to keep them in the top flight that season, was very much on. Roy's biggest mistake? Signing Kevin Davies for £7.5m: *'Oh dear, oh dear.'*

Chief culprit (among many) was seen as Roy Hodgson, who spent £7.5m on Kevin Davies, £5m on Christian Dailly and £4.5m on Nathan Blake.

### Just Kidding

Many names cropped up, because the challenge of guiding the club to safety was an attractive prospect. Blackburn aren't poor either, so there would be money to spend.

'Tony Parkes had another short stint as caretaker manager, before the appointment of Brian Kidd, Alex Ferguson's number two. Damn. I never had a good feeling about Brian Kidd – he'd had a managerial position before at a lower club, but no experience of top flight management.

'To be honest, Brian Kidd was a complete disaster for the club. He should have stayed with Man Utd. Anyway, he brought along Man Utd old boy Brian McClair, and for some reason thought he'd make a good assistant manager. Shame. Brian Kidd bought some of the worst players Blackburn have ever had, he couldn't save us from relegation, had a horrible first half of season in Division One and got sacked, to the relief of everyone supporting Blue 'n' White.'

# Ruud Awakenings

## Ruud Gullit and Chelsea

Ruud Gullit came to Chelsea as one of the greatest players on the planet, in the twilight of a career that had seen him win trophies for AC Milan and Holland. He was a big man with a massive ego and a large mane of dreadlocked hair to keep it all warm. Glenn Hoddle had persuaded him to come down to Stamford Bridge and together they masterminded the redevelopment of the west London club into one of the Premiership's finest.

When Hoddle left the club to become England manager, the call to make Gullit coach was long and loud and Chairman Bates deemed it appropriate to give the Dutchman his chance. All went well at first. The club won the FA Cup in 1997 and Gullit did well in the league. But inevitably, problems arose and these centred mainly around money. Colin Hutchinson, Chelsea's Managing Director said that when Gullit was renegotiating his salary he asked for £2m. Hutchinson said: *'Gross?'* and he said, *'No, netto, I always talk netto.'* Ruud was furious with the way the club had handled the leak of his salary negotiations. There was talk that the players had turned their backs on him and that he no longer had the support of the chairman.

*'Next week they will say, "the players didn't like him,"'* said Gullit. *'Then it will be I was "a greedy bastard". But I know for sure that it was not the players and it was not the money. What I want to know, from the club, is the real reason for this.'*

### Ruud joke

Gullit's personality undoubtedly rubbed some people up the wrong way. When he left the club they were in the quarter-finals of the European Cup Winners Cup and second in the Premiership but still he didn't have the backing of his staff. Graham Rix, who became Chelsea coach after Gullit's sacking said: *'There were many times when I just had to tell him: "You can't do this." At Leeds we were 2-0 down after just nine minutes and he told three of the subs to warm up. I asked him what he was doing, and he said he was making two substitutions. I couldn't believe it. I said: "You can't do that. You can't take two players off after only nine minutes. You will destroy them." But he wouldn't listen. He was adamant. So I said: "You'll make yourself look stupid. You are admitting that you've made an almighty mistake." He listened to that, and decided he wasn't going to make the changes after all.'*

## Playboy

Ken Bates faced questions on the manager's sacking and was quite specific. He said, *'Colin Hutchinson wasn't prepared to pay a huge percentage of his player budget for a part-time playboy manager who carried out his lucrative commercial contracts at the expense of his training – that much was obvious to everybody in his last game at Arsenal.'*

*'I couldn't believe it. I said: "You can't do that. You can't take two players off after only nine minutes. You will destroy them."'*

# Titled Gents

## Wenger and Fergie

Arsene Wenger's subtle barbs have always rubbed the Manchester United manager up the wrong way. During the 2001-02 season, Wenger scoffed at suggestions by Sir Alex Ferguson that Manchester United were the best team in England.

The Arsenal manager expressed his disappointment at United's exit from the Champions League but added: *'Only at the end of the season can you say who's been the top team. I believe this season it will be Arsenal.*
*'Perhaps Alex was referring only to the Champions League because United reached the semi-final and I'd have loved them to have won last night. It's important for English football and everyone benefits.'*
Ferguson also claimed the quality of United's football is unrivalled but Wenger laughed: *'Everyone thinks he has the prettiest wife at home.'*
Back in 1997, Wenger was annoyed to see Ferguson come on to the pitch after Ian Wright's foul on Peter Schmeichel. *'I was surprised to see Ferguson on the pitch because you can only play 11.'*

## Sweet dreams
Commenting on the rivalry between the two, Wenger said: *'People probably think I'm jealous of Alex but nothing could be further from the truth. All I will say is he had the luck to work with people at a time when they were more patient than now. He had time to build up a team and everyone can see the results. I could never expect to be given the same sort of time.'* As the title race continued to heat up, both managers were apt to chuck a Barbie at each other. During 2001-02 season, on the eve of Thierry Henry's appearance before the Football Association, Fergie said: *'Arsenal have been very clever in delaying the hearings for Henry and Vieira. It's amazing that*

Back in 1997, Wenger was annoyed to see Ferguson come on to the pitch after Ian Wright's foul on Peter Schmeichel. *'I was surprised to see Ferguson on the pitch because you can only play 11.'*

they haven't been brought to book yet. Had it been a Manchester United player who did what Henry did, it would have been Sing Sing [an American prison] for him.
*'They've delayed it very cleverly but it may come back to haunt them – sometimes you can be too clever. If we win the title, we will have done it the right way.'*
Wenger, responding, said: *'One thing that I will say is that he [Ferguson] doesn't disturb my nights at all.'*

### Wining, not whining

By the end of 2001-02, it seemed that the Arsenal manager had ended his feud with Ferguson. The pair have never enjoyed the friendliest of relationships, with their mindgames proving to be one of the annual sideshows of the Premiership.

Ferguson had said that Wenger was the only manager who never came for a post-match drink, although the Frenchman relented following Arsenal's 1-0 championship-winning match at Old Trafford. Wenger said, *'Alex was very fair. I had a drink with him. It was red wine and very nice. He recognized that we deserved our success. He was the first to say it and he supplied the wine. You cannot take anything away from him and what he has done.'*

# Rules of the Game

**While the emerging game had begun to adopt some form of structure, most people still had their own rules. When meeting for a casual lunchtime kickabout, half the time would be taken up arguing about which rules to adopt, still a common occurrence on playgrounds up and down the country, not to mention one or two Premiership stadiums.**

It wasn't until after a meeting in October 1863 when the various groups came together and formed the Football Association that a proper set of rules could be formed (see Mob Rules). Rugby footballers split from the association, not over the principle of handling the ball, but because the rugby enthusiasts wanted to continue using the tactic of cutting down opponents by kicking their shins. It is interesting to note that though the present-day understanding of the off-side rule was instituted in the 20th century, various different versions of the concept were adopted throughout the 19th century as well.

- The rules set down at the 1863 meeting made no restrictions on the size of the pitch, height of the goal or duration of the match. The pressing concern was to limit the level of violence on the field. In those days no one played in any particular position, it was more like a scene from a school playing field. Those of you who can remember those kick-and-rush, pre-pubescent school days will recall that this tactical formation is known as 'the swarm'.

# The rules set down at the 1863 meeting made no restrictions on the size of the pitch, height of the goal or duration of the match.

- It was left to the Scots to come up with a practical understanding of defence, midfield and attack, and by 1869, sides were restricted to just 11 players. In 1871, the goalkeeper was formally introduced as the player who could use any part of his body to protect the goal. Five years later, the referee – whose introduction had been utterly derided – was given the authority to send players off and halt the game.

- In 1892, the 'throw-in' replaced the 'kick-in'. That same year, a goal net was introduced to save time retrieving the ball and to substantiate claims that the ball had travelled through the posts.

- But the global game needed a governing body. In 1904, the Federation Internationale de Football Association (FIFA) was born. To this day, most of the rules introduced by the English still remain at the heart of the FIFA rulebook.

# I'm on Strike!

## Forest and Pierre Van Hooijdonk

In May 1998, Dave Bassett won the Division One title with Nottingham Forest and took them back up to the Premiership. After a miserable season in the top flight, he was forced to sell star players Kevin Campbell and Colin Cooper. Bassett decided to keep his other main asset, the Dutch forward Pierre Van Hooijdonk. Bassett, though, was less than effusive in his praise for the player. *'He's not your archetypal English centre forward,'* said the archetypal English football manager. *'They chase lost causes and put other people under pressure. Pierre just won't do it and it's no good asking him. You have to come to terms with that and make the rest of the team do some of the things he won't.'*

### The striking striker

It seems the famous Bassett psychology was lost on the Dutchman because he took one look at the team sheet and decided the lack of new players insulted the honour of an agreement he'd had with the club that were going to strengthen the squad. Unbelievably, Van Hooijdonk went on strike. Commenting on the strike Ron Atkinson, who was to take over at the club within four months said: *'I'd like to see him banned for the rest of his career. The only possible way he could come back to Forest was if he cleaned all the lads' cars for a week, did their gardens, made their tea, scored a hat-trick every Saturday and gave a year's wages to charity.'*

Forest tried to freeze Van Hooijdonk out of the game. The player who had scored sackfuls of goals in the Nationwide League thought he was better than the club he was playing for. Bassett said, *'Until the big plonker goes, then we're short of cash. If someone gave me an olive branch I'd stick it up his arse.'*

'Until the big plonker goes, then we're short of cash. If someone gave me an olive branch I'd stick it up his arse.'

### Bunged up

Van Hooijdonk saw it differently. He was defending principles. *'I am careful not to judge other people because there are too many who judge me without knowing the facts, some of whom are hardly in a position to judge anyone, like George Graham, who took bungs. And these people are criticizing me! I'm saying, hold on a minute, I haven't been suspended for a year and they are allowed to slaughter me on national TV. What is it that you say in England, the pot calling the kettle black?'* Van Hooijdonk was sold to Vitesse Arnhem in June 1999.

# Yes Dear, No Dear

## Gregory and Unsworth

It was the news no-one could believe when they heard it on the radio, least of all his manager. *'His missus clearly wears the trousers in his house. The poor lad was under the impression that Birmingham was on the outskirts of Bolton. It took him an hour and a half to get home and he found his dinner in the bin,'* said John Gregory, the Aston Villa manager, when asked why he thought David Unsworth asked to leave the club within a week of signing from West Ham in 1998.

*'When I was a player, it was a case of "pack the china, love, I'm going to a new club",'* continued Gregory. Harry Redknapp, the West Ham manager said: *'I don't understand wives getting involved. They should concentrate on looking after the kids and the house.'* Unsworth was persuaded to re-sign for a previous club of his, Everton, although the papers alleged it was because his wife wanted to stay in that part of the world. Unsworth was furious with Gregory for the cheap jibe he'd made about his wife saying: *'John Gregory was very hurt by what I had to say when I told him I was determined to leave, and the only way he could hurt me back was by saying those things about my wife. None of it was true and he was well out of order, but now I think I can understand his frustration and anger.'*
Gregory had paid £3m for Unsworth in order to replace Steve Staunton on the left back of a defensive three, but by the opening day of the season he was gone.

# 'It's not Liverpool, but it's all right if it gets us out of London. Just as long as it's not bloody Birmingham.'

### The posh villa

A wonderful play was written to record the moment for posterity under the banner *'Who Wear The Boots In This House?'* In scene One, Mrs Football Player hears from her husband, Mr Football Player, that they are moving.

Mr Football Player (excitedly): *It's done, luv, I've got me transfair*

Mrs Football Player: *Oh luv, are we going 'ome then?*

Mr FP: *Weeelllll, not exactly luv, but it is closer to 'ome, and I think you're gonna luv it there.*

Mrs FP (not too sure): *Luv it where, luv?*

Mr FP (A note of caution in his voice): *Aston Villa.*

Mrs FP: *Aston Villa? Oo 'eck, that sounds lovely.* (Tenderly) *Aston Villa. Fair rolls off the tongue, dunt it, luv. Sounds dead posh, that, Aston Villa.* (Puts her arms around Mr FP) *It's not Liverpool, but it's all right if it gets us out of London. Just as long as it's not bloody Birmingham.* (Laughs)

Over her shoulder the audience can see Mr Football Player's face take on a stricken expression.

### In the drop zone

In a strange twist of fate at the end of the 2001-02 season, John Gregory, by now managing Derby, took his side to Everton where he needed a win to avoid relegation. In a high-scoring game that was to finish 4-3 to Everton, who should score the opening goal for the Toffees? David Unsworth.

# Hoddle Must Go

## The Matt Dickinson interview

Glenn Hoddle's interview with Matt Dickinson in *The Times* produced his infamous comments about the disabled, which provoked a chorus of disapproval around the country. Those that did not demand he resign called for his sacking.

Only *The Mirror* offered an escape route for Hoddle, prompted by his reported comments that disabled people are paying for sins in a former life.

*The Sun* provided the most vocal opposition, filling its front page with the emphatic headline, *'GO'*. Its front-page comment declared: *'Glenn Hoddle must go today. If he won't resign, he must be sacked... Hoddle was already a joke with his players, who laughed at his ridiculous antics with a barmaid turned faith healer. Now he is a figure of hate for the fans.'*

*The Express* was fiercely critical, splashing with a reader poll that put dissatisfaction with Hoddle at 80 percent. Its leader said: *'Mr Hoddle's comments show him unfit to bear the responsibility of being England coach.'*

But with a spot of spiritual foresight that would make Eileen Drewery proud, the *Daily Mail* trumped them all to announce confidently the sacking of the England coach. It said the FA would tell Hoddle he had lost the faith of the nation. And its leader had a further twist in the tail:

*'It is time to bring a sense of proportion to the Glenn Hoddle affair,'* it said. *'Mr Hoddle's future should be decided by one thing – his performance as the English manager. And on that criterion he should almost certainly go.'*

*The Times*, which printed the interview that sparked Hoddle's crisis, predictably took another damning line. It said: *'The English coach manufactured yet more reasons yesterday why he should now submit his resignation – and why, if that resignation does not come, he should be removed from his post.'*

*'He is now... a bit of a laughing stock.
In the end, that may be the most
persuasive reason to reap what
he has sowed.'*

It also gave front-page space to the writer of the interview, Matt Dickinson. *'Glenn Hoddle has changed his story so many times that I have lost track. Instead of issuing a proper denial, he is in denial,'* he said.

## Not funny

*The Guardian*, no more supportive of the embattled coach, could not resist the biggest joke doing the sportswriters' rounds. *'It is hard to imagine what sins Glenn Hoddle committed in an earlier life to have been saddled with such a disabled intellect in this one,'* it said. *'He is now... a bit of a laughing stock. In the end, that may be the most persuasive reason to reap what he has sowed.'*

The *Daily Telegraph* weighed in with a doom-laden: *'The fate of poor Glenn Hoddle is almost certainly sealed.'*

But for *The Independent*, only the language of medieval times was enough: *'Sacking Glenn Hoddle is just a painless way of telling ourselves we care. So – off with his head.'*

## Mirror image

It was only *The Mirror*, which secured an exclusive interview with Hoddle, that took a supportive line. It carried the leader, *'Honest Hod is worth one last chance'*. It went on: *'Glenn Hoddle is not an evil man. Nor does he believe that disabled people are being punished for their behaviour in previous lives. Glenn Hoddle should remain as England coach with one proviso. He should never discuss his beliefs in public again.'* Within a month, Hoddle had gone.

61

# Ego Landing

## Horton, Lee and Man City

A review of the excellent *'Blue Moon Rising: The Fall and Rise of Manchester City'* by Andy Buckley and Richard Burgess (Milo Books) appeared on the King of the Kippax website, written by a lady called Sue. It summed up the insanity of an era at the club where, having ridden itself of one ogre in the form of Peter Swales, was only to be riven with another in the form of Frannie Lee. The review sparkled with humour and insight and captured the *'reluctant sigh'* of an observer who had clearly seen all this before…

'A great read, a racily written book by two professional journalists well known to many City fans. Brian Horton's *"dismissal"* is documented with comments from those involved. 'Following an evening at the League Managers' Association Annual Dinner, Brian Horton picked up the morning papers to discover he was to be sacked that day, and City were already looking for a successor – a fact, according to the national press.

'But Francis Lee tries the Pontius Pilate line in retrospect: *"Brian rang me at home… I said I knew nothing about it and hadn't even seen the papers… he demanded that I ask the board for a vote of confidence. Whether he wanted to get out because of the pressure, I don't know, but he certainly brought matters to a head….I rang all the directors and they were all in favour of sacking him."*

'Are we to understand that a Football Club's board of directors read in the papers that their manager was to be sacked before they'd even discussed it? Are we to believe that until that point they were not even thinking of sacking him? And are we to accept that the Chairman – a man quite capable of expressing his anger on other occasions and stamping his authority, as it were, on all who begged to differ – didn't have the balls to make a statement to the press in defence of his manager, of whom he says: *"I was definitely of the opinion that we should not get rid of Brian because he had done well for us. I liked him*," but meekly turned to his board of directors and asked their opinions? That's not the impression I had at the time – and I was at the Player of the Year celebration that night, attended by all significant personnel, and no-one else appeared to have that impression either. But maybe we were wrong.

### The chuckling Chairman

'This present day Mr Lee seems such a pussycat as he looks back on his time as Chairman as a successful one. Funny, not many of us noticed it at the time. However, I still believe that Francis Lee came in with the very best intentions for City, and I now prefer to remember Franny the feisty footballer, rather than the chuckling Chairman (he chuckled in silly, embarrassing radio interviews whilst the good ship City sank to its lowest point in its history).

'FHL had arrived at Maine Road as the *'saviour'* for many fans, prompting the comment from one who knew him well – *"The ego has landed!"'*

### Life of Brian

'And someone who did bow out gracefully was Brian Horton. Maybe not the world's greatest manager, but an impressive human being.

'There are lots of people quoted in this book, and some are significant by their absence, but as a small paperback it can only present a 'thumbnail sketch' of the last ten years, yet it is essential reading for all Blues.

'However, for those who are too young, or too confused, to remember what really went on, don't be suckered by the apparently fine words of people who will never admit to failure; never be honest about themselves and never fail to pass the buck. A large number of fellow Blues, cleverer than me, and including me, were suckered by them. The present regime, thankfully, do not fall into the above category, well I hope not, anyway!'

# Taylor the Turnip

## Graham Taylor and England

Nicknamed *'Turnip'* by the press, Graham Taylor was dubbed a failure after a disappointing reign as England manager. But he picked himself up and landed himself the managerial job at Molineux, taking over from Graham Turner.

This was the kind of job Taylor loved, with the chairman, Sir Jack Hayward, digging deep into his pockets at Taylor's request. Taylor spent millions but to no avail. He finally left in 1996 and was once again dubbed a failure by everyone. This was soon to change. He took over at Division Two side Watford and steered them into Division One and then the unthinkable happened – he steered them into the Premiership.

And now he's back in the managerial hot-seat at Villa. When he was lured to the England job by the FA, Doug Ellis managed to let slip all Taylor's good work. Taylor never had the cash which Ron Atkinson and Brian Little got to play with so instead he built up a team to compete with the very best. Now there were some very ordinary players in Villa's runners-up squad. Price, Gage, Birch, Ormondroyd. Hardly world class, but they gave their all for Taylor and the Villa. Indeed, if you could have taken the skill of Atkinson's squad and mated it with the commitment to the cause of Taylor's, Villa would have been unstoppable.

He also unearthed the odd gem. Take Tony Daley. It wasn't until Taylor got hold of Daley that he produced his best. Taylor was the only man who would take the risk with Paul McGrath, a player Manchester United had discharged in Ferguson's initial clearout.

# Lineker was furious as he trod off the pitch, barely able to conceal his contempt for the decision.

### Shuffling the pack

England sent to Sweden the weakest squad they had ever assembled for a major international tournament. Injuries had robbed the squad of several top players for the European Championships – including those chiefly responsible for providing the team's creative impulses in midfield – and underscored the paucity in talent available to the national side. With manager Graham Taylor, at his first major tournament, desperately shuffling players, positional assignments and team formations, England struggled to scoreless draws with latecomers and eventual champions Denmark and the much-fancied France before succumbing to Sweden as two second half goals erased an early lead.

### Euro flop

In that last match, Taylor took off national hero Gary Lineker, making his 80th and final international appearance, with almost 30 minutes to go and the score still level, stripping him of his chance to equal Bobby Charlton's England goal record of 49 and, as it turned out, England of any chance they had of advancing. Lineker was furious as he trod off the pitch, barely able to conceal his contempt for the decision.

The next day's *Sun* carried the notorious headline which is almost always resurrected when Taylor's England tenure is mentioned. *'Swedes 2, Turnips 1'* accompanied by a picture of Taylor's head superimposed on a turnip. It was the beginning of the end for Taylor, who never recovered, in part because the relentless press never allowed him to.

# Ron Returns

## Sheffield welcomes back Atkinson

Wednesday were to play Chelsea in the 1992 League Cup semi-final. Ron Atkinson had turned the Yorkshire giants into a slick passing side and suddenly everyone in the country was talking about the team from Hillsborough. A workmanlike 2-0 victory at Stamford Bridge helped them take control of the tie, and they followed this up with a triumphant 3-1 win three days later which ensured that Ron's army were on their way to Wembley, and a chance to test their mettle against Atkinson's former outfit, Manchester United. It was Wednesday's first major cup final in 25 years.

Pre-final nerves had caused a slight flutter in league form, with three straight defeats over Easter, but the Owls were still holding on to an automatic promotion place when Wembley beckoned. United were favourites to claim the silverware… but the Division Two side dominated the Red Machine, when a sweetly struck half volley eight minutes before the interval from John Sheridan cannoned off the inside of the post and into the net, giving the Owls the lead which earned the club its first major honour in almost six decades. Wednesday proceeded to collect three points in three of their closing six matches; enough to fulfil their overriding aim of an immediate return to the Premiership. The team were on a roll and Atkinson was purring.

### Heroes and villains

But a major bombshell was about to land on Hillsborough. Late in May, the day before a civic reception to commemorate the promotion and cup double, was planned, Atkinson submitted his resignation from the manager's position, intending to assume the same role at Aston Villa. The board and the players got to him and managed to talk him round. Dave Richards reminded him that he was on the brink of achieving great things at

# Atkinson's two assistants, Andy Gray and Jim Barron, joked that they preferred not to sit next to him… in case a sniper took his chances.

Wednesday. Richards and the players persuaded Atkinson to give them one more year, arguing that the Villa job would come again. They knew how much he loved that club. Atkinson's club had always been Villa, indeed he still drove past their training ground everyday on the way to work in Sheffield, but he had promised to finish the job he'd started at Wednesday. After those crisis talks the civic reception went ahead as the fans rejoiced. The following week, Atkinson was out the back enjoying the sunshine when he was visited by Doug Ellis, Villa's chairman. Atkinson admits he didn't exactly see eye-to-eye with the fiery chairman but he was made an offer he couldn't refuse and within the week, and to the fury of all those at Wednesday, he was installed as Villa's new boss.

### 'Er indoors

As fate would have it the new season fixture list threw together Villa at Wednesday on the opening day of the season. Villa's new boss could hardly disguise the dread he felt. Atkinson's two assistants, Andy Gray and Jim Barron, joked that they preferred not to sit next to him on the team coach travelling over to Sheffield in case a sniper took his chances. The fans were out in force, shouting insults at Atkinson in the car park and within a short while Villa were 2-0 down.

Then the comeback started. By the time Atkinson walked out of Hillsborough, Villa had managed to turn the game around and won 3-2. The home fans were fuming but Big Ron managed a smile. *'I've had a bigger earful from the wife,'* he said, when asked about his treatment, before spending a few days getting over the weekend at a health farm.

# Ground Control

## Ron Noades at the Palace

*'Ron Noades suckered us into accepting the sell-off of the ground to his holding company in 1987,'* writes a Crystal Palace fan on a protest website. This was written when the fans were preparing demonstrations against Mark Goldberg, but the problem never truly went away. Ron Noades still owns the ground, having left the team to fend for itself with receivership knocking on the door until the supporters decided to set up a trust fund to try and rescue the club. It is only 10 years since they were in the FA Cup final and in the top division, but financial mismanagement has hit Palace hard. Indeed, they were one of the founder members of the Premier League.

The Selhurst Park ground has never been a popular place. Even when Palace came into the top flight, under the banner *'team of the eighties'*, the Sainsbury's end was a favourite place for away supporters to leapfrog the wall onto unsuspecting home supporters and the suspicion remains that the club's big cheeses got more out of the supermarket sweep than any customer or supporter ever would.

In the nineties, just when it looked like Palace were about to go under, Jerry Lim, an Asian businessman, completed a £10.6m takeover of Palace for an unnamed consortium and sold it to businessman Simon Jordan minutes later.

The new owner, an admirer of Mark Goldberg for having the courage of his convictions when he took over at Selhurst Park, said he would put controls in place to stop history repeating itself and personally ensure they work.

He said: *'Mark led with his chequebook and ultimately paid the price. I'm not going to allow people to run away with my chequebook.'*

*'Mark led with his chequebook and ultimately paid the price. I'm not going to allow people to run away with my chequebook.'*

### Gripping Stuff

Ron Noades still owns the Selhurst Park freehold, but his grip on the future of the club was finally loosened when he agreed a new, 10-year lease for the use of Selhurst Park and Jordan stepped in.

The ground is in need of redevelopment in parts. While the club was in Ron Noades' hands there were attempts to redevelop the Main Stand, but the local council made it virtually impossible for any work to start and the plans were abandoned.

The difficulty now is that Ron Noades still sees the ground as a valuable asset to him without him having to put any money into it. Until someone buys the lease outright, Palace will remain in his grip, a steady cashflow for one person but a drain on resources for the club.

# Mob Rules

**When you munch on your pie and swill back those last tasty morsels with something wet from your friendly football vendor, consider for a moment how this beautiful game, so bulging with cause for argument, managed to evolve to the stage it's at today.**

Football in its rawest form began as a rowdy and dangerous past-time, growing from the street games in Cheapside, Covent Garden and the Strand and the Shrove Tuesday games at Derby, Nottingham and Kingston-on-Thames, that came to be known as *'mob football'*. The football field was the length of the town, the players numbered as many as five hundred and the conflict
continued all day long. But from turmoil came order and the laws of the modern game evolved.

· The FA drew up its rules for the game, including the following:
   10 - Neither tripping nor hacking shall be allowed, and no player shall use his hands to hold or push his adversary.
   12 - No player shall be allowed to take the ball from the ground with his hands under any pretext whatever while it is in play.
   13 - No player shall be allowed to wear projecting nails, iron plates, or gutta percha on the soles or heels of his boots.

· The new laws of the game made no provision for the numbers of players on each side, nor for the duration of play; these matters had to be agreed by the two captains concerned. Thus Barnes fielded only nine men against 14 when

# The football field was the length of the town, the players numbered as many as five hundred and the conflict continued all day.

they went to Penge to play Crystal Palace. On the same day a nine-a-side match took place at Kilburn between No Names and Wanderers that lasted for one hour.

- In 1863, the following clubs sent representatives to the meeting at the Freemason's Tavern on 26 October: Forest; NN (No Name) Kilburn; Barnes; War Office; Crusaders; Perceval House, Blackheath; Crystal Palace; Kensington School; Surbiton; Blackheath School. In addition, Charterhouse School sent an observer, and some unattached footballers were present. It was agreed: '*The clubs represented at this meeting now form themselves into an association to be called the Football Association.*'

- In 1872-73, spectators were not exactly made to feel at home. A rich club might build up some banked terracing with a few railway sleepers. They might even throw down a few lengths of duck-boarding in wet weather. Stands were not unknown, albeit just a patch of land with a cover. In 1873, if you had nothing better to do than watch football, then you had to take your chances.

# The X Files

## Michael Knighton and Carlisle

Chairman Michael Knighton has ruled the roost and attempted so many schemes to raise money for the club (who can forget the time he was about to sell a 25 percent interest in the club to Stephen Brown, a man who had claimed to have made £6.3m from the sale of a hotel complex in Spain, when it transpired that he actually lived in an old people's home in Peebles. He had also been working as a barman in an Indian restaurant, and his experience in sports administration was restricted to an ill-starred spell as commercial manager of Scottish non-league club, Gala Fairydean! But his most famous outburst was fuelled more by paranoia than business sense when he claimed he was being distracted from his day job by UFO's.

Then there was the time when sponsors Eddie Stobart, the haulage firm, made the side change their away strip to the trucker's livery of gold, green and red.

The most recent furore has sprung up around the plan to merge with Clydebank and take their place in the Scottish League. Most English clubs have endorsed this plan as it would be cheaper for the Scottish sides to travel to Carlisle than those in the English League. Other schemes have been a renaming of the side to *'Carlisle North End'*, to reflect their position in the country, but it was thought this would be unnecessary.

### Knighton Day

in September 1997, the Blue Army began to seriously wonder if the plot had been lost. Knighton took control of the team on the premise that the current manager's results (covering the previous 15 games) would have got anyone sacked and that he could do better himself. Out went the hugely popular Mervyn Day and in came Mr Knighton.

# This from a man who promised Carlisle United a place in the European Cup, a packed, modern stadium and the world's best youth scheme, all by 2002.

Knighton's United managed just 11 victories from 40 games and were relegated back to Division Three, finishing second bottom. He stubbornly continued his policy into the 1998-99 season until he finally appointed Nigel Pearson as Director of Coaching in December 1999. Knighton's reign as 'manager' was at an end, but his Chairmanship continued. The club now faced a dogfight to avoid dropping into the Vauxhall Conference.

### Top ten pipedream

Fans have been set against fans, boycotters against supporters, the players seemed to have formed cliques (Irish v Atkins), the club versus the press. The last four years have been the worst in the club's entire history. Carlisle have been promised take-overs that have never happened. Players that have never materialized. They have been promised results that haven't come. The club has returned to the state it was in before Knighton arrived. This from a man who promised: (a) Carlisle United a place in the European Cup, a packed, modern stadium and the world's best youth scheme, all by 2002. (b) An all-seater stadium by 2000.

Who said, *'Carlisle United have the potential to be bigger than Blackburn Rovers'*, *'Carlisle will be the place to be over the next few years'*, *'I predict that within ten years, Carlisle United will be among the ten wealthiest clubs in this country. We will be competing in Europe and have one of the finest stadiums'*, *'History is history and I'm a big believer that destiny is a wonderful thing'*.

In July 2002, Knighton sold the club.

# ALL Change at the McAlpine

## Steve Bruce and Huddersfield

Chairman Barry Rubery, (that's one *'b'*) strolled into the McAlpine Stadium a few years ago promising players, promotion and the Premiership, like so many other young chairman before him.

The fans have got used to this sort of lark and wouldn't be so easily hoodwinked but there was no denying their eyebrows were raised when Steve Bruce was brought in to replace the popular and hard-working local hero, Peter Jackson. Jackson had taken Town to its highest position in 30 years (eighth in Division One) yet that wasn't good enough for Rubery, and Bruce was given a war chest (something denied Jackson) to persuade some of his footballing mates to come and join the fun.

The actual playing staff pocketed around £6m out of a total wage bill of £6.7m. Steve Bruce (who himself earned around £200,000) had to shoulder much of the blame for bringing in players on Premiership salaries who failed to perform, namely Ken Monkou, Scott Sellars and George Donis. Bruce was forced to play some of Jackson's players, players he had told were surplus to his requirements, so the motivation levels were somewhat lower than expected.

What's worse, Town decide to sell one of their '*depreciating assets*' (Chairman Rubery's words) Marcus Stewart, a move that would allow Bruce to strengthen the team overall and a move which wouldn't have any impact on their push for the Premiership. Town received £2.7m from Ipswich (who won promotion and made a national star out of Stewart) but spent £170,000 on one unheard of midfielder and a striker who managed only a handful of games. Town lost out on a play-off place, losing their last game of the season.

# Bruce was given a war chest to persuade some of his footballing mates to come and join the fun.

### Bruce wanes

Rubery had told the supporters that team strengthening would be dependant on season ticket sales and TV revenue yet, although season ticket sales were at record levels and Town were getting decent audience share on the telly, the only team-strengthening in 2000-01 was on a player who subsequently left for *'a better standard of football'*. Moves in the summer to sell players without Bruce's approval created a crack in the relationship between Bruce and Rubery and after a poor start, one win in the first 13 games of the new season, Bruce and Town parted.

### Waste

*'The biggest mistake I ever made was believing that a great footballer would make a great football manager,'* wrote Rubery in his programme notes. *"I was absolutely wrong. Some £3m was wasted on players brought in by Steve Bruce who we have now thankfully parted company with – and that's money that could and would have been spent more wisely by a more experienced manager without an ego to feed."*
Bruce countered in radio interviews by threatening legal action but the damage had been done. The sale of the major asset, Marcus Stewart, explained Town's demise and when new manager Lou Macari failed to halt the slide it seemed inevitable that a team blessed with a splendid stadium and a decent crowd, but a lack of sound management and judgement in the boardroom, should slip unceremoniously into Division Two. Barry Rubery said he could get Huddersfield Town out of Division One within three years. On that promise at least, he managed to deliver.

# Roy McFarland Splits

## From Bradford to Derby and Torquay

In 1981 Roy McFarland had taken Bradford City up into Division Three, and the club lottery was said to be bringing in an annual six-figure sum. But one year later the club was £155,000 in debt. How could it all go wrong?

Thirteen years after Bradford Park Avenue FC had failed to gain re-election to Division Four, the Yorkshire club was in turmoil. Bradford was within 10 days of losing its football club completely. The Football League had set a target date, August 8, for interested parties to come up with a salvage package which included a minimum share capital of £150,000 and a promise to repay creditors.

The 1908 Company, which had gone into receivership at the end of June, owed 99 organisations, individuals and the Inland Revenue a total of £374,000.

And things were about to get worse.

McFarland had gained a legendary status on the terraces but whether it was the financial chaos or the overtures from Derby County's Baseball Ground, something tempted him back to the club that had given him so much success as a player. And the fans in West Yorkshire would never forgive him. They saw this as an act of treachery, leaving the club when it needed heroes not handshakes, the fans saw McFarland's departure to Derby as an indication that for them the fight for survival was futile. But out of difficult circumstances a steely determination to survive was forged.

### Clough

In May 1981 after seeing Derby win two League Championships, McFarland had joined Bradford City as player-manager. His first season in charge was a success and the fans believed that some of McFarland's experience under Brian Clough, who had been his manager during two championship winning seasons in the old First Division, would rub off on the struggling Fourth Division club.

Clough had seen McFarland as one of the first pieces of the jigsaw which would eventually give the Rams the League Championship, take them to the European Cup semi-finals and win 28 full England caps. He would certainly have won more honours – and made more than his 577 senior appearances – had it not been for increasing injury problems late in his career.

### Quit

McFarland was replaced as Bradford manager by the former Leeds United defender Trevor Cherry who took the team into the Second Division but the timing of McFarland's departure, the sudden nature of his decision to split when the club needed him most, this is the thing that sticks in a West Yorkshire man's throat. Big Roy may have done the right thing for his career but you'd be hard-pressed to find a Bradford City fan who'd wish him all the best for it.

To make matters worse, McFarland had walked out on the club after overtures from the Baseball Ground.

# Team Grudges

'Billy Bremner's behaviour was scandalous, producing one of the most notorious incidents in Wembley history.' **Brian Clough**

# London Calling

## Arsenal vs Spurs

The north London derby is one of English football's noisiest institutions and an instant barometer of each club's form. If one side is doing well in the league, they invariably approach this match with a swagger. But if one of the sides is struggling, this is torture of the highest magnitude.

Spurs were formed by a bunch of former grammar school boys in 1882. Arsenal came together four years later. Originally a south London outfit, the Gunners moved to Highbury in 1913, only miles from Tottenham's home at White Hart Lane. Inevitably, this led to a battle for the emerging football fans in the area and rivalries developed which divided the community; families, school friends and work colleagues suddenly found themselves on opposing sides. The Spurs supporters certainly saw this move by Arsenal as hostile, and the famous north London rivalry was born. Six years later the rivalry was given an added impetus when Arsenal were promoted back to the First Division, despite only finishing fifth in the Second Division. Somehow they'd been lucky enough to be at the right place at the right time as the expansion of the First Division proved sufficient to include their fledgling collection of players following the end of World War I.

### Style

Tottenham couldn't believe their new neighbour's good fortune as this was the season they were relegated from the top flight. Though Spurs may have lost ground in terms of geography they could at least take pride in the style of football they played. Free-flowing, attack-minded, adventurous football was the hallmark of all Spurs teams even in the days of cotton shirts and baggy shorts.

In the 1960s led by Danny Blanchflower and Jimmy Greaves and through the 70s and 80s with Martin Peters, Steve Perryman, Ossie Ardiles and Glenn Hoddle, Spurs exhibited a swashbuckling approach to the game. Arsenal continued with a more pragmatic approach.

# 'The "boring" tag was never more zealously thrown at the Gunners than under the reign of George Graham'

### Boring

Arsenal, on the other hand, have had to endure less flattering labels, despite being more successful than their north London rivals. *'Lucky'* and *'boring'* are the usual insults hurled at them by opposing fans. *'Lucky'* stemmed from their style of play under the great Herbert Chapman. This involved cooking up opponent's pressure at the back and then scoring goals on the counter-attack. The *'boring'* tag is a much more recent innovation, resulting from the side's success being built on defence rather than attack.

'APPEN AS HOW YOU'RE DISLOYAL, JUST LIKE ME PERISHIN' GRANDFATHER!

The *'boring'* tag was never more zealously thrown at the Gunners than under the reign of George *'What Envelope?'* Graham, the man responsible for bunging together the defensive quartet of Tony Adams, Steve Bould, Lee Dixon and Nigel Winterburn. No wonder the home fans enjoyed singing *'1-0 to the Arsenal'*. They were happy enough just to win and not at all fussed how their side went about it. Recently, under Arsene Wenger, Arsenal's brand of football has exuded class, excitement and sophistication. Some Spurs fans now moan that Arsenal have stolen their mantle as the flair north London side.

# Singing the Blues

## Liverpool vs Everton

Everton Football Club was formed in 1878 due to the growing popularity of football in Liverpool. John Houlding, an influential businessman and future mayor of Liverpool, was to play a big part in both clubs' history.

Everton began playing at Anfield Road, a field rented by Houlding from the local brewer John Orrell. As Everton strived over the years, Houlding poured in more money to build stands at Anfield. After a disagreement concerning rental between their board and Houlding, the club split into two factions. One group decided to move out of Anfield and raise money for a new stadium which was to become Everton's home at Goodison Park. The other group chose to remain with Houlding. Faced with a prospect of owning an empty football ground, Houlding decided to adopt the city's name as the name of his new club. In 1892, John Houlding founded Liverpool Football Club with the support of the Anfield loyalists who stuck with him after the rift.

The city was shocked by Houlding's move. No one could foresee the city supporting two clubs. Where would the talent come from? Houlding turned to his old chum John McKenna for help. McKenna, an Irishman with a keen interest in football was to become Liverpool's first ever manager. Entrusted with the weighty responsibility for finding talented young footballers for the new club, McKenna ventured north to Scotland where he signed ten Scotsmen for his new team. On 15 March 1892, Liverpool Football Club began its long and happy association with players, not to mention managers, from north of the border.

### Rivalry

The rivalry between Liverpool and Everton has been viciously intense since the Merseyside derbies began in 1893. Everton Football Club was originally formed by St Domingo Church School and played in Stanley Park, a venue which still hosts amateur

# The rivalry between Liverpool and Everton has been viciously intense since the Merseyside derbies began in 1893.

football matches. Having been regular members of the top division since 1954, Everton's stay in the top flight is bettered only by Arsenal, although Everton's lack of success in recent years has led to plenty of catcalling from fans just down the road.

Their nickname, the Toffeemen, is derived from the famous sweets made nearby and they are world renowned not the least because the name Everton also appears in a number of clubs in South America, inspired by travellers from Britain. verton's most successful spell was under Howard Kendall in the 1980s when they won league, FA Cup and European titles. But their chance to compete in the European Cup was thwarted thanks to a ban on all English clubs taking part in European competitions following a sickening clash between Liverpool and Juventus supporters in the 1985 European Cup final at Heysel.

# Fight Clubs

## Millwall vs Manchester City

After the first match in the annual league meeting between these two in 2000, Millwall chairman Theo Paphitis made the curious remark: *'Manchester City have a much greater history of crowd violence than we do.'* At the time many considered this an ill-conceived remark that had little to back it up in fact.

Most people with an active brain cell could see that the game was going end in trouble. Newspapers sent reporters, magazines sent undercover hooligan-watchers, and the meatheads from both clubs with brains in their backsides turned up in force in anticipation of fisticuffs.

After the game at the New Den, Manchester City manager Joe Royle made what many considered to be a few emotive and inflammatory jibes. *'We need to settle a few old scores,'* he said. To make the situation even more explosive, City refused to make the return fixture all-ticket for Millwall fans. There had been much discussion about ensuring that only genuine, law-abiding supporters were able to gain entry into the away end on the day, with ideas like only selling tickets to those with the last three home ticket stubs. Once City had declared their intention to sell tickets on the day all bets were off.

### Name calling

*'Wankers'*, *'Brain dead sickos'* and of course, that age old chestnut, *'Scum'*... there's nothing like a match between these two to get the blood boiling. Are all Millwall fans really just *'droppings from Satan's arsehole'* as one website puts it? Can City fans equally be described as *'only a few orders of magnitude removed from being the collective second coming of Christ?'*

Millwall fans have asked City supporters to consider the following: *'What do you think about those people who smash up coaches?'*

# Last season an innocent coach driver was almost beaten to death...

They want to know what should be done with those who throw coins, seats and other missiles at people whose only crime has been to pitch up and watch their team play a game of football.

Last season an innocent coach driver was almost beaten to death, and a gas canister thrown at him whilst he was parked outside Maine Road. Millwall is a club with a reputation for crowd disorder. Manchester City is a massive club with an even bigger following. Blend the two collectives together and the result is a dangerous mix of supporters who can be easily encouraged to come to blows.

### Violence

In 2000, visiting fans at the North Stand told of a constant downpour of coins and missiles, climaxing in seats being ripped out and thrown. People were led away with their heads bleeding.

Those who stayed were kept in for around 45 minutes. During this time they got constant updates from the *'highly professional stadium announcer'*, who had earlier exhorted City fans to *'ignore the fracas in the visitors' stand'*. Her explanation for fans being detained started out as *'crowd congestion'* but after some time she let it slip that a *'volatile'* situation was occurring outside.

# Northern Exposure

## Blackburn vs Burnley

Blackburn Rovers are seen as a money team with no real historical class. Burnley's image is somewhat more traditional; not very successful in recent decades but proud of their past nonetheless. Fans from the Claret and Blue half of east Lancashire are fiercely proud that the club has not tried to buy it way out of doldrums. *'Not until recently,'* the Blue and White contingent would observe, though few would see the purchases of Ian Wright and Paul Gascoigne in the fading light of their careers as anything other than an attempt to sell merchandise and a few extra club shirts.

The intense regional rivalry in the North West has created most of the grrr in this grudge. Burnley, like the other Lancashire cotton teams, Bolton, Preston and Blackburn, were effectively consigned to mediocrity when the £20 maximum wage was abolished in the 1960s. Burnley's decline was the most dramatic, partly because of its bustling and egotistical butcher-turned-chairman Bob Lord, a man immortalized in the concrete edifice that bears his name at Turf Moor. During the 1970s, the club suddenly seemed incapable of holding on to good players whilst the management in the post-Lord era of the 1980s behaved as though it was wandering about with someone else's credit card.

### Walker's millions

What really riles Burnley fans is that Blackburn sought (and succeeded) in buying success with the money of their chairman and benefactor, Jack Walker. The money from Walker's steel empire financed the purchase of Alan Shearer, manager Kenny Dalglish. and numerous other high-profile signings. And it worked. Blackburn won successive promotions and the inaugural Premiership trophy in 1995.

# Burnley were effectively consigned to mediocrity when the £20 maximum wage was abolished in the 1960s.

### Faded cotton

You cannot divorce the club's fate completely from the history of its northern location. Turf Moor is probably the best-appointed workplace in the region. But it needs a strong town to do it justice as well as a strong team. Maybe a bloated dictator would help if he were the right sort of man. It needs a local legend to foster the collective unity and spirit that has traditionally brought the boot out of players, administrators and supporters.

Blackburn's reciprocal loathing of Burnley waned during a 17-year gap from 1983 to 2000 in which the two teams' paths failed to cross. Whilst supporters of Blackburn revelled in promotion to the top division and European competitions, Burnley flirted with First and Second Division football. But the rivalry recommenced as the two clubs reacquainted themselves with their true derby fixtures in two fiery encounters in the First Division in 2000-01. Rovers emerged victorious; Burnley fans licked their wounds. And the police bought villas in Spain with their overtime money.

# Tyne and Weird

## Newcastle vs Sunderland

Who are Sunderland AFC? Or, what is Sunderland AFC? Isn't it obvious? They are by far the greatest team the world has ever seen. If you listen to the masses at the Stadium of Light or watch a video of the good old days at Roker Park, you'll know what people mean when they refer to Sunderland's fanatical support. Blind to the limitations on display they may be, but you'd never be able to call a Sunderland supporter fickle.

As far as the average fan is concerned, Sunderland AFC is one of the biggest football clubs in the world. The supporters alone are phenomenal people who follow their club with unrivalled passion and desire. Sunderland AFC, the thirteenth member of the football league, has enjoyed many successful seasons throughout its history. Most, however, came in a rose-tinted, bygone age prior to World War II, where league championships were commonplace. Since the end of the last war, Sunderland have bounced up and down between the top two divisions. However, in 1973, one of the club's greatest triumphs was achieved when they lifted the FA Cup. As a struggling Second Division side, the unfancied Rokerites triumphed over Don Revie's mighty First Division Leeds United.

### Upstarts

The view from Newcastle is somewhat different. Sunderland are perceived as a club full of upstarts. They may be capable of attracting a decent crowd but when it comes to achievement, the Geordies claim the Mackems have very little to shout about. Of course, you have to take into account that Newcastle have struggled to be anything other than bridesmaid's to someone else's wedding in recent seasons. Indeed, when Kevin Keegan took hold of the club back in the early 1990s, Newcastle were on the verge of dropping in to what would have been the old Third Division.

Sunderland themselves were relegated in 1987 to the old Third Division. It was the lowest point in the club's history and a nadir that no Sunderland supporters wish to revisit. But since then the club has bounced back under the auspices of Peter Reid.

### Expansion

When the club bade farewell to Roker Park, its proud home for 99 years, the occasion marked a turning point in their fortunes. The Stadium of Light, a 42,000-seat arena, opened for the start of the 1997-98 season.

Having bobbed up and down between the top two tiers of the English league, Reid secured promotion from Division One by beating every team in the division at least once and losing only three matches in a remarkable 46-game campaign. Sunderland scored more goals than any other team and racked up the highest ever points total in the history of English football. Reid had suddenly turned the club into a top 10 side just five years after being sacked as the boss at Manchester City.

Newcastle supporters moaned that their rivals were punching above their weight. But when Ruud Gullit sent out a below-par Newcastle side to face Sunderland at a rain-soaked St James' Park, leaving the talismanic striker Alan Shearer on the bench, the resulting home defeat appeared to have given the Mackems the last laugh. Gullit's immediate departure coupled with Shearer's subsequent renaissance, however, soon restored the Geordie smiles.

# Sunderland are perceived [by Newcastle] as a club full of upstarts.

# West Country Madness

## Bristol Rovers vs Bristol City

A city the size of Bristol should have had more success than either of these sides have managed to provide. You have to go as far back as the 1970s to find even a glimmer of notoriety to shout about on either side. Bristol City's City Service have perhaps the greater notoriety but Rovers have managed to engage in similar levels of hooliganism over the same period. Throughout the 1980s and early 1990s, casuals joined Rovers' firms like the Gas and Young Executives. They would begin by coining the away fans and then descend into mindless violence. Kids would get to the matches early to see where City fans parked their cars, and then leave early to go and wait for them.

Bristol Rovers were formed as the Black Arabs in September 1883 following a meeting of five young men at a restaurant on Stapleton Road in the Eastville district of the city. The original name was derived from the black shirts worn by the players and a rugby club known as the Arabs that played on a pitch at Purdown in east Bristol. The Black Arabs played their first match, a friendly fixture, on 1 December 1883. During their first season they played a further nine games, in which time they assumed the nickname of the Purdown Poachers.

### From Arabs to Rovers

The club became known as Eastville Rovers in 1884-85 and continued to play friendly matches for a number of seasons, changing grounds on several occasions. They joined the Bristol and District League, forerunner of the Western League, in 1892 and moved to a ground at Eastville in 1897. Professionalism and a further name change to Bristol Eastville Rovers came at the start of the 1897/98 season, with the name Bristol Rovers being adopted at the start of the following campaign.

Having competed in the Western League and the Birmingham and District League, Rovers joined the Southern League at the start of the 1899-1900 season. They acquitted themselves reasonably well at the higher level and won the Southern League championship in 1904-05. Though they remained in the competition until 1920, it proved to be the club's only success before they became members of the Football League.

## Hooligans

Asked why the Rovers support had dwindled in the nineties, hooligans' replies centred on the move by the *'Gas'* out to Bath, in which they lost a generation of Bristolians whilst the club spent ten years in exile. Only now are they recovering since the firm moved its operation back to Bristol.

*'I for one have seen them [Gas] on a good day, away to Cardiff few years ago,'* says one member of the firm on a hooligan website. *'And they aren't as bad as we make out... It's just that they could never cope with City's numbers and they know this, so they just don't seem to bother turning up. You never know, they might prove us wrong when we play them next, but I doubt it.'*

It seems that what they're left with is a collection of songs that leave little to the imagination, and too insulting to repeat here!

# Kids would get to the matches early to see where City fans parked their cars, and then leave early to go and wait for them.

# England Invade Latin America

**As the British Empire expanded from Manchester up through the ports of Liverpool and across the Atlantic to South America, so, naturally, did the men on those boats take the first steps towards creating the unique version of the game played by countries throughout Latin America today.**

Imagine a group of tired and thirsty sailors disembarking at the port in Buenos Aires. While Argentine labourers step up and unload the blankets, boots and flour brought all the way over from England they then rest for an hour before loading the boats back up with raw materials like wool, hides and wheat with which English factories will churn out more goods.

- Imagine if you can the sight of English sailors sporting hobnail boots, kicking a ball about in the streams surrounding the docks. Those men would wonder at the sight of English brawn carting a ball about in front of them and think: 'I could do better than that,' and 'when I've finished here I'm going to have some of that for myself.'

- The Latinos organized themselves into teams made up of labourers and the local English subjects. A mixture of industrial managers and diplomats would come together in an unlikely alliance to play beneath portraits of Queen Victoria. The first known game played in Brazil occurred in 1895 in a match between the British Gas Company and the Sao Paulo Railway.

While the men sported long trousers and heavy boots, they made sure their moustaches were waxed and twirled whilst their heads were covered with a sensible cap.

While the men sported long trousers and heavy boots, they made sure their moustaches were waxed and twirled, while their heads were covered with a sensible cap. As the game's popularity soared, the local players began to wear the shorts, shoes and socks being brought back from England. Boats brought with them the rules and words like score, goal, goalkeeper, back, half, forward, penalty and offside became widely used.

- The game required little money and could played almost anywhere. What began as a pleasurable pastime for those lucky enough to be associated with the Empire's expansion soon found its way into the slums. Balls were made of old socks filled with rags and stones were used to mark out the goalmouth. As the athleticism of unbridled youth got its grip round the functional restrictions of this primitive football the first signs of South American silky skill could be seen. The world noticed that a Latin American heartbeat had begun ticking in football.

# Flying High

## Brighton vs Palace

Many people do not understand why the two clubs are such bitter rivals. Here, one supporter explains his experience of the south coast grudge match.

The first Brighton game I attended was at the Goldstone in 1974 in our Division Three days. The trouble started before the game down on the seafront in Hove when a small group of Palace supporters came face-to-face with a large Brighton contingent and chased them off over the hill and far away.

This was to set the pattern for the coming clashes between the two clubs and the Palace were never found wanting.

At all the away games, the Palace support was huge and more than 10,000 wouldn't be an overestimate. The Palace Pier on Brighton seafront was always occupied by Palace fans. On match days, the pier is regarded as our own. During the games, inside the ground you'd often see disturbances down the Brighton end where some of the naughtier Palace fans had taken up residence for the game and, in general, the atmosphere was sheer bedlam with fights breaking out.

### Bedlam

Before the game had finished, the park outside would often be full of brawling fans. In the town afterwards, there would often be small flare-ups during the evening and night. Things really came to a head though when we were tear gassed – something you would not want to experience.

As for the Whitehorse end at Palace, there were indeed some of our bad boys in occupation of that end. One thing about Palace in the past was that whenever any of our number came under threat, hordes of supporters came steaming to the rescue.

# 'Tribal hatred is a very natural thing and CPFC-BHA is tribal hatred.'

*'A Brighton game is special and you'd be buzzing all week before it in anticipation. Just hope that we can meet the scum again soon.'*

### Mutual loathing

My dad hated Brighton and Mullery so much that when Mullery became our manager, my dad refused to step foot inside Selhurst. So he dragged me to Croydon FC for two years to watch them instead. He has never forgiven former chairman Ron Noades for bringing him in and, to this day, still despises Noades cause he got rid of Kember and brought in that twat.

All I heard for years was about Mullery and ripping up money in front of our fans. He took me to my first away game at Brighton in mid-80s and I swear everyone in the Palace end apart from us two had left the ground 20 minutes before the end.

You couldn't see any grass on the park opposite as there were running battles everywhere. We stayed in Brighton for a while after and when we went to get our train, the Old Bill were pulling back in a Croydon-bound train, which had been gutted by Palace fans.

*'All these lunatic Palace fans were escorted off the train back at Brighton station. I'm no hooligan but I reckon tribal hatred is a very natural thing and CPFC-BHA is tribal hatred.'*

95

# Spurs vs Chelsea

## 10 March 2002

Blue murder down at the Lane today. Chelsea exacted their revenge for the previous week's 5-1 Worthington Cup defeat, with a result that was just as embarrassing for the home side, although schoolboy errors were a contributing factor. Spurs were competing until they went 2-0 down and could argue that the linesman got a few decisions wrong – Gudjohnssen looked offside when Dean Richards calmly walked out of his half and claimed the decision that never came. In the second half, Spurs never looked like scoring and the Chelsea fans taunted their opposition with chants like *'You've got your Tottenham back'*.

The first chance came after nine minutes, when a Richards long free kick was headed on by Les Ferdinand, but Sheringham's flick went over the goal. Chelsea scored from the first corner of the game, and Sullivan was at fault for misjudging Hasselbaink's kick taken on the left. Sullivan could only flick the ball to the back post, where Melchiot returned it low, Lampard turned it on, and Gallas was allowed to slot home for his first goal for Chelsea.

**Lead doubled**

Spurs did not get into the game until the 16th minute. Simon Davies' cross reached Gus Poyet who seemed to be brought down in the box, but got no penalty. Chelsea seemed to be getting the benefit of the doubt with their challenges, as Gronkjaer's late tackle on Poyet also passed without punishment.

Hasselbaink then nearly doubled the lead. Le Saux and Babayaro combined on the left to cross. After an exchange with Gudjohnssen, Hasselbaink chipped a shot onto the top of the bar. Spurs at last got the home support excited with a bit of pressure, and should have equalised on 38 minutes, when Les Ferdinand headed Anderton's cross against the foot of the post. There was one more effort for Spurs before the break, when Ferdinand found Ziege on the left, but Sheringham's first time attempted flick went over the bar. Almost the only other chance for Spurs came soon after the interval, when Ledley King headed a Ziege free kick goalward, but Cudicini saved.

### Surprise

Within minutes of the restart, Chelsea were two up. Spurs were taken by surprise by the long clearance aimed at Gudjohnssen. Richards stepped up, but got no flag, and Gudjohnssen was allowed an unimpeded path to goal, where he coolly slotted past the helpless Sullivan.

Thereafter, Spurs had trouble clearing their lines. On 54 minutes, after Gardner and King had worked the ball inside from the left, Sherwood gifted the ball to Le Saux on the edge of the box, and Sullivan was beaten again. Richards was taken off for Sergei Rebrov, but this move only served to leave Spurs more vulnerable at the back.

After 66 minutes, Spurs lost the ball inside the Chelsea half. Gudjohnssen's pace, and Spurs' lack of defence allowed him to race on and score.

Simon Davies' 78th minute shot did find its way to goal, but a free kick was given against Sheringham for impeding the keeper. Spurs just couldn't get on the scoresheet.

# The Chelsea fans taunted their opposition with chants like 'You've got your Tottenham back'.

# Slings and Arrows

## Nottingham Forest vs Notts County

Two of the oldest clubs in the world have been slugging it out in derby games for over 130 years.

The Nottingham derby was the start of them all. Milan, Manchester and Madrid may all have their derby matches, but the oldest of them all belongs to Nottingham, England. Notts County, the oldest league club in the world (founded 1863) and Nottingham Forest, the third oldest (1865) enjoy a rivalry which dates back over 130 years.

Nottingham may be more famous around the world for the rivalry between Robin Hood and the Sheriff. However, it is the city's very special footballing derby that is the important fight for the local fans. It all started in the spring of 1866. The match was billed as the red-shirted Garibaldis of Forest versus the maroon and mustard-striped Lambs of Notts County and took place on Nottingham Forest's recreation ground.

According to the earliest Forest club history published in 1891, the Reds won 1-0 with a goal from W.H. Revis, but this appears to be disputed by a local newspaper report published on the morning after the game, that records a no-score draw.

Notts County became founder members of the Football League in 1888 and Forest joined them four years later. A crowd of 18,000 saw the first league match between the two at Trent Bridge on 8 October 1892. All the goals came in the second half and it was County who took control. Harry Walkerdine, Harry Daft and Scottish international Dan Bruse scored in a 3-0 win.

# Milan, Manchester and Madrid may all have their derby matches, but the oldest of them all belongs to Nottingham.

The last derby between the two clubs took place in the 1993-94 season when both teams were in the First Division. Nottingham Forest won 1-0 at their home ground, and in the return match, Notts County gained their revenge with a 2-1 home victory.

**Fortune**

The two sides enjoyed very different fortunes throughout the last century. Nottingham Forest enjoyed their best period during the late seventies and early eighties when, under the leadership of the legendary Brian Clough, they won the European Cup twice. Notts County would have to go back to the start of the last century to reminisce about their best periods in the game, but can happily boast of an FA Cup triumph.

By 2000, the two Nottingham sides were a division apart and despite the fact that Nottingham Forest have beaten the likes of Malmo FF of Sweden and Hamburg SV of Germany in European Cup finals, when it comes to playing derby games, anything can happen.

# With the Midlands

## West Brom vs Wolves

For the first 80 years of the club's existence, the only rivals to West Bromwich Albion's supremacy in the Midlands were Aston Villa – the only other local team capable of winning anything. No other neighbouring clubs could claim to have met one another in three separate FA Cup finals, and the league fixture regularly used to attract crowds in excess of 60,000.

But over the last 20 years it has proved difficult to hate a team you never play and, apart from the occasional cup drubbing, the teams have been in different divisions for years – although with both sides set to trot out in the same division in 2002-03 the rivalry will finally be renewed.

In order to accommodate the seething desire to have a pop at someone – anyone, for that matter – a whole new hate culture has developed, centred on Albion's Black Country neighbours, Wolverhampton Wanderers.

You might argue that this loathing was started by Albion. Selling them four key players – including their cult hero and record goalscorer Steve Bull back in 1986 – saved the Wolves from going out of business, long before their *'Golden Tit'* benefactor Jack Hayward arrived on the scene to bankroll the boys in old gold.

Now the rivalry has reached an unsavoury level unseen anywhere outside Glasgow: a Black Country derby is a true throwback to the bad old days of the 1970s. Wolves still come out onto the field to the tune of *'The Liquidator'*, the lyrics of which give the fans an opportunity to shout abuse about the Albion at the end. Efforts to stop this by the Wolves management have been half-hearted to say the least, hence the suspicion by some Albion fans that the obscenities are officially approved.

# A Black Country derby is a true throwback to the bad old days of the 1970s.

## Tatters and Dingles

There are subtle nuances implicit in this sobriquet for Wolves supporters, which locals understand but causes outsiders a lot of head scratching. In the Black Country, the term *'tatter'* means someone who earns his or her living collecting and selling bits of copper, brass and lead to scrap metal merchants. As these items are usually acquired under somewhat dubious circumstances, including midnight *'visits'* to local factories, the term has come to mean someone who's little better than a common thief.

The Dingles moniker is, sadly, meaningless to anyone who's never seen the television soap drama Emmerdale. The Dingle family are a bunch of fat, ugly, pig-ignorant thieves and petty crooks who live in a slum and do nothing but cause trouble. Any resemblance between them and the good people of Wolverhampton is completely intentional and not the fault of Albion supporters, whatsoever, honest.

♪♪♪ WE HATE WOLVES, BUT er, OBVIOUSLY NOT AS MUCH AS THE VILLA....WHO WE WOULD LIKE TO MEET MORE FREQUENTLY... ♪♪♪

# Showboating

## Leeds vs Liverpool

Forget about Mark Viduka's goalscoring exploits against Liverpool or the fact that Robbie Fowler signed for Leeds after an unhappy ending to his love affair with Liverpool, the real dramas between these two kicked off twenty years ago.

Leeds were the dominant side of the early seventies and Liverpool were an emerging superpower. The full force of the Anfield machine was yet to come but the 1975 Charity Shield confrontation brought out the best, and the worst, in both sets of teams and their management.

The showman Bill Shankly led out Liverpool for the last time – he'd announced his resignation that summer – alongside Leeds' freshly installed young manager, Brian Clough. It was strange seeing Clough lead out a team designed by Don Revie and the strange sight wasn't just felt by the fans. The players begrudged the robust management style of Clough and, judging by the performance, pre-season training had left many of the Yorkshire stars in no doubt that their futures lay elsewhere.

As the young pretender, Clough tried to engage Shanks in some friendly banter but the Liverpool supremo completely blanked him. Leeds and Liverpool had had some bitter battles down the years, but it is doubtful whether there had ever been an angrier encounter than there was that day.

## Squabbles

The trouble started early in the game. There were tasty clashes all over the pitch with Billy Bremner and Johnny Giles snapping at the heels of a Liverpool team that Shankly had rebuilt from its eminence in the 1960s. Leeds had obviously set out to win the game at all costs. The arrival of the abrasive Clough had disturbed the Leeds camp and they were in no mood to contribute to what they saw as a waste of time and a diversion from

# Clough tried to engage Shanks in some friendly banter but the Liverpool supremo completely blanked him.

the squabbles that were clearly breaking out in the north. Early in the game, a Liverpool player had pressed Giles from behind and clipped his ankle – the Irishman was never one to take such treatment lying down and turned round and lashed out at the offender. He got a booking and a stern lecture for his trouble. The game was warming up nicely.

### Sending off

That was only the precursor to the main event of the afternoon, however, as the match became ever more fraught and fractious. It was six of one and half a dozen of the other, but Clough, with his customary black and white vision, was clear about who he felt was the guilty party in the clash just after the hour which will remain the lasting memory of the game: *'Billy Bremner's behaviour was scandalous, producing one of the most notorious incidents in Wembley history. It was as if the players were offering grounds for all my criticism that they had resented so much.'*

Bremner and Kevin Keegan clashed. The two lashed out at each other and were both sent off. Remember, Keegan was the golden boy of English football and seemingly never lost his temper. Keegan has been captured forever with that picture of him walking along the touchline having thrown his shirt to the ground. Behind him you can see Bremner walking past Brian Clough, a steely glare in his eyes as Old Big Head ignores his captain and barks out orders to any members of the Leeds side prepared to listen.

# Coast to Coast

## Southampton vs Portsmouth

Most teams' rivalry stems from nothing more than regional proximity, and a desire to compete with, and beat, your neighbours. In modern times there have been fewer matches than either town would want. Portsmouth continue to be referred to as the last great sleeping giant whilst Southampton remain consistent survivors in the top flight without ever looking likely to challenge for honours. Not content with singing *'Stand up if you hate the scum'* on the rare occasions they meet, Portsmouth have a massive collection of songs they reserve just for the visits of the Saints.

### Jealousy

Although Southampton and Portsmouth football clubs are both over 100 years old, the bitter rivalry between them really took off in the early 1970s before reaching a peak during the 1980s. The main reason was jealousy. Whilst the Saints were winning the FA Cup, getting promoted and staying in the First Division, signing European player of the year Kevin Keegan, playing in Europe and finishing second to Liverpool, Portsmouth were languishing in the lower leagues, even sinking as far as the old Fourth Division. It's not clear where the name *'Scummers'* came from but some say its origins trace back to a dock strike in the 1950s when Southampton dockers refused to support the Portsmouth dispute.

The nickname *'Skate'* was born in the early 1980s. The name has many meanings but there are two plausible explanations. The first is that Royal Navy sailors – who were at sea for months on end – would often use skate fish to relieve their sexual frustrations (something to do with the shape of the mouth, allegedly). The second explanation is that skate is a *'bottom dweller'* fish. Apparently the skates at the Sealife centre in Southsea, Portsmouth, were removed a couple of years ago as people were caught *'interfering'* with them.

# Southampton remain consistent survivors in the top flight without ever looking likely to challenge for honours.

### Skirmishes

There have been about 15 significant confrontations between these two rival sets of supporters since the early seventies. Thankfully, this has tailed off in recent seasons, but below is a list of some of the worst:

1974/75: Saints vs Pompey, much trouble around the city and The Dell, referee (Clive Thomas) attacked by a Saints fan.

1982: World Cup in Spain, Saints clash with Pompey in Bilbao.

1983/84: Pompey vs Saints FA Cup 'the peak' of hostilities. 10,000 Saints travel to Pompey, many incidents of ferocious fighting around Fratton Park with mobs up to a 1,000 strong on each side, dozen of arrests and serious injuries.

1985/86: Saints Reserves vs Pompey Reserves. 100 Pompey turn up and after the game they are confronted by around 100 Saints and retreat back to central station.

1987/88: Pompey vs Saints, more clashes in and around Fratton, police out in record numbers, kept the fans mainly apart.

1987/88: Saints vs Pompey, large number of Pompey fans arrested at St Deny's station prior to kick-off. 500 police on duty, some being drafted in from Sussex, Dorset and Surrey. Surprisingly no trouble in the ground.

1993/94: Pompey vs Saints, Alan Knight's testimonial. Pompey fans attack innocent Saints fans after the game and then smash some brick walls and shop windows.

# North and West

## Preston and Blackpool

The rivalry between these two Lancastrian clubs is purely geographical. Back in the days after World War I, Alex James was a favourite with Preston North End fans for four years before his transfer to Arsenal in 1929. The move hit the football headlines when the fee involved was reported to be £9,000, a fortune at the time.

Following the departure of James, relegation to the Third Division was twice narrowly avoided but what happened later with a management committee of four under the chairmanship of the late J.I. Taylor was modern footballing romance. Holdcroft, Lowe, Harper, Rowley, Tremelling, Shankly, Gallimore and Dougal were signed and promotion was gained in 1934. The two Beatties, Andy and Bobbie (unrelated), together with Mutch, Smith, Milne, Fagan and the O'Donnell brothers were among the many Scots who came to Deepdale. North End reached the Cup Final in 1937 when they lost to Sunderland and in 1938 when they reversed the result of the 1922 final by beating Huddersfield town 1-0. The winning goal came from the first penalty awarded at Wembley, and was scored by George Mutch with the last kick of extra time.

### Finney

After the war, and until his retirement in 1960, the skill of Tom Finney was the most important aspect of football at Deepdale. His genius and gentlemanly conduct was, and still is, and example for all footballers to follow and brought great credit, not just to the maestro, but also to his home town of Preston. The honour of being made Freeman of the Borough and the award of the CBE for services to football was just reward for this footballing legend. Sadly North End's defeat, 3–2 by Albion in the Cup Final of 1954, did not result in a Cup Winner's Medal and another disappointment was in 1953 when the First Division championship was lost to Arsenal on a goal average difference of one.

# 'Preston North End are nicknamed "The Lillywhites"'

### Knob Ends

According to a Blackpool website, the reasons for the rivalry with Preston North End are simple. They write: *'The town of Preston lies just 17 miles up the M55/M6 from Blackpool and as such they are the Seasiders' nearest opponents. For this reason it is perfectly understandable that Blackpool supporters consider Preston to be their most hated local rivals.*

*'Preston supporters also consider Blackpool to be their most hated local rivals which is not so reasonable as Blackburn is only 10 miles east of them. The reason for this is that the people of Preston have not yet grasped how to read a map.*

*'Preston North End, or Nob End as they are affectionately known, are nicknamed "The Lillywhites" which originates from the way their players react to tough tackling Blackpool midfielders. Their supporters often refer to their club as PNE, an acronym made from their initials but which to most people sounds like a sexually transmitted disease.*

# Wartime Football

**During the summer of 1916, the appointed English captain wellied a football into the trenches of the German opposition before launching an attack. His regiment was unsure about the unorthodox tactic but joined him in battle only to see their leader gunned down. The sight inspired them to fight even harder and before the day was out a great victory had been achieved. An historic football rivalry with the Germans had been started.**

Two years earlier one of the most incredible stories from the Great War took place on Christmas Day. Tales of the British and German soldiers playing football together in no man's land has become become the stuff of legend. But the Christmas truce of 1914 really happened. It is as much a part of the historical fixtures of World War I as the gas clouds of Ypres or the Battle of the Somme. Yet it has often been dismissed as though it were merely a myth. Or, assuming anything of the kind occurred, it has been seen as a minor incident, blown up out of all proportion, natural fodder for sentimentalists and pacifists of later generations.

- But the truce really happened. And it happened a far greater scale than has been generally accepted. The English Bedfordshire regiment and German troops got together and agreed to play in an area not too disturbed by shells or fallen heroes. The Germans, with typical efficiency, won the game 3-2, but only after the football had been punctured when it struck a tangle of razor wire.

The Germans, with typical efficiency, won the game 3-2, but only after the football had been punctured when it struck a tangle of razor wire.

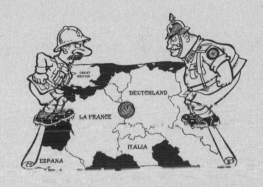

- Enemy really did meet enemy between the trenches. There was, for an all too brief 90 minutes, genuine peace in no man's land. Though Germans and British were the main participants, the French and Belgians also took part, but were presumably eliminated at the group stage. Most of those involved agreed it was a remarkable way to spend Christmas. As the game unfolded in front of them, soldiers mulled over the pointlessness of fighting. *'Just think,'* wrote one British soldier, *'that while you were eating your turkey I was out talking and shaking hands with the very men I had been trying to kill a few hours before. It was astounding.'*

- *'It was a day of peace in war,'* commented a jubilant German participant. *'It is only a pity that it was not decisive peace.'*

# Pots of Trouble

## Stoke vs Port Vale

The local derby, the Potteries clash. It is a Battle of the Bulge and a clarion call to supporters of both sides to stand up and be counted. Whenever these two meet you can tell there's going to be trouble. And it can often be of an ugly kind.

Take October 2001...

The first Potteries derby game of the season was marred by trouble, with nearly a hundred arrests. The match between Vale and City ended a draw but even though there were over 200 police on duty for the Potteries Derby, there were still ugly pockets of violence both during and after the match. Fighting spilled on to the pitch after half-time and battles between rival gangs continued in Burslem town centre later in the evening. It was nothing less than expected.

The trouble started after half time when Stoke scored an equaliser. Fighting among supporters spilled on to the pitch as it became clear that some Stoke fans had managed to get tickets for the Hamil Road End where the home supporters stand. The game wasn't stopped and Chief Inspector Vaughan Betts, the officer responsible for the policing of Port Vale matches, insisted it was a case of the minority ruining the game for the majority. Where have we heard that one before?

Worse was to come later in the evening. Throughout the centre of Burslem, fighting broke out in Newcastle Street and police say that metal bars and sticks were used as weapons. Over 80 arrests were made for a number of offences; 60 of those arrested were detained for chanting racial abuse.

## Racists

Ironically, the violence took place in the week when a campaign to eradicate racism from football was being launched. Port Vale players paraded around the pitch in T-shirts

# Throughout the centre of Burslem, fighting broke out in Newcastle Street and police say that metal bars and sticks were used as weapons.

promoting the campaign before the game; the Stoke City team wore similar shirts during a game the previous week. Organisers of the campaign were naturally disgusted by the chants.

Residents living in and around Vale Park in Burslem were said to be petrified as 'fans' fought, smashing windows and overturning cars.

Superintendent Nick Howe of Staffordshire Police said a large group of trouble-makers seemed determined to march toward the multi-ethnic area of Cobridge a mile away. He said the group was arrested as a whole to prevent further disturbances. Officers had originally been brought in to ensure the protection of the near-by mosque.

He added that his officers were specifically looking into the chants of racial abuse from the fans which mentioned the BNP and National Front groups by name.

Piara Powar, National Co-ordinator of Kick It Out, football's anti-racism campaign said, *'The fact that fans are heading towards areas to deliberately stir up hatred and violence simply endorses the idea that some football supporters will become involved in creating an atmosphere and confrontations that give the game a bad name. The individuals concerned deserve to face the full force of the law.'*

**Riots**

The Cobridge area suffered earlier problems in July of this year, when 49 people were arrested in Cobridge during disturbances among Asian youth. The trouble, which came shortly after the Bradford riots, appeared to have been sparked by rumours of a march by right wing extremists.

# Fishy Business

## Scunthorpe vs Grimsby

Grimsby and Scunthorpe are the nearest teams to each other and in Scunthorpe United fans' eyes they are the biggest local rivals, followed by Doncaster Rovers and Lincoln City.

The teams haven't played each other in the league since 1989, but when it finally happens it will be an occasion similar to all the big well-known derby games.
The rivalry between the two towns goes back to when Grimsby were part of the Humberside County. As far as Scunthorpe fans are concerned, Grimsby grabbed all the south bank development money and resources, with very little going Scunthorpe's way. And it doesn't help that Grimsby somehow manage to survive by the skin of their teeth in Division One every year.
United fans call Town fans 'codheads', 'soapdodgers', 'scum' and 'dole scroungers', while Town fans call Scunny supporters 'scunts' and 'inbreds'.

### Temper, temper

Legend has it that when Brian Laws was appointed Scunthorpe manager he took a set of Grimsby cast-offs with him. But before then he was celebrated as a man who had done something against a Grimsby player that many Scunthorpe fans would have wanted to do themselves.
'Lawsey,' as his mates know him, has something of a temper on him, or at least is famously as uncompromising off the pitch as he was on it in his Nottingham Forest days. When he left Forest to become player-manager at Blundell Park, he became notorious for throwing a plate of chicken at Ivano Bonetti, his Italian striker, for not trying hard enough. The Italian's cheekbone was fractured.
According to Laws: *'Things early on went really well. The gates were up at Grimsby, we had a good Cup run and made a few bob, and sold a couple of players for well*

# United fans call Town fans 'codheads', 'soapdodgers', 'scum' and 'dole scroungers'.

over a million pounds. Things were looking rosy. I signed a new three-year contract, and got the first Italian footballer to play in the Endsleigh League, who was Ivano Bonetti. While things were going well, we had a great working relationship. The crowds were coming to look at this Italian. 'It was a great coup for us, because on the PR side Grimsby Town FC was being mentioned in the national papers, which was good for the area.

'And the incident is quite famous now. I had to take it on the chin and let the FA deal with it, and let my advisers do the rest.

'But it all left a nasty taste, and in the end, the board at Grimsby (who had been fantastic to me) felt that it was time to let me go.'

# The Wanderers

## Bolton vs Blackburn and Stoke

Bolton began life in 1874 when the boys of Christ Church Sunday School, led by their master, Thomas Ogden, formed a football club under the Christ Church name.

*'Where were you when you were shit?'* has for some time been a particular favourite among the Bolton fraternity, a cheeky jibe aimed at the new-found-jump-on-the-Jack-Walker-bandwagon fans that popped in to see Blackburn during their championship-winning tenure in the Premiership in the 1990s.

### History

The Lever End was the area behind the goals at the south part of Burnden Park, where the biggest attendance for a match with Blackburn was 65,295 during a sixth round replay win in 1929. The largest attendance ever was a staggering 69,912. The uninitiated who visited Burnden Park were at a loss as to how such a huge amount of people once got into the ground but in those days the Embankment section alone held the best part of 30,000 and the Lever End housed 20,000 standing spectators.

Historically, Burnden Park always saw its largest gates on FA Cup days. The ground's first 50,000-plus gate came in 1907 when Everton won a third round replay 3-0 before a crowd of 54,470. Burnden saw only one other crowd of such proportion: a second round FA Cup tie with Swindon in 1914.

Things moved onto a much larger plane during the 1920s. The visit of Manchester City for a second round tie in 1922 attracted 66,442 spectators, whilst 61,609 witnessed the Trotters defeat Huddersfield in 1923. But it was Blackburn who always drew the greatest animosity. As ever, the close proximity had much to do with the tension but there were deeper roots associated with the respective teams' abilities on the pitch that led to much of the antagonism.

# As the teams came out, two barriers near the corner flag collapsed.

### Tragedy

Although Blackburn provide Bolton with the most local rivalry, Burnden Park's darkest day came during the second leg of a sixth round FA Cup tie against Stoke City.

The Burnden stand was still full of food and an estimated 85,000 were on the ground for the game. Thirty minutes before kick-off there was a crush outside the ground as people tried to get into the Embankment section. It was impossible to move along the terraces and into a decent viewing position but still they pushed their way in.

It should have been obvious that a disaster was unfolding. Some of the turnstiles were shut but spectators continued to get in either by climbing over the wall or climbing over the railway line fence. Some people decided to get out of the ground and forced a lock open. Instead of easing the pressure, thousands more streamed through the gate.

As the teams came out, two barriers near the corner flag collapsed, the crowd sunk and a number of people were trampled on. Hundreds spilled out onto the trackside and incredibly the game carried on for another 12 minutes before it became obvious that spectators had been killed. The referee led the players off the pitch and people looked on unaware of the scale of the disaster they were witnessing. Eventually 33 bodies were found and laid out on the pitch whilst first aid was given to hundreds more.

Incredibly, the Chief Constable and the referee decided to restart the game after a few thousand people had been moved to the Burnden stand. The game was restarted at 3.25pm and continued without interval resulting in a goalless draw to send Bolton into the semi-finals on aggregate.

# Spaghetti Westerns Pt I

## Birmingham, 1992–96

February 1992. Blues vs Stoke. About 300 Blues fans riot when Stoke score fans invade the pitch and mass fighting forces game to be stopped. Stoke's goalie gets punched by a Blues fan, and the referee gets attacked. Outside the ground Blues fans armed with bricks, stones and bottles ambush Stoke fans. 17 are injured and more than 70 Blues fans are held by police.

May 1992. Stockport vs Blues. 30 arrests made as rival hooligans clash in the city.

September 1992. Millwall vs Blues. 250 Zulus fight with about 300 Millwall fans at London Bridge. Fans were armed with bats, bottles and guns.

September 1993. Blues vs Villa. Rival gangs clash after game. 200 Blues fans try to ambush the Villa fans, pelting them with stones and bricks. 40 arrests.

January 1994. Blues vs Kidderminster. 40 Blues fans clash with 30 Kidderminster fans by the Clements Arms pub. Bottles and wood used.

February 1994. Millwall vs Blues. 300 Blues make the trip to London. Rival fans fight in the stands. After the game, police keep over 500 fans from clashing.

May 1994. Southport vs Blues. 100 Blues fans go on the rampage fighting local youths and pelting police with bottles. 46 arrests.

April 1994. Blues vs Stoke. Around 150 Blues fans try to attack the Stoke escort by Garrison Lane. Fighting in park as Blues fans attack middle of escort.

July 1994. Friendly. Blues vs Celtic. 200 rival fans fight outside the Dubliner pub before the game, throwing bottles and bricks. After the game, rival gangs clash again throwing bricks and stones at each other, five injured, 12 arrests.

January 1995. Liverpool vs Blues. Rival fans fight with knives, bottles and bricks, before and after game, running street battles with bricks and bottles thrown, six fans stabbed, and 30 Blues fans arrested.

April 1995. Blues vs Cardiff. Hundreds of rival fans clash in pitch battles with bricks and slabs thrown. Seats are ripped out in ground by Cardiff fans, 12 arrests.

April 1995. Auto Windscreen Final. Blues vs Carlisle. Zulu's plan a mass fight with Carlisle in Southend, a number of pubs are damaged in fighting with bottles and glasses thrown, a pub is wrecked in Paddington Station by Blues fans.

September 1995. West Brom vs Blues. Police are attacked in streets by rioting Blues fans with bricks and stones, 16 fans arrested.

November 1995. Blues vs Millwall. About 500 Zulus run riot attacking Millwall fans and the police. Six police injured, seven arrests.

April 1996. Millwall vs Blues. Police stop over 100 Zulus at Euston station and send them back to Birmingham.

September 1996. Man City vs Blues. More than 100 seats are ripped out and thrown at police and Man City fans, police are attacked, more clashes outside, eight arrests.

# Spaghetti Westerns Pt II

## Birmingham, 1996–2000

February 1997. Blues vs Wrexham. Missiles thrown by Blues fans hit the linesman.

May 1997. Ipswich vs Blues. 16 Blues fans arrested in Great Yarmouth after pelting police with bottles and bricks.

July 1997. Friendly. Blues vs Villa. Bar St Martin is wrecked as fans clash before game. More clashes as Blues fans hunt down Villa fans. Blues fans go on rampage at The Square Peg pub, 28 arrests.

February 1998. Leeds vs Blues. Fans clash outside ground throwing bricks at each other, 15 arrests.

March 1998. Blues vs Notts Forest. 200 rival fans clash at the Marlborough pub armed with clubs, bottles and glasses. Four injured. 100 more fans clash after game.

April 1998. Portsmouth vs Blues. 60 Blues fans clash with Portsmouth fans in the street after the game.

September 1998. Norwich vs Blues. 20 Blues fans attack pub full of Norwich fans. CS gas is used and barstools are thrown.

October 1998. Blues vs Huddersfield. The team coach of Huddersfield is pelted with missiles and damaged.

February 1999. Crystal Palace vs Blues. Rival Blues and Palace fans clash in the Camel pub in London. Chairs, tables and bottles thrown causing £7,000-worth of damage.

March 1999. Huddersfield vs Blues. Serious disorder before and after the game with rival fans fighting running battles.

April 1999. Blues vs Wolves. 200 Blues fans attack Wolves fans and police outside the ground, 17 fans arrested.

May 1999. Police raid homes of four Blues fans for violence against Wolves fans and police after trouble in April.

July 1999. Friendly. Blues vs Leeds. Blues fans damage Leeds players' coach.

August 1999. Blues vs Fulham. Blues fans pelt Fulham coaches with bricks and stones

September 1999. West Brom vs Blues. 100 rival fans clash before game in local pub. After the game 200 Blues fans try to attack West Brom fans. Two policemen injured.

April 2000. Blues vs Wolves. 100 rival fans clash armed with bricks, bottles, clubs and petrol bombs. After the game, Blues fans pelt Wolves fans with bricks. 17 Wolves fans are injured in the fighting.

May 2000. Blues vs Barnsley. Stone-throwing Blues fans ambush Barnsley coaches.

January 2000. 70 Blues fans clash with Wolves firm who got the train to Birmingham. Blues fans come out of the Bar St Martin throwing bottles and chairs.

November 2000. Blues fan jailed for five years for attacking Wolves' fan with a house brick during mass rioting between rival hooligans.

# Middlesbrough vs Blackburn

## 16 February 2002

The referee had a nightmare. It's that simple. Graham Barber got it completely wrong on most decisions and Graeme Souness in particular had every right to feel aggrieved.

Ugo Ehiogu headed Boro into the lead three minutes from time shortly after Blackburn had had Lucas Neill sent off for a professional foul. Ehiogu's late winner sent Middlesbrough into the FA Cup quarter-finals with a 1-0 win but this was a dour battle of wills that ended in frustration and controversy.

Souness fielded four natural centre-backs along his backline and the stand-in full-backs, Martin Taylor and Nils-Eric Johansson, never advanced down the flanks. As a result, Rovers were always struggling to find any width.

Noel Whelan had the first glimpse of a chance when Dean Windass lobbed a pass over the Rovers defence. Whelan was unable to take the ball in his stride and Taylor came across to shut out the danger.

It was 29 minutes before either side managed a shot on target, and Robbie Stockdale had to manufacture the chance for himself. He skipped inside one lunge and struck a powerful drive from 20 yards but it was at the perfect height for Brad Friedel, and straight at the keeper, too.

### Thrust

Boro boss Steve McClaren thrust two new strikers into the fray for the second half as Slovakian Szilard Nemeth and Alain Boksic came on for Mark Wilson and Dean Windass. You got the feeling that Boro wanted this more than Rovers.

The move almost worked out straight away when Nemeth burst past Johansson on the right and only Friedel's alert dive to cut out the cross prevented the home side scoring. Blackburn looked like they could do with a change up front, too. Souness was seething at

# Souness exploded and the disciplinary panel was getting ready for another meeting with the fiery Scotsman.

the way his side struggled to come to terms with Boro and when Cole's flick set Duff racing away he chose the wrong option, trying to pass to Keith Gillespie rather than go himself, with Southgate intercepting.

Souness finally made his move, bringing on Matt Jansen for Duff and the left-footer immediately made contact with a Craig Hignett's free-kick, but his flicked header sailed wide of the far post.

## Off

Then came a moment of controversy when referee Barber sent off Neill for a professional foul on Stockdale. The ref was convinced that Neill made contact with the Boro player outside the area, but Rovers protested vehemently he was not the last man. Souness exploded and the disciplinary panel was getting ready for another meeting with the fiery Scotsman.

At least the sending off roused the crowd. Boro scented victory. Nemeth powered a shot from a difficult angle into Friedel's stomach, before Robbie Mustoe volleyed into the crowd from eight yards out.

Three minutes before the final whistle, Boro seized their chance from a free-kick, awarded against Jansen for handball and then advanced 10 yards when he protested. Gareth Southgate floated the ball in and his fellow centre-back Ehiogu powered a header downwards and into the net.

There'd be no need for a replay.

# Chelsea vs Leeds

## 19 December 1999

The referee was appalling as the entire Leeds team and Frank Leboeuf did their best to make this an afternoon of shame. The referee never seemed to have much control on a match that everyone knew would be a bad tempered one. The Leeds team spent most of the match collapsing in a comedy pile on the floor every time a tackle came in. Leboeuf did his bit for the Chelsea cause by getting sent off when the back four had already been reduced to two by injury. Yes, it was that sort of game.

Quite what Harry Kewell did to warrant the French defender stamping on him is debatable, but Leboeuf had plenty of time to think about it on the long walk back to the changing room. Leeds did a good job of following O'Leary's instructions, which was clear: do anything you can to get Chelsea's players booked or sent off. Chelsea get no marks for failing to ignore the blatant cheating, and should have known better. Luca Vialli got the Chelsea fans scratching their heads when he said after the game that Leeds had the look of champions. They played like bruisers and would have done well in a bar brawl but champions? Come on, the game hasn't sunk that low has it?

### Controversy

Where do you start? How about when Lee Bowyer refused to put the ball into touch when Marcel Desailly was lying in agony from a dislocated shoulder? That was a nice touch from the Leeds boys and Chelsea were clearly going to stick the boot in to remind them about it later. With at least half the Chelsea crowd showing their true colours by wandering off for some shopping just when the team needed their support the farce was unfolding in front of a quiet stadium. Five minutes after Leeds' second goal the ground was half empty.

For the first 70 minutes, Chelsea ran the game and made Leeds look like a mediocre team of professional moaners and groaners. The turning point was the Frenchman's silly sending off. Chelsea were already shaken after first Marcel Desailly (dislocated shoulder), then his replacement, Jes Hogh (pulled hamstring), were taken off and from a team featuring a back four that were easily holding off the Leeds attack, they went to a team with a hastily-reconfigured back three featuring a recognized defender on the right (Ferrer), a £10m striker (Sutton) in the centre, and a youth team winger on the left (Jon Harley), who had never played in defence before. It didn't take much to realize that Chelsea were about to understand the true meaning of a struggle.

### Blind

Leeds raised their game and started thinking about scoring. It was as if they felt they had achieved the first phase of the game plan by reducing the opposition quota of players, now had a whimsical punt at goal that unbelievably slipped into the net. The scene was set.

The referee played his part by constantly awarding Leeds free kicks. It was getting quite interesting to see how myopic the officials could get. Chelsea mustered some resistance but Leeds just dropped back deep and flooded their penalty area with diving players. It was like watching a beginner's class on Streatham Ice Rink. An undeserved soft goal from a free kick led to further defections among Chelsea supporters' ranks but by then it was clear that with one man down and a ref who appeared to favour his puddings from Yorkshire the battle would be fruitless and the pain somewhat excruciating.

# The referee played his part by constantly awarding Leeds free kicks.

# The Ball

**Like everything else, the Chinese invented the first ball, made of leather filled with lashings of hemp. The Egyptians bundled together straw and wrapped it tightly in coloured cloth. The Greeks and the Romans used an inflated ox bladder covered with roughly sewn cowhide. Stories of soldiers using victims' heads remain extremely dubious.**

Europeans developed the idea of filling a ball with horsehair while the conquerors of America went one better with the development of latex, discovering a rubber ball could bounce far higher than its low tech predecessors. Reports tell how Hernan Cortes bounced a Mexican ball high into the air before the disbelieving eyes of Emperor Charles.

- Before the invention of the lace-free ball in the 1930s players would cut open their heads when they headed the ball. The stitching on the balls invented by Charles Goodyear stuck out and was course and hard.

- It wasn't until the 1950s that the ball's colour changed from its brown hue. On rainy days the ball was so heavy it wouldn't budge in the mud. A player literally risked his neck going up for a header. Indeed, Billy McPhail, who played for Celtic in the 1950s, claimed in court a few years ago that his pre-senile dementia was caused by repeatedly heading sodden, old-style leather footballs.
The first completely non-leather ball appeared in the 1960s. But FIFA preferred leather, albeit with a fully waterproof coating for World Cups until Mexico 1986, when the synthetic Adidas Azteca was used.

# Before the invention of the lace-free ball in the 1930s, players would cut open their heads when they headed the ball.

- The Adidas Fevernova used in the 2002 World is more accurate and faster than any other previous World Cup ball. Hand-stitched in Morocco, the ball is made of syntactic foam which consists of equal sized, highly elastic, exceptionally resistant gas-filled microcells. As a result, it can convert the applied energy evenly at every point and give the ball additional damping properties at the same time. This, in turn, makes for more effective play and a more precise, calculable flight of the ball.

- The syntactic foam is embedded in a composite consisting of several polyurethane layers, applied to a woven fabric. The outer layer of the ball is made of a particularly abrasion-resistant variant of Impranil polyurethane so that the ball can withstand exceptionally tough treatment.

# Manchester Utd vs Arsenal

## 8 May 2002

On a night of storming battles, hard tackles and tough talk, Manchester Utd surrendered their title crown to Arsenal, but not without a fight. This was the mother of storms and cups. It took Sir Alex Ferguson 10 years to secure a second domestic Double with Manchester United so you can imagine the glee on the Gunners' faces when Arsene Wenger's boys did the same feat in six.

It was a poor season for the Red Army that left them without a trophy for the first time in four years. Fergie must have turned the air blue.

A 57th minute goal from Sylvain Wiltord transformed this previously impenetrable fortress into Wenger's theatre of dreams. The sight of Kanu leaping over the Frenchman in celebration capped an outstanding moment as the crowd looked on at a team head and shoulders above the rest. It was a perfect way to finish an almost perfect campaign that not even Ferguson could argue saw them emerge as the finest team in the country. In completing one Double they celebrated another, having already beaten United at Highbury.

Arsenal also became the first team in more than a century to end a season without losing a game on their domestic travels, which in itself is some achievement.

### Climax

The game started at pace, Wiltord meeting a Ray Parlour cross with a first-time shot that took a slight deflection off Phil Neville and whistled wide of Fabien Barthez's post. United responded immediately, Paul Scholes sending a powerful drive just over the Arsenal crossbar before a Veron cross caused some concern.

It was exciting stuff, and with the atmosphere already charged by an overwhelming sense of dread, Paul Scholes turned up the temperature when he caught Edu with a nasty challenge from behind.

# It was a poor season for the Red Army that left them without a trophy for the first time in four years.

Arsenal players rushed angrily towards the United midfielder, referee Paul Durkin raced to the scene, and a furious Ferguson made his way along the touchline in obvious protest, going so far as to shove the fourth official, Jeff Winter, in the chest.

Durkin allowed Scholes a second chance by showing only a yellow card, and he then stopped short of dismissing Neville and Keane for their respective fouls on Wiltord and Patrick Vieira.

As usual Keane could consider himself rather fortunate, having nearly caught his great rival in the groin with his studs. It was somewhat disappointing to see United resort to such heavy-handed tactics. As a football team, they usually set the standard.

## Brave

A Veron free-kick was blocked by the brave head of Vieira shortly before the break, while a second attempt was driven into Arsenal's defensive wall. It was a cameo of his disappointing season.

Arsenal finally struck when a mistake from Mikael Silvestre lost possession and allowed the visitors to launch an attack. The ball eventually fell to Freddie Ljungberg on the right and, when he muscled his way past Laurent Blanc and his shot was turned into the path of Wiltord by Barthez, the French international striker drove the ball home.

Ferguson immediately withdrew Veron and sent on Van Nistelrooy, but it was to no avail. United were trapped in their worst nightmare.

# Sheffield United vs West Brom

## 16 March 2002 (match abandoned after 81 minutes)

The most contentious game in the football year took place against a backdrop of ill-feeling and tension. For the Albion supporters it was too incredible to be true. The question going round the ground was simple: how many players do you need to fulfil a fixture?

As the teams were read out at the start of the game, the mention of Andy Johnson's name caused a huge boo from the Blades' fans. Who could forget the shocking challenge from last year against Georges Santos that broke his' cheek bone and seriously damaged his eye? At that time there were threats of legal reprisals, but nothing seemed to happen. The Sheffield United fans hadn't forgotten though, and they weren't the only ones.

The game started fairly ordinarily – lots of rough and tumble and not a lot of football. Dour to watch in fact. But things livened up after eight minutes when former Man City skipper, Keith Curle, allowed Scott Dobie to get a clear run at the Blades' box. Keeper Tracey raced out to try and get there, but the pacey Dobie was first to it, lobbed the ball goalwards only for Tracey to stop it with his hands. Unfortunately for Tracey it was well outside his area – no choice for the ref but to send him off.

With Ndlovu off for a sub keeper, United opted to try a three-at-the-back approach and keep some attacking shape elsewhere. You had to admire them, at least they were still interested in playing at this stage. It took Albion 10 minutes to test them out.

### Off

By the second half, Albion were one up and then one of the Blades' fans came over to the Albion section and nicked a flag. Skirmishes were about to start on the pitch, too. After a second goal for the Albion, United manager Warnock made a double substitution. On came Santos and Suffo. It only took about 30 seconds for Santos to see his chance to remind Johnson of their previous meeting. Up they both went for a 50-50 ball. Santos got some of his foot to it but most of the challenge was aimed at Johnson who was quickly writhing in agony. The ref saw the intent and immediately red-carded Santos.

A scrap broke out in the centre of the pitch with United players seeming intent on having a word with the spread-eagled Johnson. McInnes stood in the way and Suffo gave him a headbutt for his trouble. Another red card. After a third goal, United's Brown trudged off the field and down the tunnel and with no subs left Blades were reduced to seven men. Then Ullathorne was down in his own box, and eventually, despite treatment, unable to continue. Now the question going round the ground was answered. With only six United players on the pitch there was an automatic match abandonment. And so it finished. 81 minutes gone and Albion fans confused as to whether they'd won or not.

### Hernia

Post match Warnock said Brown couldn't continue as he'd been carrying a hernia injury for a few weeks and he'd want him fit for Tuesday. Ullathorne too was injured. Had it been 11 against 11 and all subs used, would Warnock have taken two players out of the game leaving his side down to nine men? Had anyone ever seen this happen? On the radio phone-ins the jocks were struggling to understand how a manager could send out a team full of half-fit players but there you go, Warnock was standing by his decisions and the Albion would have to wait and see if they'd won the game or God forbid, go through the whole thing again in a replay. For once, some sensible person at headquarters decided that would not be necessary.

# The ref saw the intent and immediately red-carded Santos.

# Root Canals

## Man Utd vs Liverpool

Two charismatic Scots, Sir Matt Busby and Bill Shankly, created the foundations for these two clubs to dominate much of the football played in England since 1950. The former's first great side, the ultimately tragic Busby Babes, was followed in the 1960s by the Best-Law-Charlton vintage which finally won the European Cup in 1968. Shankly's Liverpool side first came to prominence in the 1960s. Into the 1970s and 1980s, the men from Anfield became the most successful British club side ever.

As a result, the rivalry between the two sides and their supporters has become intense and at times too fierce, slipping over the line from passion into violence. As the Liverpool sides of the 1970s and 1980s piled up trophy after trophy while United experienced barren years, the latter's fans built up years' worth of bitterness. Now, as United under stewardship of Sir Alex Ferguson experience the kind of dominance once held by their Merseyside rivals, their supporters rule the roost.

### Matt and Bill

Busby and Shankly, names carved in the folklore of British football, shared a common bond in an understanding of what it means to go hungry.

Both men were born into a culture of hard work and struggle, Busby in 1909 in the village of Orbiston near Bellshill, Shankly four years later at Glenbuck, barely a mile from the border of Ayrshire and Lanarkshire. Both made their mark in football management after beginning life down a coal mine. Both had to be the principle breadwinner in the house following the deaths of their respective soldier fathers during World War I.

Denis Law, who played under Shankly at Huddersfield Town and Busby at Old Trafford, said: *'Shanks was the extrovert but Matt was not flamboyant like Bill. But he was always in charge. There were people outside the club who might have thought that he was soft because he was quietly spoken or gentle-mannered but his players knew better than to try to cross him.'*

The Liverpool board directors didn't know how to handle Shanks, but his outspoken, often highly contentious views made him a god with the supporters on the Kop. On the other hand, Sir Matt was invited onto the Old Trafford board after he finally stepped down as manager in 1969. For Shankly there were to be no such honour.

But Shankly's presence is indelibly stamped on Liverpool, just as the spirit of Sir Matt presides over Manchester United in a new age of achievement by a club that rose from the dead.

# As the Liverpool sides of the 1970s and 1980s piled up trophy after trophy while United experienced barren years, the latter's fans built up years' worth of bitterness.

# Bury the Grudge

## Manchester Utd and Munich

The Pennines have seen plenty of rivalry between Lancashire and Yorkshire and the northern cities of Manchester and Leeds have shared more than a few moments of biting inhospitality since the Leeds players started swapping shirts – Cantona, McQueen, Jordan.

Then there was Leeds pipping United to the title in 1992 as well Leeds fans taunting United over the Munich air crash. This poignant article was posted on a website by a Manchester City fan and wonderfully articulates the issue of grudges using Manchester United and the Munich air disaster:

' *"Munich"* – where did it come from? Suddenly, more than 30 years after the disaster, someone comes up with the idea of referring to United fans as *"Munichs"*, and it catches on to such an extent that in long-established songs (including such good-taste lines as *"surrender or you'll die"*) City fans start using *"Munich fan"* for *"United fan"*.

'Now I personally find it distasteful, and I don't go along with the idea that MUFC plc have cynically exploited the disaster and that that justifies it. You couldn't have something like that happen without marking it by memorials and occasional references. Though whether the victims' families have always felt the memorials were appropriate – and adequate – is another matter.

'Yet it would be folly to pretend that disasters are sacrosanct; never the subject of humour. Most disasters are swiftly followed by macabre jokes, some even funny, though those who have been bereaved are less likely to see the joke, just as jokes about drink-driving fall flat if told to someone whose relative has been killed by a drunk driver. And football fans are not noted for their readiness to refrain from cruelty. Arsenal fans happily turned the death of six million Jews into an occasion to get at Spurs. United fans have in recent times had songs about Hillsborough to sing at Liverpool, and about Turkish fans to sing at Leeds.

# 'Arsenal fans happily turned the death of six million Jews into an occasion to get at Spurs.'

## The runway song

'The "runway song" has been around a long time. This is a cruel world. Giving offence is part of terrace culture, and winding up the opposition is part of the game. Some people find sick humour appealing, and the boundaries have been pushed so far that no-one even uses the term "sick joke" any more.

In a similar way, the Munich reference has already lost its power to shock. It is hardly even a reference to a disaster anymore, which is why it is pointless to point out that an ex-City player was among the dead. Obviously the club was right to apologise for letting it slip into the programme. It is offensive and inappropriate in an official club forum. But it is hard to class it as the height of bad taste, not given the depths to which humour has sunk on television.

## Funny?

'Can we actually make a mental distinction between honouring those players, crew and journalists who died at Munich and the use of the word as a term of abuse? If using the word is intended to be disrespectful to their memory, it is appalling. There are things that should transcend rivalry. If you hate Man United, clap your hands. But remember Roger Byrne, Tommy Taylor, Billy Whelan, Jeff Bent, Mark Jones, Eddie Colman, David Pegg, Duncan Edwards, Frank Swift and the others who died.'

# Judas

## Paul Ince, West Ham and Manchester Utd

No one could believe it when the by now former West Ham midfield starlet grinned out of the pages of the nation's newspapers wearing a Manchester United shirt. He had been a darling of the terraces at Upton Park and many had thought of him as a future England captain. But here he was: Paul Ince, a United player before the money had even changed hands. Ince enraged Hammers fans when he posed for a picture wearing a Manchester United shirt before he had officially left for Old Trafford following West Ham manager John Lyall's departure in 1989.

### Apology

Despite apologising in *Hammers News* eight years later and claiming that he was wrongly advised over the shirt incident, Ince had by then become Upton Park's most hated figure, loathed by Hammers fans for committing what they considered the ultimate act of betrayal. Booed and barracked whenever he has returned to play in the colours of United, Liverpool or Middlesbrough, Ince is unlikely to ever be forgiven for his actions. During one particular game between Liverpool and West Ham years later, Ince was barracked mercilessly from first kick to last by the West Ham fans.

*'Some of the things were a bit nasty but Paul has got broad shoulders and I didn't think it was too bad,'* said his manager, Roy Evans. *'Paul took some stick but he knew he was going to get it. It's the first time he's been back here for a while I've seen worse and I'm sure Paul's had worse than that.'*

This report from the match summed up the atmosphere: 'At the outset, with Liverpool stroking the ball about casually, the home fans had seemed more interested in abusing Ince than anything taking place on the park. Eight years might be a long time, but the grudges are deep in this corner of east London, and Ince bore the brunt.

'"Judas", "Stand up if you hate Paul Ince" and "You're scum and you know you are" hardly made for a warm welcome, nor did an unpunished tackle from behind from Iain Dowie. But Ince would not have minded running the gauntlet of hate if his side had taken advantage of their early dominance.'

# Eight years might be a long time, but the grudges are deep in this corner of east London, and Ince bore the brunt.

# Yorkshire Terriers

## Scarborough vs York

Scarborough Football Club was formed in 1879 when members and friends of the town's cricket team wanted an activity to occupy themselves during the winter months. Indeed, the club was called Scarborough Cricketers Football Club until 1884 and played its home games on the club's cricket ground.

York City Football and Athletic Club Limited were formed on 31 March 1922 to play in the Midland League. They bought a piece of land on Heslington Lane on which they intended to build their Fulford Gate ground.

Scarborough turned professional in 1926 and by 1969 were one of four Midland League sides admitted to the new Northern Premier League. After early jitters, Boro quickly established themselves as one of the top sides in the division. During the 1970s, the club never finished outside of the top five and won several county cups and floodlight league titles. They achieved promotion to the Football League in 1987 after winning the Alliance Premier League.

But success on the pitch was not emulated financially, due to full time professionalism. Leeds businessman Geoffrey Richmond, who secured ground sponsorship with the frozen food company McCain, saved the club from extinction.

Scarborough went on to make the Third Division play-offs in 1998 but, after a disastrous campaign under new chairman Anton Johnson, could not prevent relegation to the Conference the following season. A now famous last minute equaliser by Carlisle United goalkeeper Jimmy Glass sent the Yorkshiremen down.

Whilst York City had their own problems it was nothing compared to the struggles going on up the road. A season of consolidation followed for Boro as their first season in the Conference brought a mid-table finish. However, hopes of a return to the Football League the following season soon disappeared after a disastrous start to the 2001-02 campaign

# Leeds businessman Geoffrey Richmond, who secured ground sponsorship with the frozen food company McCain, saved the club from extinction.

which saw the club win only two of the first 19 fixtures, leaving the *'Seadogs'* at the foot of the table.

### Thinking

There are numerous Boro and York City websites dedicated to the rites passage that require a fan to slag off another. But under the banner *'Comments you're not likely to hear at the McCain Stadium'*, the following thoughts sum up the attitudes in the stands: *'I do admire the type of football York play', 'Use your height Worrall', 'Use your pace Robbo', 'The referee's having a good game', 'I wish we still had Trebble', 'Wasn't it a shame to see Johnson go', 'Oh good we've got a corner – that means we might score', 'It looks like it's a big crowd today, well over 3000', 'Scarborough's kick-off leads to another goal', 'Brodie scores from five yards', 'Hoyland's keeping up with Rod Thomas all the way', 'Well played Bullimore', 'The Shed toilets are clean', 'Aren't stewards nice', 'Not many Man Utd fans', 'Tony Parks looks his age', 'The East Stand's in good voice today', 'I see Robbo's on a diet', 'Saville scores', 'Today's Boro man-of-the-match – number two, John Kay', 'Another three points for the Boro', 'That's Robbo's 20th of the season', 'Brodie from 20 yards', 'It's crowded in here – move up a bit', 'This Boro song's good'.*

# Ego Maniacs

## Cardiff vs Swansea

Nothing enrages a grudge like a local skirmish. When the Welsh FA announced it was going to start up a proper cup competition in 2002, fans of the two principle Welsh footballing sides rubbed their hands together and thought, excellent, now how are we going to get through this one? Would it give Wales an end of season showpiece as the administrators hoped or would it be a nightmare for the police and a great day out for the hooligans of each side?

Cardiff City chairman Sam Hammam and all at Cardiff City stressed they wanted a hassle free fixture. That was before the press started running scare stories. What had been regarded as an opportunity for Welsh journalists to build a few bridges and establish some goodwill between the clubs turned into the complete opposite. According to Keith Haynes from Swansea website JackArmy, *'Neither set of fans are the closest and never will be, but like many football fans I know, a lot of proper Swansea City fans have been friendly with proper Cardiff City fans for years. No malice at all, just the usual digs when we get a result against each other. You know ringing them up at 3am and shouting 1-0 LIVE ON SKY! Just a laugh.'*

The essence of previous encounters hasn't been so much about keeping up with the Jones's, as murdering them. Among the fans, violence is not only possible, it's compulsory. It's one of the game's last bastions of regular crowd trouble. They say it's all John Toshack's fault. If he hadn't rejuvenated Swansea in the late seventies, the cream of South Wales football would never have met on the same pitch. Cardiff were always a division or two above, but suddenly they were on a par and Swansea were getting the plaudits. The fact that Toshack was a Cardiff boy just added further insult.

## Songs

Songs range from Cardiff shouting 'Jack bastards' to the Swansea contingent breaking into a rendition of 'Swimaway, a-swimaway' accompanied by breaststroke motions. This is a reference to some Cardiff faithful pitching into the sea one year to escape their Swansea pursuers.

## Chaos

Emotions boiled over when the two sides met in the FA Cup first round in 1991. Swansea won the match 2-1 and chaos broke out. Supporters showered each other with bricks, stones and metal from a nearby building site and Swansea city centre resembled a Brighton seafront battle from the film *Quadrophenia*. Swansea fans took revenge at Ninian Park two years later, just before Christmas. A pitch invasion delayed the start by 40 minutes, and having beaten Swansea 1-0 in the League, they ripped up seats and wood from the stand and went on the rampage. Front page headlines like 'Season of Hatred' and 'Night of Defeat and Destruction' said it all.

For the next four years, visiting supporters were banned from the match at either venue. They were allowed back in the late nineties but team mascots, Barclay the Bluebird and Cyril the Swan, were banned in case they inflamed the situation.

# Swansea city centre resembled a Brighton seafront battle from the film *Quadrophenia*.

# The Referee

**He is the man in black, the person dressed for mourning and the official we all think is crap and unfit for high office. But how many of us would answer this calling?**

Since the late 1800s, the referee has been the one to step onto the field of play, haul his considerable weight about the pitch and keep some semblance of public order.
A referee needs to be a person moulded from the toughest fibres, aware of mistimed tackles, oblivious to the baying spectators and without fear of the assessor in the stand awarding the visually impaired referee marks out of ten.

- No one runs about the park more than the referee. No one sweats over a decision or chases the play more than the man for whom the outcome of each match is meaningless. He is the only person involved in the game who cares neither if he wins nor loses. The merest suspicion that he has a favourite can jeopardize his standing and undermine his authority.

- In order to be a referee you must wear a shirt, shorts, socks, shinguards and footwear. Shinguards should be covered by the socks, made of a suitable material such as Kevlar, and must provide a reasonable degree of protection. It's become that sort of a game.

# Remember that coloured cards and your finger should never be waved admonishingly under a player's nose.

- In order to officiate you focus fully on the game. Acquaint yourself with every rule no matter how trivial. Learn man-management skills and pray you have the patience of a saint.

- Don't just look smart, look immaculate, both on and off the field of play. Arrive early and be seen to inspect the pitch. Shake hands firmly with the captains. Make your whistle project your personality, indicating by its varying intensity your ability to discriminate between the petty infringement and the cynical. Never treat players in a manner that would offend you if you were in their position. Speak to players firmly and fearlessly yet with a measure of politeness. Remember that coloured cards and your finger should never be waved admonishingly under a player's nose. Be aware that a questionable decision from five or six yards is more likely to be accepted than a perfectly good one from 50 or 60 yards. If out of position when giving a decision, carry on running towards the incident. Smile often – it helps to calm down an annoyed player. Remember that trouble arises more often when the ball is dead, so keep the game flowing when possible. And finally… be enthusiastic. Enthusiasm is infectious. If the referee appears to be enjoying the game, it is likely the players will enjoy it also – without giving the man in the middle too much trouble along the way.

# Welsh Rarebeats

## Chester City vs Wrexham

Chester lies only 11 miles from Wrexham town centre, although for the bitter rivalry, it might as well be one mile. The Wrexham versus Chester City fixture has gained a reputation of notoriety, and has managed to continue since the dark days when soccer hooliganism was at its peak.

Recent encounters have been subject to restrictions by the local police force, forcing all-ticket and early kick-off regulations which have adversely affected attendances but not the trouble.

The two teams last met in an FA Cup tie in 1997 at Chester, where it was reported that over 100 people on each side engaged in a mass brawl in the city centre. Natives reckon the local usual media frenzy before such games has hardly helped matters. But there is no doubt that this derby game has particularly more needle than others, as the Wales versus England issue runs through the thick of it. Wrexham and Chester supporters may work together cheek by jowl during the week, but divisions run deep, sometimes spilling onto the streets of Chester on a Saturday night. Derby games are sorely missed these days thanks to Chester City's freefall from the Football League into the Conference.

The more charitable Wrexham supporters will acknowledge that Chester City have fallen on hard times of late. The sale of their Sealand Road ground in 1990 by supermarket chain Morrisons signalled the start of their misery. The team was forced to play its home games at Macclesfield's Moss Rose ground, creating an 80-mile trip for the supporters.

## Relegation

Chester returned to the Roman city two years later to a new stadium situated on the old Bumpers Lane refuse tip. Although only a short distance from the old ground, the Deva Stadium with its paltry capacity of 6,000 captivated neither the imagination nor support of the public, and relegation christened the new ground.

# Ratcliffe annoyed many City supporters after admitting his side was useless in every department.

In 1994, Graham Barrow led Chester back to Division Two, and another local derby match became a mouth-watering prospect for both sets of fans.

Chester collapsed in 1995 under the auspices of Kevin Ratcliffe. The Deva staged a humiliating defeat at the hands of Wrexham in a live televised FA Cup third round game. Ratcliffe annoyed many City supporters after admitting his side was useless in every department. The ex-Wales international managed to take the club to the play-offs in 1997 and was also in charge during the traumatic 1998-99 season when the club almost folded due to financial problems. Ratcliffe in fact bailed the club out of trouble by paying an outstanding water rates bill.

### Wacky

In July 1999, the weird and wacky world of American tycoon Terry Smith came to Chester. He bought the club and invited ridicule by installing himself as team manager despite his complete lack of experience. Things were so bad, some Wrexham fans actually felt sorry for City.

Chester City fans now felt that their club was dying and began picketing the Deva Stadium in an attempt to force Smith to leave the club. A coffin was carried and delivered to Terry Smith and fan called George Rogers stood in the general election. It was during a picket that a few fans caught a glimpse of the club's wacky owner kicking the Variety Trophy around his office. It seemed that Terry Smith had had enough.

# So Near and Yet...

## Chesterfield and Middlesbrough

It was the kind of decision on which success and failure teeters precariously. Controversial referee David Elleray managed to bungle the decision that turned the course of the game when he disallowed Chesterfield's Jon Howard a goal that would surely have sent Second Division Chesterfield to Wembley.

It was April 1997. John Duncan's battlers, 2-1 up against 10-man Middlesbrough and desperately resisting the Brazilian genius Juninho's best efforts to turn a classic FA Cup semi-final around, looked set to make history when Howard sent his close-range shot cannoning down off an Old Trafford crossbar and at least a yard over the goal line. The Chesterfield supporters threw their arms into the air, believing that finally they were going into the big time with an improbable FA Cup final against the mighty Chelsea. With his assistant signalling for a goal to be awaded, Elleray unbelievably awarded Middlesbrough a free-kick for an infringement. But no one in the ground could work out why.

Bryan Robson's men then came back into the match, first equalizing to take the match into extra time, and then taking the lead. But the last laugh of the afternoon belonged to Jamie Hewitt who looped a last-gasp headed equaliser that took the tie to a replay at Hillsborough.

### Blame

Harrow schoolmaster Elleray insisted afterwards: *'I wasn't sure whether the linesman was indicating the ball had crossed the goal line or whether he had spotted the same offence as me.'*

# The Chesterfield supporters threw their arms into the air.

*'But it makes no difference whether the ball crossed the line or not. I saw an offence before the Chesterfield player shot against the crossbar and that's why I whistled.'*

*'It wasn't offside. I saw an offence, although I can't exactly remember what it was. In fact, there were eight or nine infringements I could have blown for before the player shot.'*

Television replays failed to spot any infringement, whilst Elleray certainly did not blow before Howard, who was clearly onside, fired in his effort.

## Defeat

Chesterfield's sinned-against striker Jon Howard refused to condemn the referee – which is more than can be said for the fans.

Howard said: *'Even I didn't think it went in, and I was in a perfect position to see. Of course it would be disappointing if television pictures proved otherwise, but it all happened in the blink of an eye and it's just one of those things that happens in football. I definitely didn't hear the whistle until well after I had shot, so for him to say it was for a foul before the ball hit the crossbar is a bit of a mystery to me.*

Spireites boss John Duncan said: *'Nobody knew in the middle of the game whether it should have counted or not, but it was never 3-1 because the goal wasn't given.*

*'I won't make a big thing of it as a referee must be sure before he can give a goal.*

Elleray said: *'I think after a game like that all the talk should be about the football, not the refereeing. It was one of the most sensational matches I have been involved in in 30 years of refereeing.'*

# Tees a Crowd

## Hartlepool vs Darlington

Hartlepool have spent all of their history in the two lower divisions of the Football League. The professional team was formed in 1908 as the Hartlepools United Football Athletic Company Limited – a long name for such a small outfit.

In 1916, the club's Victoria Park ground was bombed by a German Zeppelin, destroying the main stand. Despite this setback, the team managed to qualify for the new northern section of the Football League in 1921 and won their first league game away to Wrexham. Now, just when you thought Chelsea had the monopoly on signing players with long and unpronounceable names that you've never heard of, picture this: Hartlepool signed the Egyptian Tewfik Abdallah from Derby County in 1923. He became the first non-European to play for the club. No kidding.

Not much changed in this part of the world for the next 20 years until a narrow defeat in 1957 during a third round FA Cup tie against Manchester United's Busby Babes. The fact that a defeat could be celebrated pretty much summed up the level of achievement at the club and things didn't really get going until Brian Clough was appointed as manager in 1965. Legend has it that he visited every pub and club in the town to raise funds for the club.

Darlington have always been a quiet an unpretentious outfit. Never likely to challenge for anything other than a footnote in the end of season round-ups, their struggles have been internal, principally about money and ownership of the club. All of which has provided their local rivals with ammunition to sling back at them. As far back as 1884 (the year after their formation), they lost a Durham Senior Cup tie replay against arch rivals Sunderland, but had the match replayed as the ref had been *intimidated* by the Mackems players. The following year Darlington went and won the thing.

# In 1916, the club's Victoria Park ground was bombed by a German Zeppelin.

### Troublemakers?

Darlington are a team often overshadowed by their three illustrious neighbours: Newcastle, Middlesborough and Sunderland. On the whole, Darlington fans – like the majority of people from the North East – are all pretty friendly, and passionate about their football. However, they have a small but very game squad calling themselves the Bank Top 200, some of whom apparently fight for Middlesborough as well.

In the last derby to be played at Feethams, over 2,000 travelling supporters came to see Hartlepool create chance after chance in the opening period. But Darlington hit back and, typically, Ian Clark notched for the Quakers against the club he had previously played for.

A fan on a Darlington website asked: *'Does anyone feel, like me, that the Tin Shed concentrates too much on anti-Hartlepool songs rather then pro-Darlington?*

*'They obviously don't think about whether this will actually motivate the Darlington players, as I for one would not get the extra spur from this. I would feel a lot more pride from giving our team support than slagging off other teams (though the odd anti-other team FC song would always goes down well).'*

# Penalty Kicks Off

## Leicester vs Chelsea

29 January 2000 and Leicester were again on the receiving end of a poor refereeing decision in an important FA Cup match at Stamford Bridge where Chelsea emerged winners in an ill-tempered battle.

Goals either side of half-time from Gus Poyet and George Weah gave the Londoners a comfortable lead when, with just seconds to go, Matt Elliott produced a delicate shot that floated in.

Neither Steve Walsh nor Dennis Wise managed to finish the game, having both seen red. Walsh got sent off for elbowing striker Chris Sutton. Skipper Dennis Wise took a familiar early bath for his second bookable offence in the 90th minute for a needless handball.

The turning point of the match occurred with the score at 1-0 and just two minutes played of the second half. Chris Sutton appeared to barge his way past Phil Gilchrist, pulling at his shirt, before setting up George Weah to fire home.

## Not again

City fans only have to think back to a fifth round replay in 1997 when referee Mike Reed adjudged Erland Johnsen had been felled by Spencer Prior when it looked like the Norwegian had taken a dive. That season, Chelsea went on to win the Cup by beating Middlesborough 2-0 in the final.

All in all, it was a bad day at the office for Martin O'Neill's side. Steve Walsh contributed to the misery by getting sent off in the 60th minute for a blatant and nasty off-the-ball elbow on Sutton. It was perhaps some measure of retribution for the former Blackburn striker's part in the controversial second goal that eventually proved decisive. Referee Graham Poll booked five players in eight minutes as the red-blooded battle came to the boil midway through the first half.

### Cretin

In the bitter aftermath Leicester manager Martin O'Neill labelled Chelsea chairman Ken Bates a *'football cretin'*. A fuming O'Neill let fly at Bates' comments on his side in his programme notes. O'Neill said: *'On top of everything you get footballing cretins like Ken Bates writing in his programme notes that we'd come along and play for penalties. If that's the case he doesn't know his facts. In the two times we've been to Wembley we've never actually had penalties or extra-time or replays. So he's got that wrong. We played Chelsea here two weeks ago and played them off the pitch. We should have scored five or six. He mustn't have been at that game. He must have been inside a Chinese restaurant or something.'*

The build-up to Weah's strike saw Sutton appear to wrestle Gerry Taggart to the ground, but referee Graham Poll waved play-on and moments later Chelsea were two goals up. After the 1997 FA Cup match, Mike Reed was pilloried in the media. Former BBC Radio Five Live talk show host Danny Baker urged fans to protest against the hapless referee whose car was vandalized by Leicester fans after the game.

# Graham Poll booked five players in eight minutes as the red-blooded battle came to the boil.

# Giant killers

## Wimbledon out-psyche Liverpool

There were many who refused to believe that one of the greatest of all Liverpool teams could be beaten by the long-ball specialists who had recently infiltrated football's top flight. Most up-and-under heathens viewed a Liverpool win as essential to the future of the English game, a triumph of good over evil.

But Wimbledon took little notice of what anyone thought and, if their victory was unpopular with the purists, it remained a glorious tactical triumph. Coach Don Howe had devised a plan of stopping John Barnes getting the ball by cutting his supply lines, particularly from Liverpool's ball-playing back four.

Liverpool still fashioned chances, but found Dave Beasant in fine form, while Peter Beardsley had a goal ruled out for offside. Instead, it was Wimbledon who snatched the lead when Sanchez rose highest in a crowded penalty area to complement Wise's free kick with a looping header beyond the stranded Bruce Grobbelaar.

Beasant preserved the lead with further saves from Ray Houghton and Alan Hansen, but his crowning glory came on the hour.

Clive Goodyear was adjudged to have fouled John Aldridge and the striker dusted himself down to plant his penalty firmly to Beasant's left.

One brilliant, diving save later, the Cup was Wimbledon's as Beasant became the first man to save an FA Cup final penalty and the first keeper to lift the Cup as captain.

### Straight man

As the straight man of the Crazy Gang, Lawrie Sanchez was seldom involved in the ritualistic burning of suits and scissoring of underpants in SE19. On the eve of the 1988 FA Cup final, when his footloose colleagues unwound with a night's boozing beside Wimbledon Common, the rugged old enforcer opted instead for lights out at 10p.m.

### Patronizing

After his Wycombe side beat Leicester City at Filbert Street in the Cup, Sanchez couldn't refuse the chance to catch up with some Liverpool *'chums'* down at *Match of the Day*. He had something to clear up.

Earlier in the day, he had watched Mark Lawrenson and Alan Curbishley sniffily dismiss Wycombe's chances on *Football Focus*. For Sanchez, this doyen of giant-killing exploits, it was one patronizing act too many.

'Maybe there was a bit of history with Lawrenson,' he said. 'They were saying: "*Well done Wycombe, thanks for coming, it's a great story but see you around.*"

'But people said that before the Cup final with Wimbledon. You would have thought Lawrenson would have known better after what happened to Liverpool that year.'

The irony for Wycombe is that earlier in the season, the players renegotiated their bonus payments, reasoning that there was little chance of FA Cup success. Hence Roy Essandoh's late contribution earned them only £130 each, while winning the semi-final would have netted them just £200. If they had won the competition, each player would have got £1,000. But that wasn't going to happen now, was it!

# If [Wimbledon's] victory was unpopular with the purists, it remained a glorious tactical triumph.

# Fan Grudges

'We had a lot of death threats on the answerphone. I was frightened, but Peter made light of it.' Brenda Swales, wife of the Manchester City Chairman

# Headline Makers

## Liverpool fans and *The Sun*

On 15 April 1989, Eddie Spearitt and his son, Adam, went along to watch an FA Cup semi-final match against Nottingham Forest in Sheffield. They had been caught in traffic along with thousands of other eager Liverpool fans as they made their way across the Pennines and had just enough time to find places in the allotted terraces at Sheffield Wednesday's Hillsborough stadium. Adam was fourteen and a devoted Liverpool supporter. *'We were so excited,'* said Eddie. *'It was only when the crowd in the pen really began to build up that I got frightened.'* The creaking infrastructure at the Leppings Lane End became a bottle-neck as 5,000 Liverpool fans struggled to find a gap in the crowd and make it inside the ground before the kick-off.

When the police eventually opened the main gates, instead of directing the fans to the open terraces, they sent them into an area already struggling to contain its capacity. Eddie and Adam were crushed in each other's arms. Adam was one of 96 fans who died. The subsequent inquiry by Lord Justice Taylor left no doubt where the blame lay. *'The real cause of the Hillsborough disaster,'* he said in his report, *'was overcrowding... the main reason for the disaster was the failure of police control.'*

### Sun stroke

By the following Tuesday, the editor of *The Sun*, Kelvin MacKenzie, had convinced himself that the tragedy had been caused by Liverpool *'football hooligans'*. As he got to work on his front page he brushed aside the remonstrations of senior staff and scrawled *'THE TRUTH'* in think block capitals. Beneath it he wrote three subsidiary headlines: *'Some fans picked pockets of victims'*, *'Some fans urinated on the brave cops'*, *'Some fans beat up PC giving kiss of life'*. In the aftermath of one of football's greatest

*'The real cause of the Hillsborough disaster,'* he said in his report, *'was overcrowding... the main reason for the disaster was the failure of police control.'*

tragedies *'the truth'* as MacKenzie would have it was somewhat different.

### Smear

As *The Sun* journalists watched the front page being collated they realized something wasn't right but were incapable of doing much about it. *'The error staring them in the face was too glaring... It obviously wasn't a silly mistake; nor was it a simple oversight. Nobody really had any comment on it – they just took one look and went away shaking their heads in wonder at the enormity of it,'* wrote Peter Chippendale and Chris Horrie in *Stick It Up Your Punter*, their history of *The Sun*.

Sales of *The Sun* fell almost instantly across Liverpool as fans, not just those wearing red, were sickened by the lack of taste, judgement and perception. *'The Truth'* had more to do with distorted observations on the people of Liverpool as much as football and its problems with hooliganism, and for fans of all persuasions that was something unforgivable.

# Back Stabbers

## Liverpool fans and Roma

Liverpool's recent return to the Champions League brought back memories of a different kind for many a veteran of the mighty red machine's march across European fields in the late seventies and early eighties. As thousands of travelling supporters watched Gerard Houllier's boys do battle with Batistuta, Totti and chums, the locals were providing opposition of a different order in the narrow streets surrounding the Stadio Olympico.

Stories of gangs wielding knives, slashing fans across their backsides, stealing wallets and harassing women were rife for days leading up to the match. Italians could claim that this was par for the course now that hooligans had a firmer hold on the game in Italy than across the water in England but there were many who believed the real cause lay in events that had taken place the last time these two sides met in a European Cup competition. The history of trouble between Liverpool and Roma can be traced to 1977. Roma supporters were keen to avenge the way their city was ransacked when Liverpool had visited previously to lift the European Cup for the first time after beating Borussia Monchengladbach 3-1 in the final.

Liverpool, by now undoubtedly one of the greatest club sides England ever produced, had reached the European Cup final for the fourth time in their history in 1984. Unusually, they were to start the match as underdogs, as by one of those strange quirks of fate, the final was to be held on the home ground of AS Roma, their opponents.

## Scooter gangs

Roma had come into the game confident of victory. However, after a dour, tense game, Liverpool eventually claimed the trophy following a penalty shoot-out (4-2) and the feeling feeling on the Curva Nord was one of revenge. Press photographs of the aftermath

# What was missing were the pictures of roaming scooter gangs hunting down Liverpool supporters.

depicted jubilant supporters embracing their players, fans draped in red flags smiling the inebriated smile of a person sated on success. There were pictures of fans dancing in the Trevi fountain, lapping up the dolce vita, embracing the local ladies. What was missing were the pictures of roaming scooter gangs hunting down Liverpool supporters, stabbing and slashing dozens, many of whom were family groups returning to hotels in the area. One 13-year-old boy was almost ripped apart, needing 200 stitches in his face alone.

### Easy prey

Just as England fans will remember the experience of watching their team scrape home with a 0-0 draw in Rome to qualify for France 98, there were tales of stewards and gate attendants confiscating personal property; they amassed a stash of cameras, watches, wallets and money before the match. Just as they did in 1998, the local hire cars and coaches mysteriously disappeared after the game leaving fans stranded, easy prey for the roaming gangs on scooters.

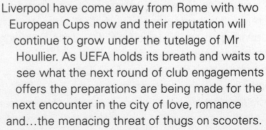

Liverpool have come away from Rome with two European Cups now and their reputation will continue to grow under the tutelage of Mr Houllier. As UEFA holds its breath and waits to see what the next round of club engagements offers the preparations are being made for the next encounter in the city of love, romance and…the menacing threat of thugs on scooters.

# Chucking Out the Cheap Seats

## Luton and Millwall fans

By March 1985, Millwall FC had made significant progress under the all-seeing eye of a fledgling young Scottish manager, George Graham. He had led the club to the top of the Third Division. Promotion looked inevitable and now the south east London outfit reached the FA Cup quarter-finals. Opponents were Luton Town at their home ground, Kenilworth Road. Viewers of local BBC news recall the presenter broadcasting from the ground itself. The crowd were already in good voice and it would have been impossible to spot the growing mob, the elite of London's football hooligan gangs and now numbering several hundred, who were steadily infiltrating the 17,470 crowd.

Luton were aware of the unenvious reputation that Millwall carried with them. The Hatters' chairman, David Evans, was a robust individual who sought the cosy corners of political involvement around Westminster, a true blue Tory. He had built a fortress of barbed-wire, steel fencing and video cameras which were designed to keep the hooligans out. This time, the hooligans were going to find out what an organized, robust police response was all about.

The statistics of the night don't do justice to what was about to unfold on the nation's TV screens. Of the 81 people injured, 31 were policemen. Thirty-one men were arrested, appearing at Luton Magistrates Court the following morning with the majority of them identifying themselves as Millwall *'fans'*.

The game was halted as early as the 14th minute, when the referee, David Hutchinson, himself a police inspector, took the teams off for 25 minutes when the first signs of problems became apparent. Hundreds of spectators spilled onto the playing area to escape overcrowding. The air was thick with violence and yet somehow the match was completed, Luton winning 1-0 only for all hell to break loose at the final whistle.

*'I could only stand in disbelief as I watched the riots and I felt like crying. Children around me clung to their parents in fear; women and pensioners vowed never to go to a football match again.'*

## Seating plan

But had the plan always been to invade the pitch and storm the players' dressing rooms? As several hundred members of London's hardest hooligan firms mounted the fencing they were covered by a fusillade of flying orange plastic chairs. The police, who had been warned beforehand that trouble might occur, charged at the onrushing mob but rapidly realized they were being outgunned by the flying orange missiles, so they retreated. On television these scenes left the viewer dumbstruck, the pictures were reminiscent of the Brixton and Toxteth riots only these were kicking off inside the enclosures of a football ground. As London journalist James Murray, a lifelong Millwall supporter, went on to describe: *'I could only stand in disbelief as I watched the riots and I felt like crying. Children around me clung to their parents in fear; women and pensioners vowed never to go to a football match again.'*

## Good Evans

That night Sergeant Colin Cooke was one of the unlucky ones. He was hit on the back of the head with a concrete block. A colleague, PC Phil Evans, gave him the kiss of life. The next day, Neil Kinnock blamed government policies and unemployment. Margaret Thatcher spoke of Victorian values, apportioning blame to family backgrounds and lack of discipline in schools. David Pleat, Luton's manager was left *'feeling empty'*.

# The Empire

## Murdoch and Manchester Utd fans

It was billed as the battle for the nation's prized sporting asset: Rupert Murdoch and the *'evil empire'* of BSkyB's attempted take-over of Manchester Utd being thwarted by a plucky group of supporters worried that their famous club would become just one more corporate arm of the mighty News Corporation, which owns BSkyB. Back in early September 1998 the announcement took the football world by storm. Murdoch's BSkyB intended to buy Manchester United PLC for around £623m (or $1 billion). At the heart of the Murdoch deal was the distillation of Premiership football's broadcast rights.

BSkyB had signed up to a five-year contract for exclusive Premiership football at a cost of some £670m and, while it was unlikely that another broadcaster could outbid Murdoch, he was worried that the escalating cost of British football would see his strategy of acquiring the massive numbers of male viewers by offering the national game unravel. The television contract with the Premier League had been referred to the Office of Fair Trading (OFT) to determine whether the packaging of TV rights was anti-competitive. If the ruling went against the contract, all TV rights would revert back to the clubs. Hence the interest in United.

BSkyB would then have to strike a deal with each club for those rights, and the clubs could seek to market their own rights or deal separately with other broadcasters.

## Sky's the limit

With BSkyB's resources many people believed their ability to bolster the playing talent at United would appeal to the club's supporters. Amazingly the fans weren't having any of it. There were a number of contentious elements to the deal. Supporters feared that the history and tradition of the football club would be further submerged beneath overriding commercial considerations. There were concerns about the wider effects on football itself and the questions of how a broadcaster and newspaper publisher could maintain independence in the reporting of its own club. Supporters started to organize against the bid. Mass demonstrations were organized in the ground and leaflet drops and petitions campaigned against the sale.

Supporters feared that the history and tradition of the football club would be further submerged beneath overriding commercial considerations.

### Unfair monopoly

The news came through on 9 April. Stephen Byers, then Secretary of State for Trade and Industry, blocked the proposed acquisition. Byers accepted the findings of the Monopolies and Mergers Commission (MMC) and the Office of Fair Trading that the merger would operate against the public interest and that it should be prohibited. The Commission had concluded that the move would reduce competition for broadcasting rights. This would have led to less choice for the Premier League itself and less scope for innovation in the broadcasting of football games. The MMC also concluded that the move would improve BSkyB's ability to secure rights to Premier League matches, and would lead to reduced competition in the wider pay-TV market.

# Beach Football

## Brighton fans vs Brighton directors

Brighton followers will never forget this particular chapter in their sometimes turbulent history. These were the days when David Bellotti was Chief Executive, Liam Brady was manager and Bill Archer and Greg Stanley wielded power in the boardroom. In 1995, things turned very sour when it was revealed that Archer, Stanley and Bellotti had secretly agreed to sell the Goldstone Ground. The outcry among the fans was deafening. If you want an example of all-out war between fans and the Board of a football club then look no further. Highlights include the abandonment of the last home match of the season due to a pitch invasion during which the goals were destroyed and the pitch torn up, mass demonstrations involving supporters of every club in the country, personal attacks, death threats… you name it, they've seen it.

In a local news report the story went like this: 'Supporters of Brighton invaded their own pitch yesterday, wrecked both goals, hurled wooden stakes into the crowd, tried to storm the players' tunnel, and forced the abandonment of the match with York City.
'The fans were protesting at the decision by the clubs' directors to sell the Goldstone Ground, their home for 94 years… and share the Fratton Park ground of Portsmouth FC, 40 miles away. Goldstone is being sold to pay off debts of £6m.
'Police had expected trouble. After the club's previous game against Carlisle, 600 fans invaded the pitch, calling for the resignation of David Bellotti, the Chief Executive. Early yesterday, supporters broke into the ground and painted *'Sack the Board'* across the pitch and directors' seats.
'Mr Bellotti and his fellow directors were told by police it was in their best interests to stay away from the game, and before play started the 12,000-strong crowd heard an announcement that no directors were present…'

# If you want an example of all-out war between fans and the Board of a football club then look no further.

### Colourful unity

All future home games were to be played miles away at Gillingham as the Goldstone Ground was being flattened. While the battle for ownership of the club continued and the club struggled to stay in the Football League – results on the pitch were dire, too – without a permanent home, Fans United was born, the idea of a young Plymouth fan, Richard Vaughan. Angered by Brighton & Hove Albion directors who had sold the Goldstone to developers, he suggested that lots of fans from different clubs should turn up at Brighton to show their support. Almost every league club in England and many from the non-league were colourfully represented on 8 February 1997. Brighton fans rank that day as one of the greatest in the club's history, alongside promotion to the old First Division in 1979 and the 1983 FA Cup final against Manchester United.

The fact that they have won promotion two years on the trot under different managers speaks volumes about their spirit. They are now happily ensconced at the Withdean Stadium back on the south coast.

# Shelf Life

## Spurs fans and Irving Scholar

Keith Burkinshaw had been appointed coach by Terry Neill in July 1975 and the Board appointed him manager following Neill's resignation. In Burkinshaw's first season, Spurs were relegated and the decision to sell Pat Jennings to Arsenal led to protests. But Burkinshaw survived and led Spurs to promotion at the first attempt and then on to two FA Cup wins (1981 and 1982) as well as the UEFA Cup in 1984. His side played attractive football and Burkinshaw looked set for a long reign until the Spurs Board was ousted by Irving Scholar, who took the club on to the Stock Exchange. Burkinshaw objected to changes the Board made to his remit and resigned, saying, *'There used to be a football club over there.'*

Scholar was a young man with a vision. He was one of the first to understand the possibility of club loyalty and replica kit sales. He took Spurs onto the Stock Market and his aggressive commercial attitude won him friends in high places but left a nasty taste in the mouths of the average supporter. On the field, there were a number of highlights. In 1983, Spurs came fourth again in the league and Burkinshaw's men, inspired by Graham Roberts, beat Anderlecht on penalties. Then there was the night Glenn Hoddle out-classed an ageing Johan Cruyff at White Hart Lane to help Spurs race into a 4-0 UEFA Cup half-time lead against Feyenoord. However, throughout that season arguments raged between Steve Archibald and Burkinshaw, and Burkinshaw and the board; arguments that started the rot that was to set in over the next few seasons.

### Pleat's seat

Irving Scholar and his board stated that the team were only a part of the business that is THFC (plc) and expenditure was needed elsewhere in other sectors. David Pleat took over the hot seat and built an entertaining side. At the back they now had Richard Gough,

# Burkinshaw objected to changes the Board made to his remit and resigned, saying, *'There used to be a football club over there.'*

the commanding centre half Spurs had been craving for years. Clive Allen scored a record-breaking 49 goals as a lone striker backed up with a five man midfield selected from Hoddle, Waddle, Allen, Ardiles, Hodge, Galvin and Stevens. Spurs lost the Littlewoods semi-final to Arsenal and an FA Cup final to Coventry and then finished third in the league. Pleat's men were doing the business on the field but still fans believed they could be given more support from the Board. Then the players started to leave. Glenn Hoddle headed off to join Arsene Wenger at Monaco, Graham Roberts went north to Rangers and manager David Pleat hit the kerb. Scholar brought in Terry Venables, the master tactician, who had achieved success out in Spain, mostly after buying Steve Archibald as Diego Maradona's replacement. Scholar watched as over 40,000 fans packed into the Lane for El Tel's first game against Liverpool. It was all an apparition. Clive Allen left in the summer and Venables brought in Terry Fenwick to organize things at the back.

## Decent venue shelved

This turnaround in fortunes signified the end of White Hart Lane as a decent footballing venue. Irving Scholar disbanded the Shelf area, brought in corporate hospitality on a grand scale and unceremoniously stuck two fingers up at the hardcore of Spurs fans in preference for snobs and businessmen stuffed into executive boxes. Scholar was never revered after that and as in his business dealings he began to understand that in football you never have much of a shelf life.

# The Football Scenes in Kes

**Kes** is undoubtedly one of the most remarkable films about education, or the lack of it, ever made. Its main theme is about giving a deprived child a crack at something. Seeing what happens is hardly groundbreaking but the dialogue and the depth of feeling in the acting bring the film to life. It is not unduly sentimental and nurtures a balanced blend between anger and comedy. It is also credited for capturing one of the funniest portraits of football on film.

Kes is the kestrel found and trained by a young Barnsley boy from a broken home. The boy, played by David Bradley, has retreated into himself, refusing to be supported by his school. But a sympathetic teacher thinks the lad's new interest might encourage him to display his real personality.

- Writer Ken Loach has always enjoyed mixing laughs with his studies in social realism but nowhere have his movies been funnier than in the chaotic schoolboy football match organized by Brian Glover in *Kes*. The PE teacher and fanatical Manchester United fan bullies opposition players and, as a partisan referee, he awards himself the dodgiest of penalties. The scene was actually shot at teacher-turned-novelist Barry Hines's old school in Barnsley. He had met Glover whilst teaching at another school.

- *'The football came directly from Barry's novel,'* recalled Loach, *'But Brian Glover was a real find and he made the film so memorable.'* A keen footballer, David

# '*I'm Bobby Charlton today, boys,*' he announces, pulling off his pristine tracksuit to reveal his Manchester United shirt.

Bradley does not have such fond memories from filming the scene: *'They had a local fire engine flood the field. Although it was August, it was bloody freezing,'* Bradley's description of how he landed his first big role is typical of the man.

- Barry Hines, author of *A Kestrel For A Knave*, was a fellow teacher in a Barnsley School. Hines made the suggestion that Glover, then aged 34, might like to play the role of bullying games teacher Mr Sugden. *'Ken Loach was improvizing a fight with loads of kids, and he asked me to stop it like a teacher would,'* said Glover. *'Well I'd stopped a good few playground fights and I had the confidence of being in the ring all those years, so I just grabbed these two kids and banged their heads together.'* Though the performance was successful Glover continued to teach for another two years.

- Glover's performance as Mr Sugden is arguably one of his greatest acting moments. *'I'm Bobby Charlton today, boys,'* he announces, pulling off his pristine tracksuit to reveal his Manchester United shirt, as he goes on to be a combined striker, referee and television commentator flattening 15-year-olds in his wake. Legend has it that the character was based on a Kirk Balk Comprehensive schoolteacher whose former student, Nicky Eaden, went on to become Barnsley's right back.

# Swales Out

## Peter Swales and Manchester City

When Brenda Swales spoke for the first time about the full horror of her husband Peter's battle to retain control at Manchester City the story could finally be fully told of how a man who had football in his blood became the target of a hate campaign that even to this day still makes the hair stand on end when the words, *'Swales Out'* get written.

Death threats, ring-of-steel security and intimidation became a way of life for the Swales family during the 1993-94 season. Manchester City's chairman was virtually under siege and the family were the frightened victims of Blues fans' anger, resentment and frustration.

Swales was bombarded with threats against his life, the family was terrorized, and one supporter even broke into the bedroom of the chairman's mother who was resident in a nursing home.

For Mrs Swales it was a time of worry and daily frustrations. *'I wouldn't let any of the grandchildren or my three daughters come round to the house,'* she told a local Manchester reporter.

### Figure of hate

*'We had security men on the gate – it was really quite frightening. We also had a lot of death threats on the answerphone. One day, when I walked to my daughter's, who lives around the corner, there were a couple of rather shady-looking characters and vans around. I was frightened, but Peter made light of it.'*

By November of 1993, the situation had worsened. City were struggling to hang on to any credibility and supporters were further frustrated by the fact that arch rivals United and Alex Ferguson had begun their glory trail. One day as the Swales' returned from a match against Sheffield Wednesday they found police at their house.

According to Mrs Swales, *'It was hard to believe, but there were police all around the*

# 'All the local pubs had received maps to our house, with a message asking people to come and sort Peter out. It was terrible.'

back garden. Apparently, all the local pubs had received maps to our house, with a message asking people to come and sort Peter out. It was terrible.'

A takeover battle ensued, led by former City striker Frannie Lee but during the course of this fight the hate campaign continued. Lee remains steadfast in his condemnation of the vicious anti-Swales campaign. *'Of course I would never – and have never – condoned any activity like that,'* said Lee, who himself later became the victim of a similar hate campaign. *'I never had any personal grudge against Peter Swales... I never fell out with him and I never had an argument with him.'*

### Sorrow and silence

Peter Swales died of a heart attack three days before City were relegated in the 1995-96 season. He had never been back to the club following the takeover and a minute's silence was impeccably observed before the final game of the season against Liverpool.

# American Psycho

## Gordon Hill, Terry Smith and Chester City

The history of Chester City and their annual forays onto the football field provide endless hours of amusement unless you happen to have been a chairman or manager of the club in recent years.

One memorable evening took place at Connah's Quay's, Deeside Stadium. The former Manchester United legend Gordon Hill had been quoted in a local paper saying that he reckoned over three-quarters of Chester City supporters would be cheering him on at the start of the season. The rest, Barrow sympathizers, wouldn't. There were those who wondered which side his eggs were on and after the pre-season friendly he would be left in no doubt what the majority of Chester supporters thought about it.

At the start of the night there was a football match. The Blues ran out bearing a reasonable resemblance to the previous year's outfit, although City fans were somewhat surprised to see Wayne Brown still propping up the defence between the sticks. Andy Porter, Steve Whitehall, Dean Spink and Jimmy Haarhof also featured as did Chris Malkin who was given a verbal battering from the stands due in the main to his willingness to associate with club owner Terry Smith and his sidekick Hill. In the ensuing report featured on the unofficial and very funny City website, *The Onion Bag*, one of football's truly great moments began to unfold...

# By full-time a lynching was looking on the cards but wisely the Old Bill had been called.

### Going down Hill

'So how did the fans react to their first collective, official sighting of Gordon Hill as City's ludicrous director of football? The majority of the 200-odd crowd were Blues followers some only entering once they were assured none of the £4 entry fee went to Chester. The usual **'Smith Out'** flags were there along with some equivalents decrying Gordon Hill and Gareth Evans. Abuse at Hill was virtually constant. Half-time was always going to be interesting. Separated from his detractors by a flimsy row of hurdles, he crossed the race-track surrounding the pitch to make for the changing rooms. Swear words and regrettably spit greeted him. If these scenes were ugly they then turned positively grotesque when he reappeared to run the gauntlet at the start of the second half. This time some spit made contact and Hill's reaction was to turn the other way and gob at another completely innocent spectator. His aim was deadly and the enraged fan, wiping sputum from his face, made to get at Hill but was restrained.

### Turfed out

'By full-time, a lynching was looking on the cards but wisely the Old Bill had been called. In all seven police cars turned up as Hill was escorted to sanctuary beneath the stand and fans were threatened with arrest if they didn't calm down. How grateful the little former Man United man must be that the Blues next excursion is behind closed doors at Turf Moor. It's only a temporary respite though as, along with Terry Smith, the man's doomed.'

# Money Men

## Swansea fans and Ninth Floor PLC

The strength of feeling that exists around Swansea with regard to the ownership of the club by Ninth Floor PLC and the subsequent attempts to offload the club for ridiculous sums of money has gone way beyond the normal boundaries of anger and resentment.

Back in 1997, Ninth Floor big gun Neil McClure strolled into Wales making promises of a 25,000 all-seater, £75m stadium. Within days that talk had been exposed for the nonsense it was. Jan Molby, the successful former Liverpool player and Swansea manager, was sacked and the club seemingly lurched from one crisis to another. Molby was too close to the fans while Ninth Floor couldn't be further from their constituency. Former Wimbledon legend Alan Cork arrived for a brief spell at the helm and then Micky Adams arrived. A likeable man, Adams began to make the team tick so you can imagine the resentment felt when after a mere 13 days he had packed his bags and left. Had Adams seen enough of the club's owners to realize all was not well? Talk that he had met McClure, Steve Hamer the back-slapping chairman and the former Fulham public relations officer, Mike Lewis, and decided he should clear off may have been wide of the mark but with those boys behind the scenes at Ninth Floor their time would come later.

## No laughing matter

Talk of floating the mighty Swansea on the Stock Exchange came and went with a torrent of laughter escorting it out the door. John Hollins came in as manager and within weeks suffered the cries of *'Hollins Out'* as he tried to muster some semblance of a rearguard action. Mike Lewis drummed up talk of big signings each time the annual season ticket reminders went out, once memorably announcing that, *'John Hollins has been locked away in his office and is busy assembling players for the new season.'* By this time Lewis was MD and had sacked Steve Hamer.

# 'The real culprit is Mike Lewis, who actually took over the club from Ninth Floor for one pound.'

### Lost in the post

Sometime later, Steve Hamer responded to the many criticisms of his time at Swansea with a statement to the Evening Post. He branded the new owner, Tony Petty, an opportunist, and attacked Mike Lewis, the man who sold the club on to the Aussie-based businessman.

Hamer resigned from the Vetch boardroom after refusing to sign the prospectus for Swansea's then planned flotation on the Alternative Investment Market of the Stock Exchange. He had become saddened by the club's capacity to lurch form one crisis to another. *'It is very tragic,'* he told the Post. *'This guy Tony Petty is clearly an opportunist but the real culprit is Mike Lewis, who actually took over the club from Ninth Floor for one pound.*

*'He [Lewis] effectively handed this club to Tony Petty without, I believe, any reference to the other board of directors. I think Mr Petty has misread the script. I don't think he understands the depth of feeling in Swansea. If I were him I'd get back on a jet very quickly and get back to Australia.'*

Lewis officially handed over control of the club in October 2001. As he walked out the door he had this parting shot: *'The knights in shining armour never came out of the woodwork. There was a lot of hot air from people saying "we won't let you down" – they did.'*

# Campbell Soup

## Sol returns to White Hart Lane

The former Spurs captain had made his controversial move over to north London rivals Arsenal in the summer of 2001, and this was to be the first opportunity for Spurs fans to voice their dissent.

Prior to the match, both sides had plenty to say about the game and a Spurs fans' website offered the following ideas for ways to voice one's opinions:

*1) Teams run out for the pre-match handshakes, etc. WHL will welcome the Spud heads with the customary enthusiasm – nothing different so far. But prepare yourself for the drum roll which will signal the start of the proceedings.*

*2) The moment the announcer starts reading out the Arse team line-up, Dan will do his drum roll (which will be clearly audible around The Lane). If you're not already on your feet, rise and turn your back on Judas. At this point, there's been a number of good suggestions on how you might occupy the time until the Spurs line-up is announced:*

*a) Remain silent until Dan signals the end of the protest with another drum roll.*

*b) White hanky/redundant Campbell replica Spurs shirt-waving.*

*c) It goes against the original 'Silent Protest' theory, but whistling is a well-recognized gesture of contempt and is perfectly acceptable.*

## Drummed out

The website continued:

*'I would also ask you to consider this – the wonderful subtlety and irony of the Goons singing the name of a player that so many of them think is absolute crap. We certainly weren't banking on Campbell playing like Ramon Vega when we started plotting this protest, but now it's happened, it's a very nice icing on the cake.'*

# Campbell took what one paper described as the ludicrous *'minute of contempt'* on the chin.

3) Protest ends when the announcer starts to call our line-up and will be signalled by Dan's drum.

Then we can get on with the business of cheering our lads on to a win and to giving Campbell some stick whenever he's involved with the play. From the moment the game kicks off, we'll all be on the same wavelength – cheering ours and giving HIM hell.

## No bottle

In a report the day after the match, the referee, Jeff Winter, decided not to mention the actions of certain fans who clearly hurled missiles at Sol Campbell. The fact that he failed to mention the beer bottle that was thrown at Campbell was more surprising. The Tottenham Hotspur Supporters' Trust condemned the actions of a minority and called upon the club to *'take the appropriate action'*. In the end, Campbell took what one paper described as the ludicrous *'minute of contempt'* on the chin.

# Leeds Fans and Turks

## Death in Istanbul

Two Leeds United supporters were fatally stabbed to death during disturbances in Istanbul city centre prior to the UEFA Cup match with Galatasaray in April 2000. On the night of the match, Leeds chairman Peter Ridsdale said: *'UEFA have decided the game will definitely go ahead, their rationale being that it has to be played at some stage. We acknowledge that on balance, and under the present circumstances, it is the right decision.'*

Matches in Turkey had become something of a tightrope for British sides since Manchester United went to *'hell'* in the Champions League. That night Eric Cantona was involved in squabbles with officials but this was something on a far grander – and more frightening – scale. Christopher Loftus was fatally stabbed in a scuffle in the centre of Istanbul after a group of Leeds supporters were reportedly involved in an argument with men in a passing van. The second man, who also died of stab wounds, was Kevin Speight. Ridsdale added: *'Tonight is going down as one of those black nights in history. It is a tragedy. One minute I was talking to Galatasaray directors to promote the friendship between the two clubs and the next minute I receive a telephone call telling me there had been some problems in town and a fan had been killed.*
*'It is obviously a horrendous situation and something I have never been through before. I was with the brother of one of the dead men when he identified the body and it is something that will live with me forever.'*

### Well dodgy
Chief Superintendent Steve Matthews of West Yorkshire Police, who travels with the club on their European trips, said: *'We had taken precautions against violence but we never expected anything like this.'*

*'One minute I was talking to Galatasaray directors to promote the friendship between the two clubs and the next minute... a fan had been killed.'*

Paul Thomas, international co-coordinator of the Football Supporters' Association and a Leeds United season ticket holder, said he had advised friends against going to Turkey because of the Galatasaray fans' reputation. *'I only heard of between 200 and 300 people going down to Istanbul and I understand the club only sold about 500 tickets,'* he said. *'Not a lot of the people I know fancied it because it is well known as a dodgy place to travel to.*

*'The fans have a bad reputation as well so I warned my mates not to go. But the worst thing is that there is never any police protection for the fans there. Even if the Leeds lot were being a problem it is their job to get in between the two sets of fans to stop anything happening. The lack of police help is a big problem for English teams playing abroad but it is particularly bad in Turkey.'*

**Further skirmishes**

The Elland Road club immediately scrapped a supporters' flight set to leave for the match on the morning of the game and all official flights were cancelled. Supporters were encouraged not to travel but despite these measures there were clashes in the city. Turkish police took statements from 20 Leeds supporters who witnessed the knife attack in Taksim Square and at least four other Leeds fans were injured in further violence.

# Smith Out

## Alan Smith and Palace

It had been a long and difficult season but eventually the man who had been so popular first time round had to go after enduring a season-long campaign of hate and vilification. It was after being booed and pelted with season-ticket stubs as he left the field, that Alan Smith, the Crystal Palace manager, was finally sacked. It was the culmination of a disastrous run that began with six straight defeats and had earned a mere six points from 13 games.

That run left Palace with little chance of First Division survival but chairman Simon Jordan's decision to appoint former Palace stalwart, Steve Kember, from within, for the last two games of the season, did the trick and Palace stayed up. Defender Dean Austin, reacting to Smith's dismissal, said: *'Something had to be done. The players have not done what they needed to in the last few months.'*

### On the line

In mid-February, Palace were mid-table, enjoying the conviction that comes with a decent run all the way to the Worthington Cup semi-finals. Alan Smith, tempted from his job as Fulham's academy director in August, had stopped the early rot of two wins in 15 games. This was the same Alan Smith who had taken Palace to the Premiership first time around – a real Selhurst Park hero.

Simon Jordan had bought the club for £10.5m. Palace, after years of struggling to stay in the professional ranks hoped that the new owner would ensure the financial difficulties that had nearly toppled the club would be avoided, but Jordan knew he stood to lose £5m from relegation. The man who had made his money in mobile phones had made a bad call in appointing Smith and now the relationship between the chairman and his manager was as bad as the one between the manager and his players.

# The man who had made his money in mobile phones had made a bad call in appointing Smith.

## Nudge, nudge

Alan Smith had criticized his own players in the media and even the interviewers seemed surprised by the tone of his comments. Then he turned around and noted with surprise that some of his players had been watching the next opponents, Wolves, *'of their own volition'*. Not that it did them much good. Palace were appalling and after the game Smith conceded: *'The game summed up our season: lots of play and chances, lack of nous and quality, shambolic defending.'*

*'I could do without what I had to put up with this afternoon. Something has to come from inside. The mentality in the club is not strong. Players need to look at themselves.'*

That something was delivered courtesy of the Spanish archer, Signor El Bow.

# Linesmen and Offside

**Everyone has a story. Everyone remembers a controversial moment. Poor refereeing decisions lose footballers medals and managers their jobs. But linesmen just get decisions wrong. They are lovingly referred to as the person on the sideline not even good enough to referee his own match. Football fans have many unprintable names for the men in black who referee their favourite game and, according to recent research in the Netherlands, linesmen really can't tell if players are offside. Well, we could have told you that.**

Assistant referees (formerly known as linesmen) viewing play from certain angles inevitably make mistakes when deciding if players are offside, says Raôul R.D. Oudejans from Vrije University in the Netherlands. Assistant referees from the Dutch professional football league incorrectly judged 40 of 200 potential offside scenarios staged by Oudejans' team of researchers.

- It's hardly surprising given that the offside rule is one of the most widely disputed laws of the game. It states that an attacking player must have two defenders between himself and the goal when the ball is passed to him. The goalkeeper is usually one of these two, leaving assistant referees to decide if the attacker is in front of the defender. Oudejans' team confirms what many fans have suspected for years. In many cases, his eyes cannot make this decision accurately.

- The problems begin for the assistant referee if he is not standing directly in line with the last defender. Put simply, the player furthest from the assistant referee

# Forwards on the far side of the pitch were almost nine times more likely to be wrongly judged offside if they ran to the left of the defender.

appears closer to the goal. So an attacker tearing down the far left wing will be halted unfairly for offside more often than his team mate on the near side. Likewise, a player cutting inside a defender on the far side of the pitch will not appear offside to the assistant referee.

- Oudejans and colleagues enlisted the help of some of the Netherlands' most talented young footballers. Two youth teams played out football scripted by the researchers to contain marginal offside decisions and three assistant referees were invited to adjudicate.
  *'We were a little surprised that such a large number of errors were made,'* said human movement researcher Frank Bakker, one of Oudejans' co-workers.

- Analysis of 200 videotaped matches from around Europe and the 1998 World Cup confirmed that forwards on the far side of the pitch were almost nine times more likely to be wrongly judged offside if they ran to the left of the defender.

- John Baker, head of refereeing at the FA, is not surprised by these results. *'We train assistant referees to line up where they stand with the second last defender and to use them as a point of reference. Standing just one metre to either side can produce mistakes.'* Not much solace here for disgruntled fans.

# Kicking out

## David Beckham and England fans

England were playing Argentina in the 1998 World Cup in St Etienne. The second half of the match was barely a few minutes old and some of us hadn't yet taken our seats. Both sides had scored two goals and the evidence in front of us suggested that this was destined to become one of those World Cup classics.

Then as Diego Simeone clattered into David Beckham the game appeared to pause as the players took time out to collect themselves. The referee, Kim Nielson stands in front of the two players and just as you imagine he's going fish out a card and book the Argentinian a sly smile emanates from beneath the floppy-haired fringe of England's No.7 and he flips his leg out, barely grazing the hind calf of Simeone. You think nothing of it, just a bit of mischief between blokes on the pitch. But the crafty old Simeone calls on years of experience and sees a chance to alter the balance of play in favour of his country and crashes to the ground as if crushed by a sack of spuds.

By now several members of the Argentina team have seen this. Gabrielle Batistuta is among those who shake the arm of Mr Nielson as if to say, *'Oi, ref, did you just see that?*

Nielson, not a man noted for his sense of humour looks at the pathetic bundle of blue that is rolling on the ground in front of him and immediately waves a red card. For a second, you think he's made the brightest decision of his life and sent off the Argentine for play-acting. For a second, you imagine justice has prevailed and common sense has won another day. David Beckham must be thinking the same thing because the look of sheer disbelief on his face when he realizes that no, it's he that must turn the bath taps on early.

# Batistuta is among those who shake the arm of Mr Nielson as if to say, *'Oi, ref, did you just see that?'*

### Hang in there

As Beckham walks alone back to the dressing room, a stone-faced Glenn Hoddle stares straight ahead, refusing to make eye contact with his player. It is an expression that suggests, *'Thanks, mate. You've just cost us the World Cup.'*. England lost the match on penalties after hanging on bravely through a second half of seething drama and intensity.

On his return to England (after a hastily arranged trip to New York), Beckham faced a wall of hate-driven reporters demanding to know if he was going to apologize to the nation. Effigies were hung outside pubs in east London and death threats were made on his phone. For that entire season, Beckham endured the taunts of football supporters wondering whether his wife Victoria received anything in her backside. It wasn't until a TV interview with Michael Parkinson was aired that a lighter side to the Beckham personality was revealed. This interview enamoured the player with it audience. The lad had ridden through the storm and lasted a lot longer on the international football stage than the manager of the day, Mr Hoddle.

### Hot spot

Beckham became the England captain and scored the last-minute goal that took his country to the 2002 World Cup finals. In the game against Argentina, the moment came when Beckham lined up to take a penalty kick that would ultimately win the game for England. Simeone was there offering advice to the captain but England had a more mature mind behind the controls. Beckham drilled the ball into the back of the net and with it went the last of any bad feeling the nation might have harboured for the villain of the piece four years earlier. For David Beckham, Golden Balls, revenge was complete.

# Saints and Sinner

## Ian Branfoot and Southampton fans

Ask any Saints supporter what they consider to be the worst time in the club's history and they'll tell you the same thing. Ian Branfoot's reign, 1991-94. P128, W36, D34, L58.

On the wonderful Saints Forever website, this offering from a correspondent sums up the strength of feeling.

### KEITH LEGG'S WORST SAINTS XI OF THE PAST 20 YEARS

*Peter Wells* – short, fat and liked dropping the ball at strikers' feet

*Mick Mills* – famous for the song, *'Oh no – Mick Mills'* often heard at the back of the Milton

*Lee Todd* – where is he now? Who the f*** cares!

*Ken Armstrong* – remember him? 6'4" of pure nonsense.

*Mark Whitlock* – a slug balancer.

*Ray Wallace* – his brothers got all the talent, he got the hairy top lip

*Steve Baker* – this man I truely hate for giving the ball away to Pom**y for them to score at the Dell, if I met him in the street now, I'd probably hit him

*Ali Dia* – I thought he had a rough ride at the Dell, if given a few more games, he could have reached the level of completely hopeless.

*Charlie George* – always injured, even sliced his finger off using a lawnmower once.

*Martin Foyle* – you felt that time stood still whilst he was running, he was that slow.

*Keith Cassells* – famous for being clean through against Luton, falling over his own feet, then got back up and scored.

*Manager* – *who else but Mr Charisma himself... Ian Branfoot.*

# Fans couldn't work out which part of *'We want Branfoot out'* he did not understand.

### Calls of nature

Such were the levels of venom and loathing directed at Ian Branfoot that each incident began to make the national news. Supporters would run up the touchline to scream abuse at his face. Fans couldn't work out which part of *'We want Branfoot out'* he did not understand. Saints fans got slated for slogans such as *'Hope you die soon'* directed at his arrogance and general stubborn nature but even when he was attacked in his car he failed to get the message. He was rumoured to have received a death threat if he failed to pick Matt le Tissier and many fans called him Ian Branflake because of the effect Branflakes had on your guts. *'That is what Mr Branflake did for Southampton FC.'*

### Alienated

According to one irate supporter, *'This person [Branfoot] did more to persuade school children in Hampshire to support Manchester United or Portsmouth than anyone else could ever have done. As things came to a head in his final season in charge, when the crowds began to dwindle, I also decided I could stomach no more and after leaving another home defeat on New Year's Day at home to Norwich I vowed not to come back until he had gone. As he had survived the first three years of his contract and somehow been rewarded with another three-year deal at the start of that season, I feared I would not see my beloved team in action for some time. I didn't have to wait too long though, I used to check Teletext each day religiously for news that he'd been sacked or kidnapped by aliens. When the good news came through the feeling of elation was unbelievable. It was like we had won something, and at the end of that season we had – our survival in the Premiership, something that had looked impossible when Mr Branfoot left.'*

# Sam Hammam and Wimbledon

## Sam Hammam and Wimbledon

He may have started out as the loveable rogue, the man who put the *'crazy'* into the crazy gang, but there are those among the faithful Wimbledon supporters who hold Sam Hammam responsible for selling off Plough Lane and seeing the ultimate giantkillers plummet from the Premiership to obscurity (via Milton Keynes). What happens, they ask, if a Safeway store is built on Plough Lane? The same Plough Lane Sam Hammam sold to line his own pockets, the same Plough Lane that the local council has let sit and decay over the past decade and has since been razed to the ground? One fan, commenting on the situation, said: *'Where does the club go then? Or will this be taken care of by one of the six potential sites people have identified by looking at an A to Z and, seeing big green areas, saying, "Oh we could build on that!" What amazes me is that the council and Sam have got away with this. If people believe Merton will help then they are wrong. These are petty-minded people who are only pandering to the desires of their electorate. These faceless wonders will be gone by the next election, and then we can all be fobbed off by the next set of community servants.'*

### Sam the Man

Hammam was the man who helped Wimbledon realize the impossible dream. After gaining entry into the Football League in 1977, the Dons clawed their way up the divisions, reaching the top flight in 1986. In 1988, the club which not so long before had been playing Southern League football took their Crazy Gang antics to Wembley, taunting the Liverpool team before defeating them in the FA Cup final. Hammam joined in the Gang's antics, initiating new players by burning their clothes, scrawling graffiti on the dressing-

# Hammam joined in the Gang's antics, initiating new players by burning their clothes and scrawling graffiti on the dressing-room wall at West Ham.

room wall at West Ham, and keeping his promise to kiss Dean Holdsworth's backside when the striker passed Hammam's target of 15 goals. After leaving Wimbledon, Hammam took over at Cardiff where he again courted publicity and was deemed responsible for a number of unsavoury headlines.

## On the move

When the news came through that Wimbledon could move to Milton Keynes, the fears of supporters who had suspected the worst once Sam Hammam sold the last of his interests in the club were realized. Back in the beginning Hammam had been the hero of the West Bank by buying Ron Noades' shares and preventing him from moving the club to Selhurst Park. Gradually though, the rumours about possible moves to places as far as Dublin became serious propositions. The fans began to suspect that Sam the Man had ideas above his station. Hammam kept it all together back then, sometimes even ringing up supporters at home or work. A move to Selhurst did ensue, however, and the flimsy remains of the club's Merton roots were further jeopardized as the Norwegian influence took hold.

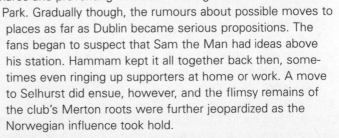

# Big Heads

## Brian Clough and Leeds fans

The man they referred to *'Old Big Head'* had never liked Don Revie's Leeds team. So it came as something of a surprise when the man who had led Derby to the league title in 1972 was plucked from relative obscurity down at Brighton to take on the biggest job in British football.

Clough's first engagement with Leeds was to be the eventful Charity Shield confrontation with Liverpool. It was to be Shanks' last game in charge of the team he had developed into the biggest challengers to Leeds. Now that Revie had quit to take on the England job it seemed odd to some Leeds fans that the board should pick a man who had been especially critical of the Revie era.

Not a man to be bothered by other people's opinions, Clough had intended to kick off his reign in a bizarre way, as he explained: *'The television pictures from Wembley, for the Charity Shield, should have been different. They showed Bill Shankly leading out his magnificent Liverpool side and alongside him, followed by the Leeds team with the glummest faces ever seen at such an occasion, there was me. Much as I admired Shanks, I didn't want to march from the tunnel at the head of the Leeds United side that day – I asked Don Revie to lead them out instead.'*

## Leeds the way

*'"This is your team," I told him, "you lead them out at Wembley." Apart from anything else, I thought it was a decent thing to do, a nice gesture towards a man who had just won the League title.*

*'"You've got the job now, Brian. I'm not coming down to lead them out. It is your privilege," he said.*

*'I was proud – and, to use Revie's word, privileged – to walk out alongside Shankly. In fact, I remember turning towards him and clapping him as we walked. But there*

*'Apart from anything else, I thought it was a decent thing to do, a nice gesture towards a man who had just won the League title.'*

*was no sense of togetherness with those who walked behind me.'*

### Having a laugh

Clough arrived despite the fact that a number of the players thought they should be given a crack at the job, in particular John Giles. Clough brought in Duncan McKenzie from Forest and McGovern and O'Hare from Derby. Within 44 days he had dismantled one of the finest sides in English football history but there were still sufficient numbers in the old guard to have the last laugh.

They say *'player power'* cost him his job. Manny Cussins decided to back the team that had brought home the cups for the last few years rather than the man he had hoped would continue the success. Clough left with his contract paid up, and could afford to take a drop down to Nottingham Forest where he went on to win the league, League Cup and European Cup in the same period that Leeds were slipping further and further from the top. So he got the last laugh after all, then.

# To Elland back

## George Graham, Leeds and Spurs

Graham's mistake in the eyes of the fans was the fact that he'd signed a four-year contract. The fans also felt aggrieved that it was Leeds who had lifted Graham, in their eyes, off the football scrapheap, after he'd served his 12-month ban imposed for taking bungs. The fact that he had Arsenal in his blood made the move to Spurs even harder to swallow.

You couldn't have asked for a less forgiving fixture than the league match between Spurs and Leeds in what was effectively Graham's last game in charge. Both sets of fans berated him, Leeds supporters had to be calmed down at half-time by the Chairman, Peter Risdale, and Spurs supporters simply couldn't believe that a man with so much Arsenal history in his blood could be coming to *'save'* them.

### O'Neill? Oh no!

Three names were in the frame for the vacant post: David O'Leary, Leicester boss Martin O'Neill and former player, Gordon Strachan, then at Coventry. With O'Leary appearing to rule himself out of the job, heightening speculation that he was following Graham to Spurs, O'Neill emerged as the front-runner. While Strachan's heritage was steeped in Yorkshire-folklore, at Highfield Road he had hardly set the world alight, despite having a considerable transfer purse.

What followed was the appointment of O'Leary and Eddie Gray on a temporary basis and a three-week game of cat-and-mouse with Leicester for the services of O'Neill. Leicester admirably refused to entertain Leeds' formal advances. Leeds remained undeterred, stirred by O'Neill's claims that he wanted to speak to the Yorkshire club. Peter Ridsdale eventually called long-overdue time on the saga and O'Leary was offered the job until the end of the season.

# You couldn't have asked for a less forgiving fixture than the league match between Spurs and Leeds for Graham in what was effectively his last game in charge.

### George who?

By the time Manchester United visited in April, O'Leary had put pen to paper on a permanent deal which put the novice right up there with the top earners. In an amazingly short space of time, O'Leary had displayed the credentials of the manager Leeds had craved. Unafraid to use the overflowing talent which had come through the Youth Academy, O'Leary unleashed the likes of Alan Smith, Jonathan Woodgate, Paul Robinson, Matthew Jones and Harry Kewell and advocated a style of play that went down well with the faithful at Elland Road. Now the worries over Graham's departure were a thing of the past and Leeds were looking like serious challengers for the title. To have gone from dismay to such dizzy heights so quickly was beyond the dreams of any Leeds' supporter but each time the traitor Graham returned with Spurs, they made sure he never forgot what they thought of him.

# The Firm

**Cult British film director, Alan Clarke, best known for violent movies like *Scum,* featuring a young Ray Winstone, and *Made in Britain* with Tim Roth, was the first to explore the hooligan phenomenon. Clarke's 1988 film *The Firm* is notable for two reasons. One is Gary Oldman's trademark, barely-under-control performance as Bexy: a respectable real estate agent, husband and father by day. But by night he is the vicious hooligan leader of the Inter-City Crew (ICC), a loose group of friends who play football and drink together.**

The film's second notable attribute is the make up of the gang. Although hooligans have historically been characterized as working-class white boys, Clarke casts the ICC as a group of multi-racial and cross-class individuals, in which Bexy and several other members represent the middle class. By doing this, it is apparent that Clarke's film is attempting to portray the real face of hooliganism.

- *The Firm's* plot follows three distinct stories: the ICC's rivalry with two other firms; Bexy's attempt to unite his fellow hooligans and lead them against German firms at a forthcoming European tournament; and Bexy's personal addiction to the buzz of hooliganism and the way it impinges on his respectable middle-class life. Because of this, he keeps his trophies from his fighting at his parents' house.

- The fight scenes are the film's key element, asking the question: why do these men with seemingly normal lives feel the need to maim each other at the week-

# The fight scenes are the film's key element, asking the question: why do these men with seemingly normal lives feel the need to maim each other?

end? Clarke's explanation is simple: for hooligans, it's all about the fight. While Bexy finds relative happiness in his married life and fatherhood, he desires the bonding rituals of the firm and the fights to provide meaning to his existence, however irrational and self-destructive that path may be.

- The scenes in which Bexy elicits the support of his rivals under a banner of a truce touch on a more modern approach to organized football hooliganism in which firms offer to support each other overseas in the national cause. Websites now provide both the hooligan and the authorities with a massive archive of footage and footnotes to events abroad and are the main recruitment point for bringing hooligan elements together.

Like much of Clarke's work, *The Firm* has a documentary feel to it. Especially realistic are the short and brutal fight scenes. Equally notable is the film's final scene, which shows all the hooligans in a bar in Germany, downing litres of beer in their Union Jack T-shirts and chanting the jingoistic anti-German line, *'Two World Wars and one World Cup'* at a bunch of television reporters. It is Clarke's final comment on the idiocy of hooliganism, the media who fan the flames and the ugly Englishman abroad, vainly trying to fly the flag of a fallen empire.

# Club-hopping

## Reading and Mark McGhee

That evening, 12,000 Reading fans greeted McGhee with what can only be described as a constant torrent of highly vocal abuse which left the former Elm Park boss visibly shaken.

His new team, Wolves, comprised of multi-million pound talent were no match for the power and passion of the Royals on and off the pitch. After an initial burst, the Wolves' fans remained muted as a wall of noise cascaded from all sides of the ground.

It upset McGhee so much that during the post match interviews the talk was not of the performance of the Wanderers team but of the anger he felt towards Reading fans. Why were they so hostile to him? What had he done to deserve this? He had left the football club in a healthy state and had done his job.

### Mark my words

As a Reading fan summed up: *'Under McGhee, Reading was transformed from Third (nearly Fourth) Division cannon fodder into a sleek First Division outfit. On an extremely limited budget and with the expertise of Colin Lee as coach, McGhee assembled a side that oozed class.*

*'For supporters bought up in the Ian 'Route One' Branfoot era this was revolutionary. Players passed to each other! They scored goals! The defence looked rock-solid! Away games became watchable without large intakes of alcohol!*

*'At every stage of his career, McGhee came across as a manager you could trust and respect. Here was a man who kept his promises.*

*'In 1993, at the supporters club AGM, he said Reading would win the Second Division title and the Royals duly romped home. At the 1994 AGM, he said Reading would make the First Division play-offs. Mark had spoken and Reading were indeed the pride of the Thames Valley as both Oxford and Swindon fans looked on jealously.*

# 'For supporters bought up in the Ian "Route One" Branfoot era this was revolutionary. Players passed to each other! We scored goals!'

### Little wonder

'It was obvious that Reading were going to find it difficult to hold on to one of the hottest management teams in the country and it surprised no one when Leicester became interested following the departure of Brian Little to Aston Villa.

'Everyone thought at the time that McGhee's intention was to shake up Madejski and to give himself a little more bargaining power in the transfer market. Leicester at the time were destined for relegation. Reading were on the up. It was no contest.

'We loved him and he loved us. The town breathed a huge sigh of relief when McGhee agreed to stay.

'Relief turned to horror, however, as the radio gave a different story. McGhee had had a change of heart the next day. Leicester beckoned and he was off.'

195

# Loan Ranger

## Scarborough and former chairman, Anton Johnson

Scarborough FC were formed in 1879, and have enjoyed some success in the lower divisions. Four FA Trophy finals (and three victories) at Wembley in 1973, 1975, 1976 and 1977, promotion to the Football League in 1987 and a place in the Third Division play-offs in 1998 were all worth shouting about. But under a new chairman, Anton Johnson, things went very badly wrong, and the Yorkshiremen were sent back to the Vauxhall Conference.

Anton Johnson, a former butcher from Essex, once borrowed £40,000 from the PFA to bankroll his ownership of struggling Scarborough. Nothing wrong with that you might think but in fact, there is a story behind Scarborough's traumatic collapse from play-off semi-finalists to relegation candidates, which should serve as a warning to clubs all over the country. Scarborough fans, in fact, blame their plight on a man who bought the club in the summer of 1999 and then dropped it like a hot potato just a few months later. Anton Johnson, who was censured by the FA in 1984 for having conflicting interests in Bournemouth, Southend and Rotherham, took over and promised the earth. He left in November 1999 amid claims that he had failed to keep up instalments to buy the club, and with supporters insisting he had never shown the slightest interest in the club.

### Bitter

According to Jonathan Cooper, co-editor of the Scarborough fanzine, *Two's Company, Five Hundred's A Crowd*: *'There's no question that the fans blame Johnson for the way things have gone. The bad form has just been a side-effect of what happened in the boardroom. We can't understand why he did it. Why take over at a club, show no interest and do nothing? It doesn't make sense. We hardly ever saw him at matches or at the club and we are very, very bitter about what he did.'*

# Anton Johnson, who was censured by the FA in 1984 for having conflicting interests in Bournemouth, Southend and Rotherham, took over and promised the earth.

Fans contacted the FA to complain about Johnson and eventually ownership of the club reverted to former chairman, John Russell. When asked at the time about the new situation, Cooper replied:

*'Things are improving. We could survive. And at least we are in good hands. We would rather have John Russell in charge with no money but good intentions than Johnson promising lots of money but with bad intentions.'*

# City and United

## Some personal views

Few football rivalries can split a city so decisively than Manchester United and Manchester City. United have had everything to crow about in recent years, but with City back in the Premiership for the 2002-03 season, Kevin Keegan's side have a chance to redress the balance.

Ask a Manchester United fan what he or she thinks of the rivalry with City and you'll get a response like this: *'Once a highlight of British football, the rivalry between Manchester's two teams in the 1990s became ludicrously one-sided as United won everything in sight and City plummeted to the Second Division.'*

United made a mockery of the phrase, *'Anything can happen in a derby game',* with the consistent stuffing of City on every occasion the teams met. It's always good for Manchester when the derby game is resurrected but it's nothing like the occasion it was. It hasn't always been like this. In the 1970's, City were sometime title challengers, while United plumbed the murky depths of under-achievement. They once won the title over United in 1968 on the final day, but the television and media virtually ignored it as United's European Cup final was being played the following week.

The City fans' bitterness at being overlooked by the press is part of a long history of being overshadowed by their more exciting, glamorous neighbours. No matter what City did, everybody was always more interested in United. Although City fans would never admit it, City are Manchester's second team – by a long way. In Europe United are usually referred to simply as *'Manchester'* – they are the only team foreigners recognize as coming from the city. Contrary to their fans' belief, City are a big club, but not a massive one. I mean, if they're massive, what does that make United, Barcelona and co.?

# In the 1970's, City were sometime title challengers, while United plumbed the murky depths of under-achievement.

## Proximity

City fans always go on about how they are Manchester's true team and no United fans come from Manchester. However, the one million people who filled the city's streets to see United's treble-winners homecoming shoots that argument down. Also, their stadium, Maine Road is further away from Manchester city centre than Old Trafford. It must be hard coping with being a City fan. Most live in denial, cursing the mighty Red's exploits at every opportunity. United fans don't hate City as much as they used to. Who cares about a team that's played the likes of Macclesfield and Walsall for three years when Manchester United have been playing Juventus and Real Madrid?

## Humiliation

Now, were you to listen to City supporters…

*'After four years of utter humiliation and degradation, our team bounces back to achieve glory by returning to the Premiership. City are back. Yes, I will repeat it again. Manchester City are back. They are in the Premiership. Next season they will be playing Manchester United and Arsenal. Not Grimsby Town or Tranmere.*

*This report absolves City from the various farces of the past five years. We can now forget Alan Ball, Steve Coppell, Frank Clark and Phil Neal. We can consign Gerry Creaney, Ged Brannan, Nigel Clough, Barry Conlon and many, many other non-entities to the backs of our minds, mere blips in what has really been a good last 100 years for City! The memories of defeats by the likes of such footballing aristocrats such as Wycombe Wanderers, Lincoln City, York and Crewe will all fade in time. The last five years should literally be seen as a "restructuring process", rather like a snake shedding it's skin.'*

Player 9

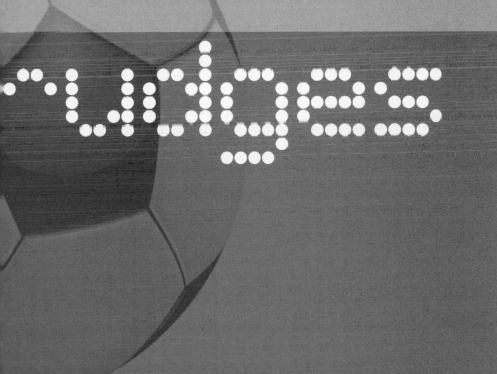

'I f*****g hit him hard. Take that you c***'

Roy Keane on his 'tackle' on Alf Inge Haaland
(vs Manchester City, April 2001)

# Head Case

## Duncan Ferguson

On the morning of Tuesday 24 November 1998, Newcastle awoke to the news that Duncan Ferguson was about to sign. Ruud Gullit had made his first signing and you couldn't get much bigger than Big Dunc. At 6' 4" and nearly 15 stone, the fiery Scot was one of the most feared players in the Premiership. Born in Stirling on 27 December 1971, he started his football career at Dundee United in 1990. He soon became an international and three years later joined Rangers for a then British record fee of £4m.

Duncan Ferguson has scored goals wherever he has gone in his career. An old fashioned style centre forward, his height and strength have made him an ideal target man. But on more than one occasion he has demonstrated a head for aggression to match his head for goals.

In 1994, Ferguson head-butted Raith's John Mcstay during a match and was later arrested by the police. He was sentenced to serve a three-month prison sentence and was also given a 12-match ban by the Scottish FA. Duncan then went on loan to Everton, agreeing to sign permanently for £4m. He eventually served a six-week prison sentence in April 1995. After all the legal battles and rows with the media Ferguson turned his back on international football, settled down, got stuck in at Everton and became a cult figure. In June 1998, he married snooker star John Parrot's sister. A talisman at Everton, he scored 42 goals in 133 games before making a shock £7m move to Newcastle United in November 1998. He suffered frustration during his spell with the Magpies as a spate of injuries saw him struggle to stay in the side. Ferguson returned to Goodison Park in the summer of 2000 for £3.5m in a protracted transfer, but his second spell on Merseyside has been also dogged by injuries.

# Duncan Ferguson caught two burglars in his house. The only surprise was that just one of them ended up in hospital.

*'Good judgement comes from experience. Experience is most often the result of bad judgement,'* says Duncan Ferguson in hindsight.

### Hands-on approach

Who tries to burgle the house of one of the tough nuts of football? That was the question everyone was asking when the news came out that Duncan Ferguson had

caught two burglars in his house. The only surprise was that just one of them ended up in hospital. The other one must have managed to carry all that was in his pants to get away. Ferguson was forced to miss out on the next match against Spurs after he cracked a hand hitting one of the intruders. Everton manager Walter Smith told Everton's official website: *'With the injury being so fresh it is causing Duncan a fair bit of discomfort. We will see how he is on Saturday.'*

### No comment

Since returning to Everton, the often-injured Ferguson continues to refuse interviews with the press. On a rare interview on behalf of his boot sponsors he answered the journalist's questions with a simple *'yes'* or *'no'* to complete one of the dullest Q&A sessions ever recorded. When David Moyes took charge at Everton he made Ferguson captain and was rewarded with a string of goals by his skipper in the first three games following his appointment, helping his side move away from the relegation zone. Ferguson continues to reject calls for a return to international duty and all enquiries for media interviews are referred to his agent for brief consideration before being rejected.

# Prisons and Screwdrivers

## Mickey Thomas

Getting 18 months in jail over a counterfeit currency scam wasn't the lowest point of Mickey Thomas' long and controversy-laden career. That came when he discovered his cell-mate had killed two people – then cut off their heads. The rest of his sentence seemed like a doddle.

*'The first place I went, Walton prison in Liverpool, was tough, but after that I had it quite comfortable inside,'* said the ex-Welsh international who was sent down in 1993. *'I made sure I had the best of everything: whatever I wanted to drink, plenty of days at home and, towards the end, I even had my own car.'* Thomas's life behind bars was so cushy that the *News of the World* filled a front page with a photo of him swigging from a champagne bottle and a story warning that the picture *'will enrage every law-abiding Briton'*.

## John Thomas

In 1992, he was stabbed with a screwdriver while fooling about with his former sister-in-law in his Golf GTi. *The Telegraph* ran a headline that said, *'Wife Was Bait In Sex Trap For Football'*. In 1993, Thomas was unlucky to receive a custodial sentence, especially one of 18 months, for passing dud £10 and £20 notes to trainees at Wrexham, his club at the time. But he was lucky that, unlike other celebrities who have been banged up, most of the wardens liked and looked after the long-haired winger, and his jokes and dressing room tales ensured the other inmates – and the guards – were friendly.

Judge Gareth Edwards had condemned the player's self-image as a *'flash and daring adventurer'*.

*'The judge made an example of me,'* says Thomas. *'He was enjoying it: a full house, with all the media there. If I'd been anyone else, I probably wouldn't have gone to jail.'*

# In 1992, he was stabbed with a screwdriver while fooling about with his former sister-in-law in his Golf GTi.

Now 47 – he played until he was 41 – Thomas is hardly short of work as a pundit, radio host and raconteur. *'I've had a great life out of football. I played 22 years professionally and never had to beg for a club. I had all the big clubs after me. Despite all the off-field stuff, I had respect.'*

## That Friday feeling

Thomas' industry, flair and eye for goal meant some manager was always ready to sign him, regardless of his disciplinary baggage. Most lived to regret it. Ron Atkinson couldn't believe it when he announced he was quitting Old Trafford. *'Ron said, "Why do you want to leave? Nobody wants to leave Man United. Stay and we can win things."'*
Perhaps his non-conformism explains why such a talented and hard-working player won very little: a Third Division championship with Wrexham and the Second Division title at Stamford Bridge. 'Winning things is probably nice but it doesn't make you a better player. But, pushed, he admits, that, *'though I don't wish I'd buckled down and accepted discipline a bit better, I do regret not staying longer at Man United, Everton or Chelsea, especially United, who won the Cup twice in the four years after I left.'*
Yet he also explains with perverse pride how he quit the club because, *'I couldn't handle the pressure – 60,000 at Old Trafford is a lot of people to please – and because, as a United player, your life's not your own.'* He took solace in alcohol.
*'I'd open a bottle of wine on a Friday night and sit up drinking until three in the morning to calm my nerves for next day's match. It helped me relax and get to sleep but didn't affect my performance as I was so fit.'* Thomas is not bitter about his life – except for his treatment by the judge.

# Cups and Saucers

## Cantona and the Manchester Utd commercial department

A surprise £1.2m signing by Manchester Utd in November 1992, Eric Cantona was not manager Alex Ferguson's initial target when he bid to increase the Red's goalscoring output. Having failed in his £3.5m attempt to land Sheffield Wednesday's goal machine, David Hirst, Ferguson was subsequently successful in his bid for the 26-year-old Parisian. It was a moment of sublime good fortune that would change the fate of Manchester United forever. Ferguson could not have dreamed just how great and glorious a catalyst Cantona would be for his developing team.

Cantona's career included a French Cup win with Montpelier and a League Championship with Leeds United, who pipped United for the title in 1991-92.
His first appearance for the Reds was against Benfica in Lisbon, in a friendly match to mark the 50th birthday of the great Portugal player, Eusebio. Cantona's class was never in doubt, but an apparently unpredictable and often outspoken Gallic temperament was, to some degree, the reason behind no less than eight different moves in the space of 10 years which had seen the French international adapt to many types of play, but not always the individuals in authority, most recently at Leeds, where he left amid recriminations on both sides.

### Impressive cult

He quickly settled on the big stage at Old Trafford. His subtle skills and flair for the unexpected made United supporters clasp him to their hearts as a cult hero and his contribution to successive Premiership titles was an immensely significant one. Not only had he created a fresh dimension in attack by his vision and self-confidence, but he also proved an inspiration to his talented team-mates who responded with their own skills and enthusiasm to his uplifting and unique brand of unforgettable magic.

Eighteen Premiership goals and four in the FA Cup was Eric's *'magnifique'* contribution to the Red's Double-winning season. With his trademark turned-up collar and shirt worn outside his shorts, the fiery Frenchman cut an impressive figure throughout 1993-94 and fully warranted his PFA Player of the Year award.

# With his trademark turned-up collar, and shirt worn outside his shorts, the fiery Frenchman cut an impressive figure.

## Mind your own business

But off the pitch things weren't quite so rosy. *'The secret of our success is to treat the fans with respect and provide them with top quality merchandise. We have over 800 products available,'* said Edward Freeman, from United's Merchandising department.

Cantona couldn't stomach the way the game he loved was driven by money. But what really annoyed him was the way his face was splattered over United's commercial offerings. It cheapened him. *'At that time they thought that merchandising was more important than the team and the players. When the business is more important than the football I just give up, rather than be treated like a pair of socks or a shirt.'*

According to Sir Alex Ferguson, *'The commercial side of the club was something that Eric couldn't cope with. There is a better communication now between the commercial side of the club and the players.'*

# Kop That

## Souness and Thompson

As a boy he supported Liverpool from The Kop. Then he got out there on the pitch, became the club captain and picked up the European Cup. It doesn't come much more romantic than that. Phil Thompson lived and breathed Liverpool, it was a big consideration for Kenny Dalglish when he made him reserve coach. *'I had Ronnie Moran and Roy Evans with the first team and Phil was the ideal age to work with the reserves and teach the younger players the traditions of Liverpool.'*

But in 1992, an acrimonious parting of the ways saw Phil Thompson ousted from the reserve team job. Dalglish had gone and Graeme Souness had been brought in from Rangers. Thompson still felt bitter about his captaincy when it was handed to Souness by Joe Fagan but he still gave everything for Liverpool.

Having been ousted from behind the scenes, an ugly court case was avoided at the last minute with an out-of-court settlement. Former Red, Sammy Lee, who had been eeking out a playing career in Spain, was appointed new reserve team coach. Thompson and Souness were never to see eye-to-eye again.

### Head-to-head

Whereas some people may have grudges against teams for sacking them, Thompson carried on caring for his beloved Reds. He worked on Sky and Radio City, and his passion for Liverpool was shown there. The board then decided to sack Souness but at the eleventh hour changed their minds and settled on a compromise. Roy Evans was appointed assistant manager at the start of the 1993-94 season, a clear message to the boss that Evans was being groomed to take over. Evans' spell brought little success and after pairing him with the Frenchman Gerard Houllier, Liverpool eventually allowed the lifelong fan of the club a crack at the job on his own. Now he needed a coach. Thompson was

# Whereas some people may have grudges against teams for sacking them, Thompson carried on caring for his beloved Reds.

appointed and when Houllier fell ill, took over the managing of the club on an 'acting' basis. Souness had by now become manager at Blackburn, and the man he had fired when the pair were together at Antield was to go head-to-head with him for the first time. Honours were shared in a 1-1 draw.

### Canny Kenny

Commenting on Thompson after Houllier was taken ill, Dalglish said, *'Phil was a tremendous reader of the game. He was an intelligent footballer and very good in the air. I sensed he would do a good coaching job.*

*'Tommo's feelings for Liverpool were well known and there was no doubt that bringing him back into the club would guarantee a man who would be enormously loyal and would bleed for the club. That loyalty and intensity of feeling have been important over the days since Gerard was taken ill.*

*'When I left the club in 1991 and Graeme took over, Phil lost his job. It was not necessarily a reflection on him but a new manager very often wants his own people around him because they make him feel comfortable.*

*'Phil was devastated. I have talked about his background and how much he loves the club. So to be told he was no longer wanted would have been a huge disappointment. His world would have been turned upside down.*

*'When Gerard was appointed as the sole manager in 1998 and took him back, it was made clear to Phil he was being appointed because Gerard wanted somebody around him who knew the club and was passionate about it.'*

# Fouls

It's every referee's nightmare: what should he do if the ball bursts during the taking of a penalty kick? The United States Soccer Federation (USSF) has published a book called *Advice To Referees on the Laws of the Game*, a companion to the *Laws of the Game* which explains many of the finer points and applications in detail. The book states, under the Penalty Kick section 14.7, that, *'If, after the kick has been taken, the ball is stopped or interfered with by an outside agent, or if it bursts on its way to the goal, the kick shall be retaken.'*

## Penalty kick

A penalty kick is awarded when a player commits a foul or handles the ball inside his own penalty area when the ball is in play. Examples of how a player could give a penalty kick to the opposite team include:

- Cruelly pushing an opponent.
- Kicking an opponent.
- Tripping an opponent.
- Tackling the opponent to get the ball,
  but touching the opponent before making contact with the ball.
- Spitting at an opponent.

## Free Kicks

There are two types of free kicks: direct and indirect. A direct free kick is awarded outside the penalty area. The direct free kick is awarded for the same rule breaches as in the penalty area. An indirect free kick is awarded when the goalkeeper inside his own penalty area commits an offence other than the ones which will result in a penalty kick, or the opponent commits the offence inside the penalty area of the rival team.

If a goalkeeper touches the ball with his hands when it has purposely been kicked to him by a team mate, an indirect free kick is awarded to the opposing side, offering a great opportunity to score a goal. Similarly, if a goalkeeper keeps the ball in his hands for more than six seconds before throwing or kicking it to one of his team mates, the referee will award an indirect free kick inside the penalty area.

# Back Stabbers

## Le Saux and Fowler

The papers reported it like this: *'Two England internationals have been charged with misconduct after ugly scenes during Chelsea's 2-1 Premiership win against Liverpool at Stamford Bridge last Saturday.'*

*'Graeme Le Saux and Robbie Fowler have two weeks to prepare a defence to the charges. Chelsea have already confirmed that they intend to support Le Saux over the incident, which ran for ten minutes in the second half.*

*'A foul by Le Saux led to an argument between the players and continued after another disputed free kick. Le Saux refused to restart play while Fowler did not move ten yards back. Fowler responded by making more comments and showing his bottom repeatedly to Le Saux, who complained to the referee. Both players were booked – the away support targeted Le Saux for abuse throughout the match and the defender's temper boiled over.*

*'As play moved on, Le Saux was caught by television cameras striking Fowler on the head from behind. The blow has been played repeatedly by television but no official took any action. There was another confrontation between the two in the players' tunnel after the bad tempered match.*

*'Le Saux faces a four-match ban on the television evidence and Chelsea's disciplinary record is poor this season. However, the decision to charge Fowler over his comments and gestures to a fellow England international could be the more far-reaching decision. Fowler appeared the innocent party at the weekend but the FA have decided to make some stand against his ugly abuse of another professional. The Players' Union has yet to comment on Fowler's abuse of Le Saux.'*

## Unforgivable behaviour

Graeme Le Saux revealed in an interview some months later that he was unable to forgive and forget Robbie Fowler's *'offensive behaviour'* during their run-in at Stamford

# Fowler responded by showing his bottom repeatedly to Le Saux, who complained to the referee.

Bridge – even after publicly making peace with the striker. Both players made partial apologies to each other as the Football Association carried out an investigation before handing Le Saux a one-match ban and Fowler a two-game suspension last season. But Le Saux didn't see that as the end of it: *'It's not the sort of thing you can just forgive and forget, or can laugh about,'* he told BBC Radio Five Live.

*'What Robbie did was very offensive to myself, my family and maybe even to gay people as well. It was a very serious statement and something I found totally unacceptable... When you start getting into very personal areas, it's out of order and judging from the support I got and the reaction of all parties both in my profession and outside it, so did other people... I wasn't going to accept that kind of thing, just laugh about it and almost say, "that's OK, you can treat me like that."'*

**England expects**

England boss Kevin Keegan was forced to intervene ahead of the Euro 2000 qualifier against Poland and both players shook hands in front of him to show that they would put their country before any private dispute.

*'It was very difficult for Kevin because he inherited this problem and it was probably the last thing he wanted,'* said Le Saux.

*'He told us he wanted it settled quickly. He wanted harmony within the team, not players at each other's throats. I'm sure he was looking at me when he said that because I was the one who reacted on the pitch and I was the one who had a problem with the original incident.'*

# Hot Striker

## Cantona leaves Leeds

Howard Wilkinson was a hard man to satisfy. Although a disciplinarian, he was undeterred by headstrong characters if he believed that they could offer a new dimension – few could have imagined Vinnie Jones knuckling down so well. Now Wilkinson had become interested in another maverick, French international Eric Cantona who had walked out on his club, Nimes, vowing never to play football again – the latest chapter in an often rancorous career.

In the event, Cantona came to England and had a trial with Sheffield Wednesday, who could not make up their minds, but Wilkinson had seen film of Cantona in action and liked what he saw. Whatever the Frenchman's temperamental flaws, he had skills that were rare in the English game, enough for the Leeds' manager to make a snap decision and sign him on loan.

Cantona made a big impression at Leeds, helping them to their first league title since the seventies when Don Revie was in charge. The Yorkshire side had battled all the way with their rivals Manchester United and you could hear a pin drop when the news came through that Leeds had sold the player many thought essential to future success to the enemy across the Pennines. There were rumours that Cantona didn't get along with the players.

### Not-so-happy Chappy

According to his team-mate at the time, Gordon Strachan: *'Eric had made up his mind that he couldn't relate to big Lee Chapman as a player. He found it hard to understand how Chappy played and Chappy found it difficult to understand him. We had to play a certain style... it was very hard... we didn't have megabucks to change the whole side just to suit Eric Cantona. Hard work made us tick – and no lack of*

## 'Eric had made up his mind that he couldn't relate to Lee Chapman as a player.'

skill, but sometimes when we went away from home, Eric just couldn't understand what we were at. It frustrated him, there's no doubt about that.'

'When we went to Rangers, he just didn't produce a performance. There were a lot of places he didn't produce. We needed a bit of help... we needed to be met a wee bit. It might have bought some time for him to meet us, and we might have been able to bring in some better players to play with him. He had just made up his mind he wanted to leave; there was no way he wanted to stay. Nobody had anything against him personally. He wasn't a problem to get on with.'

Wilkinson telephoned Sir Alex Ferguson to ask if Denis Irwin was available for transfer. Fergie stated that he was looking to buy players, not sell. Wilkinson asked if he would be interested in Cantona and rest, as they say, is history.

# Fit For the Job?

## Houllier and Fowler

Back in 2002, Liverpool were rumoured to be chasing another striker. Many observers thought it was a pity Phil Thompson wasn't charging round the training ground encouraging Robbie Fowler. If anyone needed some motivation it was the former hero of the Kop, a player who had done so much for his team but was seemingly falling out with the management. For some reason, the Reds had decided that young Fowler was surplus to requirements and had decided to go after the grumpy Turkish striker, Hakar Sukur. Gerard Houllier stated that if he picked players on past reputations, then Roger Hunt and Ian Rush would still be getting a game. Nice line that, Gerard.

Fowler was leaving the field with a face filled with spanners – and that was if he was lucky to get off the sub's bench. But there was no denying that his performances had been rusty of late. Had he no-one to blame but himself? Where was the form of the player who had finished last season so emphatically at Charlton? What had happened to the flicks, the dummies and the runs through the middle that tore defences apart?

### Fans' favourite

The fans on Liverpool's many unofficial message boards were split on the issue. Some feared that Houllier had an ego problem with Fowler. Worried that his obvious empathy with the crowd distracted the player from doing his job. Concerned that a player carried more clout with the fans than the manager. Some said that this was clearly nonsense, but could it be true? Houllier was bright enough to realize that some players would always be crowd favourites. The manager was there to make everything work and to take the blame when it didn't.

# Fowler was leaving the field with a face filled with spanners – and that was if he was lucky to get off the sub's bench.

Other fans sited the case of David Ginola, a player Houllier simply refused to pick once he became the French coach. Ginola was clearly a class player, but look what had happened to the French team after his cock-up against Bulgaria in qualifying for the 1994 World Cup! Houllier understood that it takes a collection of players not a talented individual to make a team truly great. At Manchester United, no player was bigger than the club. And while the manager was in charge, that meant doing things his way. Fowler seemed to believe that the support of the fans and his mates in the team could justify his selection.

## Fit the bill
Houllier maintained that a fit Fowler would be a part of his plans. Fowler maintained that he was already fit, but could only get match fit, by playing. While Liverpool could only watch the saga unfurl with amazement, Chelsea, Leeds and Newcastle wondered if they could scrape together a few quid and lure the best finisher in the country over to their place. Within the space of a few more months the answer was *'yes'*, and Leeds lured the Reds' icon to Elland Road for less than £10m.

# B List

## Sutton and Hoddle fall out

Chris Sutton began his football career as a trainee at Norwich, making his full-team debut as an 18-year-old against QPR in May 1991. His tally of 43 goals in 127 appearances – some of which were as a defender – at Carrow Road caught the eye of Kenny Dalglish, then manager of Blackburn.

The £5m switch to Ewood Park catapulted the striker firmly into the spotlight, and the 'SAS' partnership with Alan Shearer not only helped Blackburn to the Premiership crown, but also encouraged talk of international honours. Although the duo enjoyed spectacular success at domestic level, they were never given the opportunity to show what they were capable of on an international platform.

When Sutton then finished joint top scorer in the Premiership along with Michael Owen and Dion Dublin in 1998, there were those who touted him as a certainty to feature at the World Cup. But a much-publicized fall-out between Sutton and Glenn Hoddle ensued after the England manager selected the forward for the 'B' squad.

It was a demotion that Sutton was unwilling to accept, but he says that he would have no qualms about turning out for his country again. *'It would have been nice to have extended the partnership I had with Alan Shearer at Blackburn into the England squad but there are a lot of other good players out there and I suppose it just wasn't to be.*

*'I'm not really bothered if I get picked for England again or not. If I get back into the England team then it would fine, but it's certainly not the be all and end all.'*

## Chile factor

When Glenn Hoddle looked back at the incident in his World Cup Dairy he wrote:
*'One player who wouldn't be involved then, nor at any time while I remain national coach,*

# 'Once I saw what the World Cup was all about it dawned on me. I was very disappointed I wasn't there.'

was Chris Sutton. He choose to withdraw from the "B" squad because he thought it wasn't good enough for him. He told me so in a telephone call. It wasn't a long conversation. I think his manager at Blackburn, Roy Hodgson, tried to persuade him to change his mind.

'He totally misinterpreted what a "B" game was about. In contrast to Chris, Paul Merson did himself a great deal of good in that "B" game against Chile. Chris let himself down and that's the end of it.'

## Sorry saga

Sutton eventually offered to bring to an end the ongoing saga of whether he would play for England under Hoddle's leadership.

Sutton said: *'If Glenn wanted to clear the air behind closed doors and if I was selected for another "B" squad then I would play. I still feel I was right in what I did at the time, but with hindsight I might have made a different decision. Once I saw what the World Cup was all about it dawned on me. I was very disappointed I wasn't there.'*

But Sutton wasn't expecting much from Hoddle and this was trotted out almost as an afterthought, a means of giving himself a get-out clause. Later, Sutton added: *'I might have to wait until the next England manager comes along before I get back into the squad.'*

# Naughty Boy

## Peter Storrie

Peter Edwin Storey was born in Farnham, Surrey on 7 September 1945. Storey served Arsenal for 16 years, making over 500 first-team appearances in league, Cup and European competitions and a further 200 at various other levels. He was a strong-tackling and creative player who could function equally well at full-back or in midfield.

Storey joined Arsenal in May 1961 as an apprentice and while at the club, won honours as old Division One champions and FA Cup winners in 1971, FA Cup runners-up in 1972, League Cup runners-up in 1968 and 1969 and winners of the European Fairs Cup in 1970.

Although an England schoolboy international he never received full international honours and was transferred to Fulham in 1977 for £11,000, with whom he ended his playing career. One of the core players among the Arsenal Double-winning team of 1971, Storey was involved in an amazing punch-up during their European journey the previous season. It was an event that bonded the team and helped to create a Double-winning spirit.

In the Fairs Cup first round in September 1970, the moment came off the pitch after a match in Rome against Lazio. The Lazio team, together with some of their fans, had lain in wait for the Arsenal players. When the brawl started, manager Bertie Mee was already on the coach, but not for long. Almost immediately Mee, Storey and the rest of the players were out there in the street laying into their attackers. Mee landed a decent left hook and as Bob McNab recalled: *'There had been a few in the team not too sure about Bertie, not too clear whether he was one of us or one of the bosses. They made up there minds that night. He came out game as a pebble to slug it out with the lads. They loved him for it.'*

Storey would always respect what Mee had to say for himself from that point.

# Having admitted boozing and womanizing during his playing days, the madness took over for Storey when he hung up his boots in 1977.

### Hard luck Storey

As the hardman of a midfield that included Charlie George and George Graham, Storey had incredible stamina and strength. He was the player Arsenal relied upon to shore things up, much like Patrick Vieira. Arsenal's physio for over 20 years, Fred Street, said: *'Storey was a fierce competitor, always wanted to play, even when he was injured.'* Having admitted boozing and womanizing during his playing days, the madness took over for Storey when he hung up his boots in 1977. You know when a player is struggling when one of his post-career entrepreneurial schemes is based in the Jolly Farmers' pub in Caledonian Road, Islington.

### Naughty boy

Where to begin with the legendary Arsenal enforcer? 1979: he received a suspended jail sentence for running a brothel (the Calypso Massage Parlour, Leyton High Road). 1980: he was jailed for three years for financing a plot to counterfeit gold coins. 1982: he received two six-month jail terms for car theft. 1990: he was jailed for four weeks for importing 20 *'obscene'* video tapes inside the spare tyre of his jeep. 1991: he was given a 28-day suspended sentence for swearing at a traffic warden. Not all bad then!
Not necessarily the worst of the football bad boys, however, considering the diversity of his crimes, but possibly the most notorious. He was last heard of doing a driving job in south London.

# The Scarf

**The sixties saw a spectacularly colourful change in the way football supporters displayed their allegiance to their football team. Supporters became more organized with co-ordinated displays of scarf and flag waving, chants and slogans. And they became more mobile too. By 1964, the core of troublemakers was perceived to concentrate in groups with no allegiance to either team, and could no longer be characterized simply as hardcore supporters.**

These groups identified and named themselves separately from the teams, and used match days as venues for violent confrontations with rival groups. Fans were bundled into trains and, in the days when replica shirts had yet to take off, the only way of telling who was going were was to observe the colour of the scarves hung from the train windows.

- Inside the stadium the sport of *'taking ends'* emerged as the favourite pastime of young male supporters. The idea was to charge at supporters of the rival team, driving them away from their viewing area behind the goal and capturing as many of their flags and scarves as possible. Both sides were quite partial to throwing a few kicks and punches before the police stepped in. Once the charging supporters had commandeered their positions, they would sing a hearty rendition of the team anthem, raise the club scarf and then scarper before the Old Bill chucked them out of the ground.

In the 1970s, the *'ultras'* began to adopt the fashionable look of European terrorism, notably influenced by the Red Brigade, Baader Meinhoff and the IRA.

- Over in Europe the rituals varied. Non-violent, law-abiding fans wore scarves around their wrists like kids going to rock concerts while the *'ultras'* distinguished themselves by adopting a new way of supporting their teams. From the Brazilian *'torcidas'* came the use of drums and horns, from English soccer fans, the *'scarf effect'* (massed scarves raised and waving) and chanting. The support came to be considered as part of the strategy and tactics used to win a match – often referred to as the *'twelfth player'*.

- In the 1970s the *'ultras'* began to adopt the fashionable look of European terrorism, notably influenced by the Red Brigade, Baader Meinhoff and the IRA which all sported the scarf wrapped tight around the face to prevent recognition. Ultras took to this menacing style in droves.

- In tragedy too, the scarf has taken centre stage. Tied to a post or the gates of the club the scarf is a way of paying tribute to those who have suffered.

# Tough As Old Boots

## Billy Bremner

The core of Don Revie's great Leeds side was the midfield blend of Billy Bremner's commitment and Johnny Giles' skill. Bremner, though, was also skilful and his passing, leadership, never-say-die attitude and eye for goal made him one of the game's great midfielders.

As a boy, the Scot played for St Modan's High School and Gowanhill Juniors (Stirling) and, after being rejected by Arsenal and Chelsea for being *'too small'*, he joined Leeds in December 1959. In his early days, he often brushed with football's authorities but gradually matured and collected many honours. He won the first of 54 Scottish caps in May 1965, adding to Schoolboy and Under-23 honours, and was one of Leeds United's most capped players. He's been the most successful skipper in the club's history, leading them to two league championships, an FA Cup win and two Inter Cities Fairs Cup triumphs. He won the 1970 Footballer of the Year award, as United narrowly missed out on a unique treble of league, FA Cup and European Cup.

Bremner moved to Hull City in September 1976 for £35,000, and ended his playing career after joining Doncaster Rovers in November 1978, where he played a handful of games. He led Doncaster to promotion to Division Three on two occasions and returned to Elland Road as manager in 1985.

### Pumped-up Ball

Whether it was Keegan or Porterfield at Wembley or Alan Ball against Arsenal, Bremner never shirked a tackle. The fiery redhead was the heartbeat of the Leeds team and if it looked like he wasn't interested then how could he expect others to be? The Scotland and Leeds captain inspired people and wasn't intimidated by anyone. In 1972, he clashed with Alan Ball at Wembley. Another red head, Bally clattered Bremner to the ground from behind, smashing through his legs. With the Leeds captain on the floor, Bally walked

# Bremner was on his feet, hands raised and it took several Arsenal players to hold the England player back.

away and then appeared to hear something and come back. Immediately Bremner was on his feet, hands raised and it took several Arsenal players to hold the England player back. No love lost there, it seems.

**Worldly wise**

Don Revie rated Bremner as one of the world's greatest players. He recalls:
*'He was quick over 10 yards, could see things out of the back of his head, he could put balls between people, he could lift games out of nothing he could play one-twos and set things off and then tackle back if he or anyone else had made a mistake.'*

According to Brian Clough, in a television interview in the seventies: *'He was a better captain than Revie was a manager and it can be argued that Don Revie is the best manager in the Football League. He is doing on the field what Don Revie does seven days a week. When they trot out on that field on a Saturday, Billy is just carrying it on.'*

# 'Ouch! That Hurts'

## Vinnie Jones and Gazza

Vinnie was a product of the evolution of the game into the nineties as football required more strength and endurance around the pitch. He would give everything to the team and take no prisoners. The fearsome approach to his football was something he carried with him from his days standing on the terraces, shouting at the players to give everything they had. *'I knew what they wanted, I could identify with the supporters,'* he always said. While Jones was known more for his snarl than his smile he was a warm-hearted man off the field, generous to charities and a family man. But in the early days, he undoubtedly played up on the image of a neanderthal beast, one-way traffic in the world of intimidation. Even when he went to court for scuffling with his neighbours it wasn't the usual drunken antics of a contemporary footballer but an argument over the placing of a pig sty that had caused the row. Jones liked to cultivate the image of an English country squire in those pre-Hollywood days, a far cry from how he started out.

### Quiz master

*'He's incredibly loyal. Ask him to jump off the stand roof and he'd do it,'* said Arnie Reed, his physio at Wealdstone. *'He always grabbed the quiz book on our coach trips so that he could ask the questions. That way he didn't have to answer.'* Sam Hammam, his chairman at Wimbledon, called him a *'once-in-a-lifetime human being'* while John Fashanu called him *'The Madman'*. Vinnie was born in 1965 and enjoyed a successful spell at Wimbledon before moving on to Leeds, Sheffield United and Chelsea. He played 231 league games, scoring 23 goals, but it was his tally of yellow cards and sendings off that really made their mark on British football.

# But in the early days, he undoubtedly played up on the image of a neanderthal beast.

### Ball skills

*'Believe it or not, Vinnie's a very disciplined lad. We asked him to do a job on Gazza and he was first class,'* said Wimbledon assistant coach, Don Howe. The pictures that went round the world made both players famous. Gazza, still playing for Newcastle United and more famous for his love of Mars Bars than anything else was being marked by Jones. *'In non-league you could get away with it,'* said Jones of that incident. Jones is famously pictured grabbing Gazza's testicles, and as each frame flows he appears to give them a swift twist to the right. Indeed Jones looks like he's grimacing more than Gazza.

In fact, Gazza was actually marking Jones on that occasion. They had had plenty of banter during the match as you'd expect and Wimbledon were looking to make something of a free-kick on the halfway line.

*'He was giggling until I stood back and trod on his toe,'* said Jones as he recalled the moment again. Shortly after the pictures landed on the desk of every newspaper in the country, Gazza came south to play for Tottenham. Terry Venables, the Spurs manager, told him he'd be playing for England within six weeks and sure enough he was. Jones had to wait for many year before his international call up for Wales.

# Chop, Chop

## Ron Harris and Eddie Gray

Ron *'Chopper'* Harris played 655 league games for Chelsea from 1962 to 1980. Whether he was hunting down George Best or hacking at the heels of Rodney Marsh, Harris was a committed and forceful character who would be detailed to do a *'job'* on the opposition's better players. In the 1970 FA Cup final, Chelsea had missed him in the first match and the Leeds winger, Eddie Gray, had made a monkey out of his temporary replacement, Dave Webb. In the replay, Harris was back and Leeds, and Gray in particular, would never forget it.

### Coming to blows

The 1970 FA Cup replay was a no-holds barred encounter that John Hollins described as *'brutal and violent'*. And Hollins was right in the middle of the X-certificate action as Chelsea squared up to Leeds' tough guys like Billy Bremner, Johnny Giles and Norman Hunter to lift the FA Cup with a 2-1 triumph.

He said: *'I always tell my young players, "If you think modern football is tough, just look at a video of that final." It was a pitched battle.'*

In fact, David Elleray recently re-refereed the game by video, applying modern rules and attitudes. He produced six red and 20 yellow cards.

Hollins went on: *'I've never known a game like it in all my years in football. I was hit by someone. Someone else hit someone else. That player kicked someone else and he hit someone else.*

*'But the referee, Eric Jennings, let everything go. He didn't book anyone. Our Eddie McCreadie went through on Bremner with a kung-fu style challenge. His foot was at waist height and I never saw Billy move out of the way so fast.*

*'Ron Harris came through so high on Eddie Gray that "Chopper" ended up with Eddie's shorts on his studs! Ian Hutchinson and Norman Hunter started trading*

# 'Ron Harris came through so high on Eddie Gray that "Chopper" ended up with Eddie's shorts on his studs!'

blows and continued even as the ball went up the other end.

*'I went to take the throw-in from which David Webb nudged home the winner and they were still at it!'*

## John's punchline

Chelsea won the replay against a side feared throughout the world.

*'I still don't know how we won it,'* said Hollins. *'Leeds should have won that game 5-0. My favourite memory of the first game is taking up three feet of Wembley turf with my first tackle.*

*'It was like a ploughed field because they had held the Horse of the Year show there a few days earlier. Leeds could certainly play a bit, but they also had a mean streak. Believe me, we matched them kick for kick and punch for punch in the replay.'*

# Scots Grist

## Dave Mackay and Billy Bremner

Edinburgh-born Dave Mackay made his name in the magnificent Heart of Midlothian side that dominated Scottish football in the late 1950s. In March 1959, Tottenham Hotspur paid a fee of £30,000 to bring him south of the border. Along with Falkirk's John White and Dundee's Bill Brown, Dave Mackay was one of a trio of Scots signed in that year. Bill Nicholson had started to assemble arguably the greatest club side ever to play in the English League.

With Irishman Danny Blanchflower already established at White Hart Lane, the Londoners could boast a midfield that would be instrumental in powering Spurs towards the league championship and FA Cup.

The legendary team of 1960-61 was to sweep all before them, winning their first 11 games. It was to be a further six games before Spurs were defeated, at Sheffield Wednesday. An amazing 16 victories on opposition soil was proof of the side's attack-minded philosophy.

In this incredible season, more than two million spectators witnessed *'Super Spurs'* become the first side of the century to complete the historic league and Cup Double. Although other clubs would repeat the feat in later years, it should be remembered that Spurs, unlike the vast international-laden squads of today, used only 17 players – and three of those only once.

### Roll out the barrel

One of the most enduring photographs in football, shows a rugged, barrel-chested Dave Mackay's reaction to a foul by fellow Scottish international Billy Bremner. With arms wide apart in protest of innocence, the young Leeds grafter is pulled by his screwed-up shirt towards the uncompromising Mackay.

# With arms wide apart in protest of innocence, the young Leeds grafter is pulled by his screwed-up shirt towards the uncompromising Mackay.

You need only look at that image of Dave Mackay to realize the stature of the great man. Dave Mackay's fearlessness, drive and will to win was remarkable. At only 5'8", the Scotsman looked like he was chiselled from granite and a journalist once remarked that, *'his tackling could have earned him a good living felling trees.'* Remarkably, Mackay was never sent off in his illustrious career.

### Heart and soul

According to Terry Venables, who played with him at Spurs: *'For me, he was one of the most charismatic characters I'd ever seen. He was rugged and tough but he had the greatest one touch. He was so confident, superhumanly so. He'd come out at the start of the game carrying a ball for the kickabout and he'd throw it to the opposition and say, "Go on, have a kick now, 'cos you're not going to get one when the game starts!"'*

Bill Nicholson called him the complete professional and heartbeat of his team and Mackay is proud of his records. He was told to leave the field only once. *'But I told the ref that I thought it was a bit dubious and he agreed with me and changed his mind,'* he recalls with a smile.

# Rovers Revolt

## Le Saux and Batty

UEFA were urged by the FA to take action over an on-pitch fight between Blackburn team mates, Graeme Le Saux and David Batty in Moscow in November 1995. The England international pair fought with each other after four minutes of Blackburn's 3-0 Champions' League defeat by Spartak Moscow. Blackburn manager Ray Harford gave them both massive club fines of two weeks' wages, but the FA weren't prepared to let it go at that.

A spokesman said: *'We were very concerned about what happened in that match and we feel something must be done.*
*'However, the match comes under the jurisdiction of UEFA and we will be writing to them asking them to investigate the incident.*
*'Unlike the FA, UEFA does not usually accept video evidence, so much will depend on what their official observer and the match referee saw. But we are of the firm belief that action must be taken.'*

### Fighting talk

The amazing scenes in the Luzhniki Stadium prompted Harford to rush out of his dug-out, gesticulating wildly, as the punch-up started 30 metres away from him.
Batty and Le Saux went to claim the same ball and ended up colliding into each other. The pair squared up and angry words quickly turned to actions as Le Saux threw a punch that caught Batty in the throat. Batty retaliated and Sherwood piled in as an aggressive peace keeper, using his forearm to prevent a possible follow-up blow from Le Saux.
*'We've got to keep punching on,'* said the Blackburn boss, Ray Harford, unwittingly, after Batty and Le Saux's on field punch-up.

# Angry words turned to actions as Le Saux threw a punch that caught Batty in the throat

Blackburn had been flying the flag for England in European competition during that season, albeit at half mast, with only one point and one goal from five games. But this pitch battle, on the European stage, brought another blow to British football's reputation, having only in recent seasons been allowed back into European action.

## Rule of thumb

Graeme Le Saux was in trouble with the FA again following a red card against Sunderland five years later. Le Saux was dismissed after appearing to swing an elbow at Sunderland's Kevin Kilbane, who was also red carded for a push on the England man in retaliation. However, Le Saux was seen raising a sarcastic 'thumbs up' at the assistant referee who was just yards away from the action and it's also said that he verbally abused the official. In the build up the 2002 World Cup, pundits argued among themselves about Sven Goran Eriksson's reluctance to pick the disruptive player. One camp argued that he was a naturally gifted wide midfielder/defender with a left-foot (a rarity among the England candidates) and that he had never been sent off for England so we should ignore his temperament. While this argument carried some persuasion, Le Saux effectively ended the discussion with an horrendous challenge on Leeds' Danny Mills that had Sky Sports analyst Gary McAllister wincing in his seat. Le Saux never made it into England's squad after that.

# The Kick About

**There are several things to consider in the history of the kick about. It has been established that national leaders and gentlemen of the cloth tried to ban the *ad hoc* meetings of players on a field and the spontaneous outbreaks of a social malaise they called *'football'*.**

At school, the less enthusiastic members of the teaching profession would frown at the seemingly random way all the crap players ended up playing on one side and so asked the better lads to even things up a bit. Even those lucky enough to have been brought up in the confines of a suburban house with sufficiently large back garden to fulfil a football fixture will recognize the onset of that heart-sinking moment of panic when the ball sails towards the greenhouse and sends a shower of broken glass over the prize tomato plants. There is more to a kick about than simply pitching up and getting on with it. Pitfalls and hazards lie round every corner.

- The first, and most important consideration has to be the choice of venue. Will it be a field of dreams or a mudbath of nightmares? It is the essential part of any kickabout and without it much of the fun would be lost. Most public parks and playing fields are nothing more then windswept mud-ridden battlegrounds politely called a field. A quick study of these environments will reveal that few, if any, possess what could technically be referred to as goalposts. It is for this reason that items of clothing, specifically jumpers knitted by grandmothers, are frequently used as alternatives. Even when the weather is seasonably inclement, the jumper is retained as the goalpost of choice while the players seek the sanctuary and relative dryness of nearby foliage.

# A quick study of these environments will reveal that few, if any, possess what could technically be referred to as goalposts.

- The second important aspect of this noble pursuit is the solicitation of an opposition. Be very careful with this one for it is important to choose wisely. Challenge a set of lads who look good enough to give you a game but not hard enough to give you a hiding, and you're off to a good start. It is important to maximize the time you and your buddies have for the kickabout by playing a team that compares favourably with your own strengths. There is no satisfaction in walloping a collection of under-achievers and nothing more frustrating than playing a game that is too one-sided.

- If you find it hard to rustle up an opposition, the pragmatic thing to do is either allow both teams the luxury of a *'rush goalie'* or, failing that, read a copy of *How to Win Friends and Influence People*. As a last resort, try *'three-and-in'*, a game which should act as bait for any passing football enthusiast who will note the sparse numbers and offer his (or her) services without fear of rejection.

- Finally, make sure you bring a spare ball. There's always one smart arse who thinks it's funny to hoik your ball into a tree, the nearest cowpat-infested field or oncoming traffic. If you going to play to win, you have to make sure you have the equipment to play to the finish.

# Come In, No.1

## Mark Bosnich and Manchester Utd

*'If I can blend into the background and nobody notices the change that'll be fine by me,'* said Mark Bosnich on his arrival at Manchester Utd as the highly regarded replacement Sir Alex Ferguson had been seeking for Peter Schmeichel. Mark Bosnich was born of Yugoslavian parents in Australia, and first joined United as a non-contract player in 1990. He was a student at Manchester Polytechnic when he made his first senior appearance, as deputy for Jim Leighton, against Wimbledon, towards the close of the 1989-90 season. As a fun-loving member of Aston Villa's side, he had several run-ins with the FA, most notably when he was fined £1,000 after making a Nazi-style salute during a match with Tottenham at White Hart Lane.

His career at United was limited to just 34 appearances in two seasons and Sir Alex Ferguson, not noted for his patience with playboy footballers (as Dwight Yorke can testify), found a nice warm spot on the sub's bench for his maverick stopper until someone was prepared to cough up the £40,000 weekly wage bill Bosnich somehow managed to negotiate for himself.

### Flare ups?

On his first day at United, 15 July, 1999, Bosnich made it clear that he saw himself as the No. 1 keeper. And yet within minutes he was in trouble in a Birmingham lap-dancing club. By October, Ferguson had begun to pick the reserve keeper, Van Der Gouw as first choice. Some felt the stand-in bore a resemblance to a seventies porno star but Bosnich was the one suffering from a Playboy image.

# He was fined £1,000 after making a Nazi-style salute during a match with Tottenham at White Hart Lane.

By November the doctors were worried about the Aussie keeper's weight. Things were getting bad. During the end of November stories began emerging that Fergie was after another keeper, the Italian, Massimo Taibi, and the sorry saga of Bosnich's second spell at United was getting worse by the minute.

### Resolute blue

By January Bosnich was sunning himself in Brazil for the inaugural World Club Championships. Still no sign of a first team place. There were still plenty of snide remarks about the Australian's weight and come the summer, Fabien Bartez was on his way to United. On January 1, 2001 Bosnich's New Year's resolutions would have been *'Stand up to Fergie'*, *'Get my place in the side back'*, *'Show everyone how great I am'*. By the end of the month he was playing for Chelsea.

# Legs Have It

## Danny Mills and Graeme Le Saux

The press reported the terrible tackle that could have finished Mills' career like this: *'Danny Mills today accused Graeme Le Saux of receiving preferential treatment from referees after he escaped with just a yellow card for his horrific two-footed lunge on the Leeds defender.'*

*'The England right-back was left with stud marks from his knee to his hip after the first-half clash with Le Saux during yesterday's ill-tempered 0-0 draw at Elland Road. Leeds manager David O'Leary described the tackle as "disgraceful" and was so angry that referee Paul Durkin only booked Le Saux, that his furious protests resulted in him being sent from the touchline.*

*'Mills said he did not believe Le Saux intended to hurt him but suggested that had it been the other way around, and he had gone in two-footed on the Chelsea captain, Durkin would have sent him off.*

*'The Leeds man said: "I'm not particularly disappointed with the tackle. These things happen in football. Sometimes they are one-footed, other times you get caught with two. The thing that did disappoint me, if it was two-footed as I believe, and the referee and linesman saw it, that Graeme didn't get a red card for it. I think if that had been me doing the same tackle there'd have been no hesitation, I would have been straight down the tunnel. Unfortunately it's out of my hands. I'm not sure he particularly meant it. We were both going for the ball, I beat him to it and I've been caught. It's up to the referee to make the decision. It's gone now, the referee has got to live by his decision. Whoever looks at it will judge him on that. It was a tackle for the referee to deal with. It's a difficult thing to say without sounding like people are picking on me but it seems to me that referees look at certain players differently."'*

# 'Stung by accusations of cowardice they played with aggression and seemed determined to prove they have fighting spirit.'

### Boiling point

'Referee Durkin, who consulted with his assistant before booking Le Saux, refused to comment on that incident but when asked why he had banished O'Leary to the stands said: "That's between me, Mr O'Leary and the FA."

'After facing severe criticism for letting six first-team stars, including Le Saux, miss Thursday's 2-0 UEFA Cup defeat in Tel Aviv, Chelsea welcomed back four of their stay-aways for the Leeds game. Stung by accusations of cowardice they played with aggression and seemed determined to prove they have fighting spirit.

'At times it threatened to boil over and although referee Durkin made five bookings, and sent O'Leary off, there could have been many more cards shown.'

### Red mist

'Le Saux's tackle was the most controversial error he made. However, Le Saux looks likely to escape with the yellow card he was handed even though TV replays showed the tackle on Mills was a red card offence.

'The FA's video review panel cannot change the decision because it can only rule on incidents missed by match officials. And while red cards can be rescinded if the referee agrees to look at a sending off again, the FA say there is no precedent for a yellow card being upgraded to red.

'The FA, however, might want to call both clubs in for peace talks ahead of their next Premiership match... Yesterday's clash took their disciplinary record for their last 11 meetings to 71 yellow cards and five red.'

# Booted Out

## Ronaldo blows out Nike

Des Lynam flapped at his papers, raising both eyebrows like his puppet-master was having difficulty controlling those famous follicle strings and suddenly you knew a moment of great drama was upon us. The World Cup final show had only been on for 20 seconds and nobody knew if Ronaldo was going to play. World Cup finals simply didn't get this exciting!

There were two different team sheets in the great man's hands, one with the world's finest player's name present and one with it missing. The question was, what was going on? Rumours spread that the Brazilian doctor had argued with some of the players that the goofy-toothed star was unfit for the final and several of the players were alleged to have thrown punches in the dressing room. Stories circulated that Ronaldo had reacted badly to medication, possibly had an epileptic fit, and then again, others claimed his paymasters, Nike, had demanded he play, even if it meant borrowing Des Lynam's puppeteer for the occasion. As the players came out, the Brazilian hero was there in his silversurfer Nike boots, waving to the girlfriend and wishing he was some place else. If he touched the ball at all it was to take a throw-in and the boy from Rio de Janeiro could only sit back and watch as a balding superstar from the streets of Marseilles knocked in two goals for the French and set the streets of Paris on fire with joy and not a little conspiracy speculation.

### Order of the boot

In a leaked document before the 1999 Brazil vs Barcelona friendly laid on by Nike for some of its corporate chums, the details of Nike's reputed £200m Brazilian sponsorship deal became clearer. The deal states that Nike can dictate when, where and against which sides the world's most famous football club will play five times every year until 2006. The contract states that the team must be the full strength national side. The small

# There were two different team sheets in the great man's hands, one with the world's finest player's name present and one with it missing.

print makes clear that Ronaldo's presence, regardless of form, is a necessity. The game between Brazil and Nike-sponsored Barcelona, the biggest club in the world, was Nike's finest corporate showpiece. The contro of the show was, despite being plagued by injury, Ronaldo, whose personal sponsorship with Nike is £10m a year.

**Mystery man**

In 1997, a deal between Ronaldo and his former club, Barcelona, broke down, allegedly over the way Nike and the club would split the £30m needed to keep him there. Ronaldo was then linked to other clubs. Eventually, again in mysterious circumstances, Ronaldo signed for the £125m Nike-sponsored club, Inter Milan. According to Jose Texeira, Ronaldo's childhood friend from their slum in Rio, *'Ronaldo has no say, no idea what he's doing. He is controlled by the businesses.'* Asked to comment on the rumour that Nike ordered the World Cup favourites to play Ronaldo for their own commercial advantage in 1998, a Nike spokesperson replied at the time, *'Nike wants to emphasize that the reports of such involvement is absolutely false.'*

# Bad Boys

## A league of their own

In an article for *FourFourTwo* magazine, a table of bad boy behaviour was drawn up. It offered a refreshing examination of the lunacy of footballers, something that is less frequently seen now that players get paid so much for doing something we'd all love and enjoy. These snippets are regurgitated here for no better reason than to make sure we haven't missed anyone…

**Tommy Docherty** (1977) leaves his wife and four children for an affair with Mary Brown, the wife of Manchester United's physio, Laurie. Ultimately they were to marry, but not before he is sacked by the Old Trafford club. **David Pleat** (1987) is cautioned three times for kerb-crawling, forcing him to resign as manager of Spurs. **Norman Hunter and Francis Lee** (1975) punch and kick each other during Derby's 3-2 win over Leeds at the Baseball ground. They are sent-off, then start up all over again in the tunnel! **George Graham** (1995) is found guilty by the FA of passing a *'bung'* to agent, Rune Hague to sign John Jensen and Pal Lyndersen and is sacked by Arsenal. George is also banned from football worldwide for 12 months. **Stan Bowles** (1977), before playing for England against the Netherlands at Wembley, is offered and accepts 200 pounds to wear Gola boots during the match. Later the same day, he is offered 300 pounds to wear Adidas boots. Stan accepts this also and turns out for the match wearing one boot from each company! **The Dutch World Cup squad** (1974) on the eve of the final with Germany have four men named in the German tabloid *'Bild Zeitung'* as having a party with naked women in the hotel swimming pool before an earlier match with Brazil. Initially denied as German sportsmanship, it was later suggested it happened, but that the *'Bild'* had paid the girls to do it. Nevertheless, Johan Cruyff's wife Danny is so worried she kept him on the phone all night before the Final match! **Inter Milan** (1971-72) in the European Cup were 2-1 down in the second round away tie versus Borussia Mönchengladbach, when a member

# All five players were given a ban, and Billy never played for Scotland again.

of the crowd threw an object which hit Roberto Boninsegna. He falls to the ground and is treated by the physio. The only thing was all that was thrown was an empty Coke can, which was swiftly swapped for a full one, which was given to the referee. Boninsegna and Inter go on to lose 7-1. The club's president, Ivanoe Fraizzoli pleads for, and wins, a rematch of the tie in Berlin. This game is drawn 0-0 and Inter Milan went through.

### Front-page news
**Alfredo Di Stefano** (1963), while a player at Real Madrid, was kidnapped by the Venezuelan Liberation Front, whilst on tour in their country. He is held for two days, but treated well, and released after having succeeded in getting publicity for their cause.
**Trevor Brooking** (1991) and West Ham United Managing Director **Peter Storrie** launch a bond scheme to raise £15m for the Hammers to make the stadium all-seater, as required by law. 15,000 bonds selling at £500, £750 and £975 pounds were put up for sale. These guaranteed the purchaser priority for a season ticket for 50 years. The supporters arranged protests ending in a goalmouth sit-in at the 1992 Arsenal home match. Only 300 bonds were sold and the scheme was withdrawn.

### Shit happens!
**Billy Bremner** (1976) along with Scotland team-mates **Willie Young, Joe Harper, Pat McCluskey** and **Arthur Graham**, all break the 1a.m. curfew after some heavy drinking. The celebrations followed a 1-0 World Cup qualifying away win in Denmark. The next day the players argue with the SFA officials and allegedly, Billy (bless him), defecated on the hotel bed of one official, John MacDonald, who promptly punched the Scottish captain on the jaw. All five players were given a ban, and Billy never played for Scotland again.

# Stud Marks

## Roy Keane and Alf Inge Haaland

The rivalry between these two midfielders dates back to Haaland's time at Leeds, when Keane suffered a horrific injury while trying to trip up the Norwegian during a game at Elland Road in November 1997.

It was a reckless challenge by Keane and he suffered badly for it. Cruciate knee ligament damage kept him out of the game for a year. During this enforced absence Haaland chose to rile the Irishman further by claiming that he had found it *'funny'* that Keane had suffered a career-threatening injury as a result of the foul. During other outbursts he also claimed to *"hate"* all Manchester United players. Predictably, Keane never forgave Haaland for this and specifically for accusing him of faking injury while he lay on the floor writhing in agony waiting for a stretcher.

In his autobiography he described the moment he settled an old score with Haaland when the two came face to face in the Manchester derby four years later.

*'I'd waited long enough. I f*****g hit him hard. The ball was there (I think). Take that, you c***'* , Keane was quoted as saying in extracts in *The Times*.

This time, the tables were turned. The Manchester City midfielder aggravated a knee injury in the tackle by Keane, and has barely started a game for the Blues since. Haaland had spent almost a year in and out of operating theatres and specialists' treatment rooms. He returned to training in City's pre-season preparations prior to their Division One title-winning campaign only to break down again. Another operation kept Alfie out until the end of the year 2001 and, after four games as a substitute in the early part of 2002, he again required his knee – dubbed *"The Roy Keane Memorial Knee"* by one City fanzine – to be given more treatment.

# 'I'd waited long enough. I f*****g hit him hard. The ball was there (I think). Take that you c***.'

## Insults

Keane's book revealed how he added insult to injury by taunting Haaland while he lay stricken on the ground.

'*And don't ever stand over me again sneering about fake injuries, and tell your pal (David) Wetherall there's some for him as well,*' Keane was quoted as saying in book extracts. Keane was sent off for the tackle – and in the book he claims: '*I (didn't) wait for Mr Elleray to show the red card. I turned and walked to the dressing room.*'

## Ill-advised

Gordon Taylor, chief executive of the Professional Footballers Association, said: '*Whilst it may make good copy and profits for the book publishers and the writer, it puts Roy in a bad position. He could face action from the FA, if not possibly legal action from Alfie Haaland. We tried at the time to calm things down between the two as we've had too many player versus player cases. We don't want that to happen again, but this has just opened up old wounds again at an unfortunate time. I think Roy has been ill-advised and his comments are ill-judged. Roy hardly needs the money and I just think he could do without all this.*'

Taylor also feared it could stoke up ill feeling between United and City supporters for the new season.

'Some people are sheep and some are wolves. There are a lot of sheep over there and probably I am a wolf.' **Roy Keane**

# Molly's Alone

## Roy Keane and Mick McCarthy

'*Roy Keane is history,*' said Mick McCarthy in a packed press room after the Manchester United captain had walked out on the Irish prior to the start of the 2002 World Cup. The Irish captain had been hauled up in front of his players over comments made in an Irish newspaper. According to Keane, '*He said that if I couldn't respect him then I shouldn't play for him and that's when I walked out. When I left the room I felt I was on my own.*
'*Some people are sheep and some are wolves. There are a lot of sheep over there and probably I am a wolf – that's my honest assessment.*'

The problem had started with a series of arguments about the training facilities the Irish FA had supplied the team. Keane had taken one look at the rock hard pitch, in parts only barely covered with grass, and thought, '*Jesus, it's never like this with United!*'
Then the freight carrier that was supposed to shift specially selected drinks for the Irish to consume in the sapping heat got lost somewhere between Dublin and Japan. There was talk that team sponsors KLM had had something to do with that one, and making the team travel via Holland did seem a little unnecessary.
The Manchester United captain avoided the media by leaving his hotel by the back door to travel to the airport, where he spoke briefly to a BBC reporter. Keane was quoted as saying he had absolutely no regrets about the row with manager, Mick McCarthy, that led to his dismissal. He said his conscience was clear.
The Taoiseach, Bertie Ahern, offered indirectly to help resolve the row, making contact with both the FAI and Roy Keane through a third party and offered his '*assistance*' if either side felt it could make a difference. Clearly neither did.

*'Some people are sheep and some are wolves. There are a lot of sheep over there and probably I am a wolf – that's my honest assessment.'*

### Irish stew

Des Casey, the Honorary Secretary of the Football Association of Ireland said there might still be a slim hope of resolving the row but that never seemed likely. He said any chance of a compromise would require a very sincere apology from Roy Keane and a willingness by Mick McCarthy and his squad to accept such an apology. It was at that point all parties thought, *'Yeah right, you're joking aren't you?'*

### Not all that Keane

The row between the two men had more to do with a long held grudge between the former Irish captain, now manager, and Keane. When the players had been out for a few drinks while Jack Charlton was in charge, McCarthy had caught some players, including Keane, breaking a curfew. A row had developed in which Keane made it quite clear what he thought of McCarthy: *'A few years back in America, when we played in the World Cup, there was an argument between us when Mick was still captaining the team,'* said Keane. *'A few of us got drunk out there and Mick had a go at us on the team bus. I turned round and told him where to go.*

*'In those days he was always sitting next to Jack Charlton and the lads joked that he was just after the manager's job. But Mick's last words to me following the altercation were: "I'll get you back some day. It may not be now or even next week." Eventually, this week, I feel he has got his revenge. I really do.'*

# Spanish Archer

## Kevin Keegan and Bobby Robson

Kevin Keegan was never going to be the same man after a devastating tournament that nearly cost him his place among the greats of the English game, but getting dropped by the new England coach, Bobby Robson, after his disappointing display in the World Cup in Spain in 1982 must rank as the worst moment in his career. Only one of Kevin Keegan's 63 England caps was earned for representing his country in the World Cup finals. As skipper and leading goalscorer in *'Ron's 22'* for the tournament, the double European Footballer of the Year was expected to fire England's challenge. Sadly, a back spasm in the squad's opening training session ruled him out of all but the last 27 minutes of England's six-game, unbeaten and ultimately doomed bid to reclaim the Jules Rimet trophy.

So keen was Ron Greenwood to keep news of Keegan's injury from the press that he arranged for the curly-haired dynamo to travel overnight by car to Madrid from the squad's base in northern Spain, and then on to Hamburg by plane where he would be manipulated by his club doctor. The flying visit did the trick and by the time Keegan arrived back in Spain, he was ready to play in England's make-or-break phase two match against the tournament hosts.

### At the double

Rather than pick Keegan and the equally experienced Trevor Brooking from the start, Greenwood opted to stay with his unbeaten line-up, meaning Tony Woodcock got the nod over the frustrated Kev at the Bernebeu. But with the scoreline goalless and 63 minutes on the clock, Greenwood made a double substitution, throwing on the deadly

# Keegan slammed the turf in frustration, Brooking looked to the heavens and England were as good as on the plane home.

Keegan-Brooking double-act. It was almost a masterstroke. In the dying minutes of the match, the pair combined to fashion a clear-cut chance for Keegan to head home.

He missed. Keegan slammed the turf in frustration, Brooking looked to the heavens and England were as good as on the plane home. It was Keegan's last appearance in an England shirt.

### Off course

After the World Cup, Bobby Robson took charge and clearly the former Ipswich manager had decided to make a fresh start. He didn't speak to the players during the summer and yet when his first squad was announced the name most people still expected to see pencilled in as captain was missing. Keegan had been dropped without warning and the nation's favourite was about to take an enforced sabbatical of nearly 10 years.

# Drink, Drugs and Drudgery

## Scotland 1978

*'We're on the march with Ally's Tartan Army,'* was the cry in 1978. They carelessly left out *'on the first plane back from Mendoza'*. It's hard to imagine now, but back then, Scotland fancied their chances at winning the World Cup – and with big name players culled from the Liverpool, Forest and Leeds sides that had done so well in the preceding years, you could see why. Over 25,000 tartan-clad punters turned up at Hampden to bid farewell to the World Champions-elect as they circled the pitch in an open top bus – many of the squad sporting the free perms gifted to them by a fitba' daft hairdresser. The bookmakers made them fourth favourites to win. Really.

In the opening game, Peru weren't expected to pose any real problems. Initially things actually went quite well, Scotland dominated the first 20 minutes and went one up through Joe Jordan. It looked like the Scots were on the fast track to the final in Buenos Aires – but not for long. Ally McLeod had done little or no homework on his opponents. *'We'll play to our own strengths,'* he'd said, ignoring the opposition completely. Peru liked to sit back and hit on the break, and so they did – three times! The game finished 3-1 to Peru.

The team took a savaging from the Scottish press. Denis Law said, *'We have no chance!'* But things were about to get much worse.

### Fever pitch

*'Wee'* Willie Johnston was considered one of the key players in Ally MacLeod's squad that travelled to Argentina in 1978. But Johnston was sent home in shame after failing a drugs test. The outside-left, as they used to call them, protested his innocence, claiming he had taken pills for hayfever. Yet it was apparently not the first time he'd taken

# He was banned for a year from international football but achieved lifelong notoriety.

Fencanfamin (try saying that after a few swigs of Buckfast) pills before a match. With typical gallows humour, some Scots suggested they were tranquillizers but in actual fact Johnston was one of the few who performed well in Scotland's dismal performance against the mighty Iran. He was banned for a year from international football but achieved lifelong notoriety.

### Rough justice

*'Mr McLeod is Mr Big Mouth'* screamed the Argentine headlines. The team managed a pathetic 1-1 draw with Iran (thanks to an own goal by the Iranians) and the pictures of die-hard fans who had made the trip all the way to Argentina turning on their team, flicking V-signs at the players as they left the park, were beamed round the world. Anonymous stories emerged from the team headquarters of disarray, discord and that old favourite of Scotland squads – late night bevvy sessions.

It seemed the squad had become regular and valued customers at their local nightclub. One particularly heavy session ended with Alan Rough and Derek Johnstone staggering back to the hotel in the wee small hours, but by the time they got there the gates were locked so they had to vault the walls. Once over, the pair were apprehended by irate gun toting guards. However, Alan Rough saved the day, uttering the immortal words:

*'Don't shoot me, I'm the goalkeeper.'*

# Dodgy Tackle

## Argentina and Cameroon

The most common score in World Cup opening matches was 0-0. Cameroon started as if they intended to avoid one form of disgrace – losing – but that didn't stop them from putting the boot in. Maradona performed theatrics, his hands spread open like he was playing charades (*'Is it a play, a film, a book? No, it's a booking!'*), Caniggia came on as sub and thundered past the opposition only to dive as impressively as Greg Louganis in the penalty area. Meanwhile the Cameroons gave us their interpretation of the *'tackle'* in various guises, most of them involving martial arts. Massing and Kana-Biyik were the two to go in this match but any number of alternatives were auditioning for the part. What was so remarkable here was that after 10 minutes the Africans realized that the World Champs were hopeless, the team a pale reflection of its leader – overweight, stodgy, bereft of imagination and always complaining – so that when Omam-Biyik rose like a man on a winch to nod the ball past Pumpido two out of five people watching on the planet lept with him, thrilled that the World Champs were all beat up.

### Seeing red

The Africans had 23 minutes to hold out for possibly the biggest shock in World Cup history. With three minutes to play Caniggia broke down the right in a desperate bid for an equalizer. The striker evaded one heavy challenge and, as he fought to keep his legs, was caught around his crown jewels by Benjamin Massing. The burly defender had almost spliced the Argentinian in two and, having been booked earlier in the game, did not hang around to see the French referee brandish a red card.

# Meanwhile the Cameroons gave us their interpretation of the *'tackle'* in various guises, most of them involving martial arts.

### Smiling assassins

What we loved about the Cameroons was their attitude. As they launched into every tackle, intent on breaking something they seemed to stare ferociously at the player they were facing and then turn to the cameras and grin. It was as if they shared a global-loathing of the opposition. The Argentine players finally had something to complain about. After years of cheating, bullying and fighting their way through World Cups they were getting beaten up, and beaten on the biggest stage.

None of the Argentine players will ever have nice things to say about the Cameroons, who by now had overtaken Brazil and Germany to become the second-worst disciplined side in the history of the World Cup with six dismissals in four matches. But the rest of the world fell in love with them.

# MilLa Time

## Higuita gifts Cameroon

As goalkeeping mistakes go it was a shocker. Colombian keeper Rene Higuita (he of the famous 'Scorpian kick' overhead clearance at Wembley) indulged his silly antics once to often in the second round match against Cameroon at the 1990 World Cup... and got punished.

After 90 minutes of dull, pointless football, Cameroon and Colombia decided to make things interesting. Roger Milla scored for the Africans and the game opened up. Rene Higuita, the Colombian goalkeeper and a man bearing a remarkable similarity to any number of eighties soft rock drummers – I'm thinking Foreigner, Styx and Journey in particular here – began to stray from his goal area. First as a casual bystander, admiring the ridiculous splendour of Valderamma's coifurred hair, but then, as extra-time dragged on, joining the back four as a sweeper, knocking the occasional back-pass about and throwing in the odd step-over for good measure. And then calamity, actually fluffing a pass and presenting Roger Milla with the ball. Milla, a man some 15 years his senior, a man who understood that a place in the last eight of the World Cup was at stake, a man with a smile on his face and a grin that said, *'Son, that was one stupid thing you did just then,'* cantered off in search of his destiny and slotted the opportunity home, 2-0 to the Africans. Colombia pulled one back but it wasn't enough and Higuita, towelling down after the match dwelt on the vast gulf in living standards back home. *'It was a mistake,'* he said, *'as big as a house.'*

### Hippy hippy shake

Even a 38-year-old couldn't miss as he cantered off in the direction of goal to slide the ball into the net. They say old men never know when to hang up their dancing shoes and clear off the floor but if one man deserved his go at wearing grandpa's disco slippers it was Milla. He trotted off towards the corner flag and held his shorts up with his left

He trotted off towards the corner flag and held his shorts up with his left hand while pointing to God with his right. Then he started to wiggle his hips as he lowered his backside so that his buttocks were merely inches off the floor.

hand while pointing to God with his right. Then he started to wiggle his hips as he lowered his backside so that his buttocks were merely inches off the floor. In the background the seats were totally empty except for one man sporting a Tom Selleck moustache, scratching his nose looking on in amusement. *'He's the oldest swinger in town,'* said the ITV commentator. Old, but thankfully still living.

### Mad moment

The Colombians couldn't believe the insanity of their keeper. Everyone likes a joke and a laugh but to throw away a World Cup dream by showboating – there was nothing funny about that. The heat left the players exhausted and miserable. The journey back to Colombia would be a long and lonely one for the keeper as he sat at the back and considered a life to come, a life as *'Billy-no-mates'*.

# The Eyes Have It

## Bob Wilson and Maradona

Bob Wilson was the friendly face of football broadcasting. The first man to make the step up from player to presenter, Wilson had been a favourite with the viewers since those narrow, focused eyes first came to our screens presenting, appropriately enough, *'Football Focus'*. Was there nothing in this world that could ruffle the feathers of this Arsenal goalkeeping great? Whenever a moment of madness happened, *'Uncle Bob'* would be there to put both sides of the story. He represented balance and, like all good keepers, he oozed calm. Nothing, it seemed, could fluster the man who held the fate of football in his un-gloved hands. At the 1990 World Cup, Wilson was getting more of the limelight and sharing more of the lead presenter role with Des Lynam – another unflappable man. As we tuned in to watch one of the matches that you have on while you boil your veg and make sure the chips are baking in the oven it was hard to imagine anything out of the ordinary might occur.

### Flying pig

Even before the previous World Cup in 1990, Maradona was struggling with drugs. He had so much cortisone injected for back complaints by friendly personal *'physicians'* that he had developed alarming symptoms of heavy drug use; bloated features and an irascible personality. Over-reliance on these medicines prevents the normal process of healing, causing joints to fuse, growth to be stunted and, in extreme cases, induction of psychosis. In their opening match at USA 94, Argentina were playing Greece. Considering the stringent immigration rules regarding drug abuse it's perhaps saying something about the stature of the diminutive former Napoli player that Diego Maradona was allowed into the country at all. After 60 minutes, Argentina began a series of one-twos around the Greek penalty area like they had entered a plate-tossing competition and were doing

# 'If he came at me like that I'd have punched his face in,' said the normally placid Bob Wilson.

badly when the ball fell to Maradona who calmly slammed the shot with his left peg into the net. Maradona, not content with being swamped by a plague of blue-shirted teammates, went in search of a TV cameraman so that he could show the world exactly what it meant to score that goal. Maradona was flying, he was ecstatic, and when he finally reached the cameraman's lens it became clear, he was high, in fact, on ephedrine (a cocaine derivative) as we later discovered.'

*'If he came at me like that I'd have punched his face in,'* said the normally placid Bob Wilson. At the end of the match a FIFA official disguised as a nurse held Diego's hand and led him off in the direction of the drug-testing unit. The rest, as could be said about Diego himself, was history.

## Bad form

Without Maradona, Argentina were soon eliminated. By this stage in Maradona's career, years of drug abuse were beginning to take their toll. He returned from his ban to play for his home club, Boca Juniors, until his retirement from football in 1997. Wilson went over to ITV in the mid-nineties and it looked as though the two men's paths might cross once again when Argentina played England in the 2002 World Cup. By now the footballer was a broadcaster, having taken up the mic shortly after the Greek game. The prospect of these two gladiators battling it out on the TV gantry proved too much for the Japanese hosts, who told Maradona they wouldn't let him into the country because of his previous form. Although a change of heart enabled Maradona to be present at the match, Wilson stayed at home, averting another international disaster between the two countries.

# Football Advertising

The commercial power of football took the world by storm throughout the 1990s with sports clothing companies such as Nike achieving incredible success by saturating the advertising market during major tournaments. At the 1996 European Championships in England a series of billboard adverts turned our idolization of players like Eric Cantona on its head and became synonymous with the zeitgeist of the occasion. Where football continued to shake off its embarrassing image was on the silver screen, where the memory of Kevin Keegan urging lovers of Brut aftershave to *'splash it all over'* haunted Soho-based copywriters for more than a decade.

In 1998, an advertising phenomenon changed the nature of the media forever. The sound of the music, the quickness of the feet and the smooth feel about everything to do with the football action made viewers want to curl up in front of the 1998 World Cup in France and feel that everything was cool. All the advertisers needed was a World Cup winning side. But for that they would need to wait another four years.

## The Nike Airport Ad

- It started with a swinging piece of samba, a tune that informed you it was playtime. The Brazilian team were due to film this Nike advert on a beach in southern France but when the plane was delayed they began fooling around in the airport departure lounge. Thankfully a few bright sparks took a film crew and some

# With the goal opened up before him, the buck-toothed hotshot contrives to hit the post.

decent lighting with them so they could capture the true genius of the talent on display.

- The scene opens with Romario hanging up the phone to his agent whilst Ronaldo, Denilson and the boys set up a goal made out of bits of aluminium piping and some canvas strips borrowed from queue barriers. Then the camera cuts to a scene outside and Brazilian boys are negotiating the baggage trucks, booting a ball under the wing of a Jumbo jet.

- An ageing granny convention looks on, since one of them swears that Ronaldo is the spitting image of her favourite cartoon character, Goofy. Back in the lounge, Romario, having prised his mobile phone from his ear and, like the rest of the squad, sports shades on a freshly cropped skull, drills a pass through the metal detector unit into the path of Ronaldo.

- This is the world's best player we're talking about, not some lackey on his lunch-break and yet, with the goal opened up before him, the buck-toothed hotshot contrives to hit the post. He holds his head in mock shame. A coup for Nike.

# Death Penalty

## Pearce and Waddle, Italia 90

Stuart Pearce had already clattered the ball against the legs of the keeper when Chris Waddle stepped up to the spot. Waddle, sporting a new haircut that suggested he'd been wearing a hard hat round the top portion of his head at the time of clipping, placed the ball and, well, sort of waddled back to his mark. This only increased the tension as the starting point for this endeavour was at the tip of the *'D'* outside the penalty area – enough time for slow-motion stills of his team-mates to be picked up by cameras in the centre-circle, some of player's heads bowed, some of them instructing waiters to provide them with refreshment in case the interval curtain was about to come down abruptly. Waddle began his run. He seemed to approach the ball like a triple jumper, his legs eating up the turf as he engaged the ball like a man hitting the final board determined not to get a red flag. As his left leg hit the ball on the fifth stride he must have been thinking about getting that extra height all jumpers need to maximize their marks because the ball seemed to be aimed at someone in the upper tier. The ball flew over the bar and England were out. *'Stuart Pearce is bawling his eyes out and I thought he was a really hard man,'* observed Brian Moore on the telly. Gazza was in tears and across the nation we were crying in our beer.

### Slash of the day

*'You obviously do what you can to make the lads feel better but nothing you say means very much,'* said Gary Lineker after the match. *'A miss like that is going to stay with you for a long time, maybe forever.'*

Hugh McIlvanney writing in *The Observer* said, *'It would be scant consolation for Waddle to know that the wild slash of his left leg which seemed in more danger of*

*'Stuart Pearce is bawling his eyes out and I thought he was a really hard man,'* observed Brian Moore on the telly.

*sending the ball out of the Delle Alpi Stadium than into the net was almost certainly an irrelevance. Pearce had already failed and the instinct that enabled Peter Shilton to dive the right way for all the four penalties taken by the Germans had done him no good against the quality of their striking. He was scarcely favourite to do any better with the fifth kick had it been needed.'*

**No dice**

*'Shilton,'* continued McIlvanney, *'who went into last night's third-place decider with Italy in Bari as the most impressive goalkeeper in the tournament, would find it hard to keep a smile off his 40-year-old face if he heard some of the fancy tributes to his 23-year-old German counterpart, Bodo Illgner, that were occasioned by the saving of Pearce's penalty. According to the eulogists, that stop was testimony to the young Bodo's iron nerve and owed much to a brief but intense study he had made of the English kickers while they waited to have a go at him.*

*'This romantic version of events is worrying only because it suggests that people are willing to see the shoot-out as a serious extension of the game, to be dignified by detailed analysis. In fact, it is first cousin to a roll of a dice and should be done away with without delay.'*

# Broken Bottle

## Hoddle drops Gazza

Glenn Hoddle knew after the friendly against Belgium that he wouldn't be taking Gazza to France 98. The dead leg, the cut on the head, these could be healed. What stared back at him was his player's inability to curb his excesses.

The day of reckoning came and each member of the 28-man squad was given a five minute slot to see the boss in the training headquarters at La Manga. Hoddle reasoned that the unlucky six would want to be out of there quickly so planes were chartered to take the axed players back to Birmingham with a news release already prepared to hit the streets by that Sunday night. Ian Walker, Phil Neville, Dion Dublin, Nicky Butt and Andy Hinchcliffe were all unlucky but possibly not surprised to see the thumbs down from their manager but the last name on the list of players due in to see Hoddle at 5.30 that evening must have been dumbfounded.

Paul Gascoigne had been out on the golf course and Hoddle received a call telling him his player was already half-cut. And the meeting hadn't even started. There was a loud bang on the door and it was obvious that Gazza had sussed what was happening. He was blotto and sat down muttering, *'I don't believe this.'* When Hoddle retorted, *'You're not fit enough,'* Gazza began to cry. The player shook Hoddle's hand but seemingly snapped as he made his way to the door booting a chair with his bare feet then punching a lamp sending shards of glass everywhere. Hoddle expected another mauling in the press but despite the affection for the player the public seemed to sense that their hero had run out of gas. What he needed now was time, and that was in very short supply.

### Serious drinking

Later, in his Diary of the World Cup, Hoddle revealed, *'I thought about trying to talk to him but knew I couldn't, not while he was in this state. I stood there and he turned*

# The player shook Hoddle's hand but seemingly snapped as he made his way to the door booting a chair with his bare feet then punching a lamp sending shards of glass everywhere.

as if to go again, then came back with a barrage of abuse.' The coach said that he had been concerned with Gascoigne's attitude since England's defeat by Chile at Wembley that February. Those concerns, which focused on the player's mental state as well as match fitness, became serious doubts as Gascoigne failed to cut down on drinking.

### Out of this world

In an open letter to Glenn Hoddle's 22 players heading for France Gascoigne urged them to go on and win the World Cup without him.

'What difference can one kebab make?' he wrote in The Sun. 'I'm trying to get over the disappointment of not making it into the 22 and of course coming to terms with it and I will miss use... I feel I've let youse down because of two nights out with pals.

'But I don't see how one kebab can be the difference between beating one or three men or running from box to box or scoring a goal.

'I wanted Regan [his son] to see me play for England in the World Cup – now I don't know if he'll ever see me in an England shirt again. That breaks my heart,' he said.

Gascoigne added: 'I'm so fed up. I'm trying hard to smile but you won't see the laughing and joking Gazza for a long while.

'The worst thing is the embarrassment. I can see pity in everybody's eyes in the street.'

# National Villain

## Bilic blanks Blanc

The villagers were outraged and the mayor was preparing a protest sign proclaiming: *'No to injustice, solidarity with Laurent Blanc.'*

The residents of Blanc's home village were seething that their favourite son was banned from playing for France in the World Cup final against Brazil. Blanc had been automatically ruled out of the final when he was sent off for pushing Croatia's Slaven Bilic in the semi-final, but the over-reaction to what was seen as little more than tap was widely condemned throughout the football world. *'When he went down I thought he was dead,'* said a disbelieving Sir Alex Ferguson.

*'I feel like I've been robbed,'* said Blanc's father Gilbert. *'After an unhappy, difficult night his morale has improved. He told me he would prefer that he was unhappy and not on the pitch for the final than that the team had been knocked out because of his mistake.'*

Bilic was booed from start to finish in the third-place play-off, from the moment his name was announced over the loudspeaker system at the Parc des Princes. When he was finally presented with his bronze medal, the player kissed it and waved it at the crowd. More boos and deafening whistles ensued. But he stayed unrepentant. *'I don't feel like a cheat; I'm not a cheat,'* he said after Croatia beat the Netherlands 2-1.

## French revolution

The harsh-looking dismissal, after Bilic went down as if pole-axed, struck a chord of sympathy and outrage in France for a favourite player who scored the golden goal that beat Paraguay and put France into the quarter-finals.

Bilic played for England's Everton, and said later that he had expected harsh treatment in Everton's first game after the World Cup. Indeed he slammed British tabloid reporters for what he felt was an incident blown out of proportion.

# The harsh-looking dismissal, after Bilic went down as if pole-axed, struck a chord of sympathy and outrage in France.

The 29-year-old also denied that he had apologized to Blanc, whose name was present in the stadium on several small banners festooned from the upper tiers.

### Laurent order

*'Win it, for you, for Laurent, for us,'* said one. *'Allez Les Bleus, the World Cup for Laurent Blanc,'* said another.

*'They react to the stories in the press,'* said Bilic defiantly. *'I'm disappointed with the English press, because they were the first ones to start all this. In the French press, they all said that it was enough reason to be sent off, then the English started, and they took it from England.'*

*'The bottom line is I don't care about the blame, because he hit me in the face,'* he added. The Croat said he would like to ask Blanc how he would have reacted to being hit and went on to claim people were making a fuss simply because it was the World Cup final.

*'This is the tabloids who like a big story, and they didn't have it because England is out,'* he said.

# Dutch Capped

## Platt and Koeman

England fans I'm sure will remember Rotterdam on 13 October 1993. If not, then let me jog your memory with two words – Ronald Koeman. Ah, so now the penny has dropped and the recollections of that remarkable night in Holland come flooding back! As if it wasn't bad enough at the time, it was later immortalized in the Graham Taylor documentary, *'England Manager – The Impossible Job'*.

Holland were playing England in a vital World Cup qualifier and while both nations had one further game to play, it was almost a winner-take-all, loser-stay-home scenario. A victory would all but put the nation on the plane to the USA, while defeat would leave them needing a last game miracle. Things were going fairly well for England after 58 goalless minutes when David Platt latched onto a long through ball and had a clear run on goal. As he approached the edge of the penalty area, he glanced at the outcoming keeper and was then cynically hauled back by Ronald Koeman.

Whether the foul was inside or outside the area, Koeman should have walked so imagine England's fury when the ref fished out a yellow card. Four minutes later at the other end, Holland earned a free kick on the edge of the area and who was their free kick expert? Ronald Koeman! Commentator Brian Moore summed up the feelings of a nation when he said, *'Wouldn't it be ironic if a player who shouldn't even be on the pitch, steps up and scores.'*

## Flipping cocksure

Up stepped Koeman and hit the wall, however the ref awarded a re-take. By now Moore was screaming, *'He's going to flip one, he's going to flip one!'* and the rest is history as Koeman clipped a beauty over the wall and into the far corner. Dennis Bergkamp scored ten minutes later, Holland won 2-0 and played in the 1994 World Cup finals.

# Platt glares at Koeman who struts around the pitch like a posturing cock. *'Do I not like that!'* screams Taylor.

Manager Graham Taylor was being recorded for a TV documentary, *'England Manager – The Impossible Job'*. Taylor's words to the FIFA official on the touchline during the aforementioned documentary were spot on when he said, *'Your mate [the ref] has cost me my job, I just wanted you to know that.'* A disbelieving Phil Neal sits next to Taylor, mimicking every word his boss comes out with. Platt glares at Koeman who struts around the pitch like a posturing cock. *'Do I not like that!'* screams Taylor.

### Mr Angry

England can't believe their misfortune. Still unable to come to terms with events, the players are mulling about on the pitch looking for someone to blame. What they need is direction, what they need is help. On the bench, Taylor has now lost the plot completely and wants to have it out with the FIFA official running up the line. He fails to appreciate that the game could be retrieved but in hindsight you can't blame him for being so angry. We were all flipping furious, and that was just watching it on the telly.

# Aztec Cameras

## Mexico deny Belgium penalty

The choice of venue for the ninth World Cup was a two-nation contest between Argentina and Mexico and at a FIFA congress during the 1964 Olympic Games in Tokyo, Mexico, already selected as hosts for the 1968 Olympic Games, were granted the tournament. However, there were many delegates, particularly from Europe, who were unhappy with the choice of venue, largely because of Mexico's high altitude and the problems it might cause. Fortunately, most teams soon acclimatized to the thin air and intense 100°F (37°C) heat.

In the first round, Mexico played Belgium. The host nation had a free kick awarded and the ball was chipped in to Valdivia who swiped at the ball like a late night brawler taking a swing at a lamppost. At the same time, one of the Belgium players collides with the Mexican which gives the impression, at least from one side of the ground, that the striker's inability to connect with the ball might have something to do with the Belgium, and not his own paucity of skill. Obviously the Argentinian referee thought so. The Mexican players clap their hands and point to the penalty spot and the referee blows his whistle. The camera cuts to Angel Norberto Coerezza, the hapless ref who then seems to stumble as he walks towards the Belgium goal, shoving their right-back towards the ground. Suddenly the poor man is surrounded by Belgiums.

## Poke in the groin

Now the Belgiums are not noted for their aggression, indeed chocolate lovers around the world won't have a bad word said about them. And yet here they are, seven of them plus the goalkeeper, who is considerably taller than anyone else on the pitch, bundling the referee across the six-yard line and into the back of the goal net. They are livid. By now the ref has been joined in the melée by his linesman who appears to poke one of the

# And yet here they are, seven of them plus the goalkeeper… bundling the referee across the six-yard line and into the back of the goal net.

Belgium defenders in the groin with his flag. Next to the goal, a gang of photographers start clicking furiously. The ref goes up to one of the snappers and asks, *'What do you think?'* at which point the Belgium mob disperses in disbelief.

## Stretcher point

Meanwhile Valdivia is still on the ground. Remember, there was no hard contact with the Belgium defender. The only thing that can be broken is his pride but a mass of doctors and stretcher bearers are surrounding him, making sure he'd be fit to continue. The Belgium keeper, Piot, leans over and asks him if he'd like to step outside but it's no use, the player has succeeded on conning the ref and the Belgians go on to lose the match. The first Mexican World Cup was rated by many to be the best of all time. Fair play dominated and no player was sent off during the whole tournament. If the Belgians had managed a decent complaint rather than weakening their case by jostling the ref, perhaps that statistic would have been different?

# Gazza's Tackle

## Card costs him final place

Against Holland, Gazza had become a overnight star at Italia 90. They'd said he was daft as a brush but the Dutch sweeper wasn't laughing when Gazza made Ronald Koeman look like a mug. It took one little piece of magic – the kind not seen by a European player since that Dutch master Johan Cruyff inflicted similar misery on Sweden in 1974 – and suddenly England were in with a chance. This was the match that saw player-power take centre stage with Bobby Robson agreeing with his players to go 3-5-2 with the Geordie joker at the heart of everything. Even Gullit, Rijkaard and Van Basten look ordinary by comparison. Having bossed the midfield, Gazza held up the ball outside the Dutch penalty area in the second half, swivelled, dragging the ball with him past an amazed Koeman and crossed at the by-line only for Lineker and Bull to both miss it. Back home we were gob-smacked. With one sweet gyration of his hips, Gazza had made English hearts miss a beat and begin to dream of a nation in full World Cup flight. John Travolta had nothing on this.

In the semi-final against the Germans, Gazza was again running the show. He made Matthaus look ordinary. After 90 minutes of nail-biting football it was 1-1. Gazza marched to the England end and applauded the fans. In the first half of extra-time, Gazza was still sharp, slipping a pass that almost put Peter Bearsdley through. The Germans were ragged and holding on.

### Ham roll

The two Steve's, Bull and McMahon, were warming up on the running track when Gazza went off on another dribble. He bumps past one German, threads his way past another.

# Without hesitation he makes the most of the unnecessary tackle and begins to roll and moan, and roll and moan some more, right in front of the ref.

The ball has just escaped his foot and he over-reaches for it with his left. You can see the thought in Berthold's mind as he advances onto the Geordie's outstretched limb. Without hesitation he makes the most of the unnecessary tackle and begins to roll and moan, and roll and moan some more, right in front of the ref. Gazza just gets up and ruffles the fella's hair, still smiling.

**Tears of a clown**

The German captain Matthaus storms up to Gazza and gives him an earful. It's been a great game, but the Germans seem determined to spoil things. By now Berthold is bizarrely holding his face as if someone has punched him in the mouth. The referee has been conned and fishes out a yellow card for Gazza, a second booking that means he will miss the World Cup final should England get through. Gazza is distraught. Suddenly all the humour and good nature has gone from his face.

Gary Lineker points to the bench to say Gazza's lost it. But Gazza didn't lose it, he managed to recompose himself and got stuck in once again. The tears he cried at the end made him a fortune in comedy waterworks products but the spirit that carried him through after that booking was what really endeared the lad to the nation's heart. Could anybody be bothered to watch the Argentina-Germany final?

# Greatness

**There aren't many moments in the history of England's national side that stand out. For that we must thank our commitment to exporting the game to all corners of the globe and thus increasing the competition. This lack of success has harboured a collective grudge that borders on the defeatist, especially now that the likes of Brazil and Germany seem to stumble across success almost by accident. But there have been times when both those sides have had to stand back and admire an Englishman's predatory talents.**

The words remain an inspiration to this day. Into the last minute of extra-time; England winning 3-2 against West Germany; Geoff Hurst bursting down the right; tired legs all round; Nobby Stiles looking like a bare knuckle fighter who had just lost a bout; the moment captured in glorious black and white; Bobby Moore's pass splits the defence; Hurst hurtles towards the West German goal; *'There are some people on the pitch,'* begins BBC commentator, Kenneth Wolstenhome; *'They think it's all over,'* he adds, as Hurst pulls back his left foot, aims for a patch of goal behind the ears of Tilkowski in goal; *'It is now!'* proclaims Wolstenhome as the ball almost bursts the back of the net.

- Comedy shows, politicians and newspaper headline writers have all parodied it. Yet it is still remarkable that Wolstenhome's words were unrehearsed, merely an audible distillation of a wonderful moment, so emphatic, so gloriously significant – perhaps the last great act of a dying empire – that both the event and narrative that go with it have become one.

# Wolstenhome's words were unrehearsed, merely an audible distillation of a wonderful moment.

- Bobby Charlton said he was amazed when the victorious England team finally left Wembley that day. The streets were seemingly packed for days with people cheering them on. *'Imagine what would have happened it we'd lost,'* he said.

- Four years later, the England team travelled to Mexico and were up against the greatest team to have ever graced the World Cup finals – the 1970 Brazil team. But it was England that left the tournament with one of the defining images – Gordon Banks' save.

- Brazil against World Cup-holders England always looked like a classic, that for once lived up to the hype. Bobby Charlton recalls that as Pelé headed the cross towards the right hand corner he shouted *'goal'*. But Banks had other ideas. To see the save now is to be reminded of a man completing the most arduous of yoga routines, digging deep into his soul, searching for the will to stop the ball crossing the line. With elegant poise and lightning speed, Banks flicked the ball over the crossbar to keep England's World Cup dreams alive. The save dumbfounded Pelé and all those watching. It remains one of the greatest feats of acrobatics ever witnessed on a football field.

# Oi, Ref!

## Jack Taylor and the Germans

The Olympic Stadium in Munich, Fortress Germany, not a place for an English ref to be giving the opposition a penalty in the first minute of the World Cup final! In 1974, Jack Taylor was on the spot when he awarded a kick to the Dutch. Johan Cruyff had wriggled through three German tackles and quite clearly been shoved off the ball in the box by Berti Vogts, who had shadowed his run from the centre circle like a canny U-boat commander. The Kaiser, Franz Beckenbauer, was livid, throwing his arms in the air at the ref screaming *'dive, dive, dive'* but to no avail. As Neeskens slams the ball past Sepp Maier in goal an amazing puff of white powder trails in the path of the ball as if he's brought a musket with him to make sure of the job and the ground erupts. The Germans hadn't even touched the ball but they went on to win 2-1 with goals from Paul Breitner, another penalty, and fittingly Gerd Müller, playing his final match. Müller's goal took him past Juste Fontaine of France as the all-time leading World Cup goalscorer with 14 goals. This remember, was the World Cup final where kick-off was delayed when they forgot to bring out the corner flags at the start. Jack Taylor had a reputation as a man who didn't suffer fools gladly and yet even the popular Englishman could get things wrong and suffer the wrath of the players and the crowd...

### Offside whistle

West Germany are awarded a free-kick on the edge of the area and swing the ball out right. The Dutch are standing flat admiring each other's seventies blond barnets. Gerd Müller pounces on a cross that has the Dutch defenders raising their arms and before you can say, *'Tony Adams'*, the ball has been slipped into the back of the net. Sublime

# The Kaiser, Franz Beckenbauer, was livid, throwing his arms in the air at the ref screaming *'dive, dive, dive'* but to no avail.

control and power. But what's this? Taylor has blown for offside and the goal is disallowed. The crowd seem too busy hooting their horns to make any discernible remonstration with the ref but the German manager, clad in golfing regalia roplote with hat, is furious.

### Winners

Holland throw everything forward in search of an equalizer. But Sepp Maier and the German captain Beckenbauer look to have the game under control. Neeskens fires a shot inches wide and a volley is saved brilliantly by Maier. The equalizer never comes and West Germany win the Cup for a second time.

As Beckenbauer, holding the new FIFA Cup aloft, acknowledged the cheers, the Dutch had the consolation of knowing that they had been beaten by the only team in the competition who truly had the talent to do so – even if they had not always shown it.

# Oi, Ref! Pt II

## More World Cup blunders

Kuwait were never likely to set the world on fire, well not in the world of football at any rate. But in the heat of Valladolid in 1982, Kuwait's Prince Fahid saw plenty to get steamed up about. France were the opposition and were sauntering to an easy 4-1 win when the Arab team had a goal disallowed.

Now we've all been here, even at rank amateur level and there comes a time in every match when you need to look at the scoreboard and say to yourself, *'This really doesn't matter that much.'* Let's bear in mind that Kuwait were never going to qualify. Let's remember that Trevor Francis still had it in him to sneak a goal past them in the next match and let's recall that France, even by their high modern standards, were a pretty tasty outfit. So leading your team off, the most massive of remonstrations, simply smacks of petulance.

We all know the type. *'I've had enough of this, I'm off.'* The French were not amused. Whenever a player gets booked for dissent, someone in the ground is bound to say, *'And what was the point of that? How many times has a referee changed his mind?'*

Once, just once, you should say, in Valladolid in 1982, when referee Miroslav Stupar of the Soviet Union reversed his decision. A few minutes later, France scored a fourth goal that was allowed to stand. The Kuwaitis were almost certainly going home anyway. Yet they had moved that mountain and got the referee to change his mind.

They even offered to lend the Kuwait side one of their players to even things up. The spirit of the team had been lost, and with it, any chance of a Kuwaiti shock!

Eight years later, Prince Fahid was shot dead by invading Iraqis as he attempted to defend a royal palace. Protests were led by General Norman Schwarzkopf.

# Thomas, the eternal pedant, was sent home, allowing him to nurse the bruises from the coins that had hailed down on him.

### Doubting Thomas

Who can forget the Brazil vs Sweden match? With the game at 1-1, the Brazilians were awarded a corner with a few seconds to go before 90 minutes were up. They hadn't taken it as the clock reached the end of normal time, but no sooner had the ball been flighted into the box than it was in the back of the net. However, referee Clive Thomas, a man seemingly never far from controversy, decided that stoppages had amounted to less than 15 seconds and had blown as the corner was delivered. He'd whistled an instant before Zico connected, and the result stood at 1-1. Thomas, the eternal pedant, was sent home, allowing him to nurse the bruises from the coins that had hailed down on him

### Butch sees red

The day had started with temperatures above 100°F in the shade. As the first half of England vs Morocco was drawing to a close, Bryan Robson went up for a ball and landed badly on his already damaged elbow. While Bobby Robson adjusted his midfield to compensate for loss of his captain he couldn't quite understand what Ray Wilkins was doing getting caught offside away on the far corner of the pitch. Wilkins rarely ventured past the halfway line, indeed his nickname was *'the crab'* because of his fondness for doing things sideways.

As the referee from Paraguay indicated a freekick Wilkins seemed to petulantly throw the ball in his direction. Wilkins, who had never been sent off in an international couldn't believe the colour of the card now in front of him. It was red, and England were down to ten men.

# Good, Bad, Ugly

## Maradona madness

Against Belgium in the 1986 World Cup semi-final Maradona had already scored one goal when he received a pass unmarked inside the Belgium half. Gerets, the defender, had rated their chances of stopping Maradona as one in ten and you could sense the players backing off him. As the pass is collected on his left foot the two men supposed to keep him quiet back off, drifting into where they think he's going to thread the ball. Maradona, sensing their fear, fakes a pass with his left shoulder and nudges the ball inside right, his pace and control taking both him and the ball past the defenders like they aren't there. By now he's been joined by two more defenders, one of whom whips out his camera and stands there like a tourist admiring the exhibition. Maradona's not the kind of man to ignore such defensive lunacy so he skips past blondie and darts to his left. A third of the Belgium team are trailing in his wake. Now he's inside the penalty area and really drives on. You can see his arms pumping to give him the momentum and this forces the last defender to turn inside out, unable to simply back-peddle with the ball carrier. Maradona can now nudge the ball further away from his foot as the defender isn't looking for a split second, enough time to reach the six yard box, slap in a shot across the goal and celebrate. Sheer brilliance, and all done inside sixty seconds. Easy isn't it?

### Hand of Sod

After losing their first match to Cameroon, Argentina could have been on their way out of Italia 90 as Kuznetsov's header flew towards their net. With the referee standing ten feet away, Maradona knocked the ball away with his hands. Had the Soviet Union taken the

# Caught in a storm of pleading eyes and hand gestures the ref scurried backwards for his own safety, only to find all his exit routes blocked by square shouldered defenders with mad eyes.

lead, either from the header itself or from the penalty they should have been given, then who knows what could have happened? Referee Erik Fredriksson was sent home for his mistake. Whether he bumped into the Soviet Union team at the airport is not recorded.

**Argy Bargie**

Italia 90 was not a spectacle worthy of acclaim. Nobody said that football was the winner, because it wasn't. The main reason for this was Argentina. Carlos Bilardo's reigning champions kicked, punched and spat their way to the final, where they behaved like juvenile delinquents. On 84 minutes, aggrieved by the award of a penalty to the Germans, the entire team surrounded the ref. Caught in a storm of pleading eyes and hand gestures the ref scurried backwards for his own safety, only to find all his exit routes blocked by square shouldered defenders with mad eyes. One by one the players buffeted him, deliberately positioning themselves in his path then holding their arms up in innocence after impact. But the penalty stood. Andreas Brehme scored, and Germany won the World Cup.

# Aldridge Lets Fly

## Hot heads in America

Jack Charlton's Republic of Ireland side had already made their mark on the 1994 World Cup by beating Arrigo Sacchi's Italy in their opening Group E match. For slightly different reasons they ensured nobody would forget their participation in the States.

Six days after their Italian heroics in the Giants Stadium, Ireland were up against Mexico, as well as the heat, in the Citrus Bowl, Orlando. Things weren't going to plan as Luis Garcia scored twice for Mexico. With defeat on the cards and time ticking on, Jack Charlton was keen to throw on striker John Aldridge for Tommy Coyne, but a mix-up by the officials saw Coyne leaving the field and Aldridge refused entry to the game. The fourth official, sporting a yellow hat and a terrible fluorescent blue sports jacket, asked Aldridge if he had *a problem?* and was met by a torrent of abuse not seen since QED's *John's Not Mad* documentary in 1988. If anybody missed the tale of the Galashiels boy suffering from Tourette's Syndrome, then this more than made up for it.

In a little over five seconds Aldridge let rip with a flurry of 18 expletives in broadest Scouse before taking to the field. He was pointing his finger into the face of the officials and shouting *'You know don't you? You know? Three minutes it's been!'* Four minutes later he was on and his impact was almost immediate as he rose highest in the Mexican box to power a downward header past Jorge Campos.

## Ecky thump

The disease was clearly catching as Charlton joined the tirade on the cowering official. Jack walks up to the man in the yellow hat and begins pointing at his left palm like there's a specific set of requirements down there that need attending too fast. The official

# In a little over five seconds, Aldridge let rip with a flurry of 18 expletives in broadest Scouse before taking to the field.

is doing well not to lose his cool at this stage and starts shoving papers in Jack's belly before putting his arms around the considerably taller Englishman and loading him away. Jack's body position is all wrong if tho official is serious about shifting the former centre-half and Jack looks like he's about to thump the fella.

### Heated argument

Bearing in mind the searing heat, the argument fizzles out reasonably quickly as lots of officials bearing a passing resemblance to Mickey Rooney gather round Big Jack and tell him he's now banished to the stands. In the background, a bloke chewing gum and with enough capital letters plastered on to his hat to give him a sporting chance in a game of Scrabble, tries to decide if he should intervene and arrest Mr Charlton, while the bloke in the blue jacket and yellow hat saunters off to find himself a job at the local comedy burger store.

That Aldridge goal proved to be vital, because although Ireland lost the game 2-1, they qualified for the knock-out stages on goal difference after drawing with Norway a few days later. They subsequently went out in the second round to the Dutch, 2-0.

# Wine Buffs

## Battle of Santiago

Italian or Chilean? A tough choice in Sainsbury's and the choice of Chile as the venue for the 1962 World Cup finals caused plenty of controversy too. Some believed that Chile didn't have good enough stadiums or transport infrastructure to cope with such a large-scale event. However, things passed off fairly smoothly in terms of the organization of the event.

The main problem at Chile 62 was bad behaviour on the pitch. The early stages of the World Cup in Chile made all the wrong kind of headlines. There were several brutal, ill-tempered games in the group stage. By far the worst was an encounter between Chile and Italy that became known as *'The Battle of Santiago'*. The Chileans were spoiling for a battle and great resentment had been built up prior to the match by Italian newspaper reports describing Santiago as a rundown city, redolent of *'malnutrition, prostitution, illiteracy, alcoholism, wretchedness'*.

For its part, the Chilean press had made much of accusations that Italian players had been taking drugs. There was also irritation at the Italians' use of South American players with Italian passports. Predictably, the game ran riot in an orgy of violence. As early as the seventh minute, English referee Ken Aston sent off Italy's Ferrini for hacking down the Chilean centre-forward, Landa. Later, he expelled David for a retaliatory kick at the head of the Chilean outside-left, Lionel Sanchez. Sanchez, the son of a boxing champion, had broken the Italian captain Huberto Maschio's nose with a punch. In the absence of any official sanction against Sanchez, the Italian player punished him with a martial-arts kick. Armed police came on to the pitch on three occasions to try to restore order. Chile won 2-0, but the thuggery overshadowed any football that was played in the match.

# 'I wasn't reffing a football match, I was acting as an umpire in military manoeuvres.'

## All guns blazing

As the final whistle went, photographers, police and spectators ran on to the field and more fighting broke out among the players who held their arms up in front of them like the professional followers of Queensbury Rules. Ken Ashton looked for the safety of the tunnel but a group of Italians surrounded him and clapped ironically as they barged into him. Aston was later credited with inventing red and yellow cards. Although he had served his country during World War II with the Royal Artillery, nothing could have prepared him for this. Aston later commented: *'I wasn't reffing a football match, I was acting as an umpire in military manoeuvres.*

The press accused Aston of being *'hostile and provocative'*. The respected French paper, *L'Equipe*, wrote: *'The feebleness of the English referee Mr Aston, who never succeeded in hiding his lack of authority beneath an imperturbable front, and who was too conscious of "the voice of the people", succeeded in transforming a lively match into a street fight.'* Which was a bit harsh. '

## Reffing hell

In the opening game, between Chile and Switzerland, in the Chilean national stadium, later to become notorious for the slaughter of opponents of General Pinochet's coup, Aston had asked to see the five footballs provided for the pre-game kick-about. All of them were peeling and shabby and although Aston sent off for a new ball, it didn't arrive until 10 minutes into the second half. He was also famous for cautioning a Swiss player, remarking afterwards: *'Six stud marks on a man's thigh is good enough for me.'* Aston, who had strained an Achilles tendon during the *'Battle'*, refereed no more games, but limped around Santiago for the rest of the tournament.

# Maradona's Defence

## A view from a Marxist

In an article for *Living Marxism* after the 1994 World Cup, writer Eddie Veal decided it was time to defend the corner of Diego Maradona and set out a case for his defence against the English players and media. Terry Butcher had famously asked Maradona if he'd cheated when they stood together after the 1986 quarter-final to give urine samples. He says that Maradona always denied he had cheated. Then at the 1994 World Cup, Butcher said the fat man shouldn't have even been playing after they found he was still using drugs. Veal, however, says that isn't the real issue…

'*"We"* could not win the World Cup, since no British team had even qualified for the finals in the USA. So the British media decided to restage the glorious Falklands War instead, with the Argentinian captain Diego Maradona cast in the role of the Belgrano. Maradona was kicked out of the World Cup after failing a drugs test. He was found to have traces of the banned substance, ephedrine, in his blood stream. He might have taken it to combat a summer virus. He might have taken it to help him shed weight fast before the World Cup finals began. But one thing is for certain, he did not take it to make him play the kind of football with which he has bewitched the world for a decade. They have not invented a drug that can make you play like Maradona. If they had, even England and Scotland could have qualified for the finals with the aid of a local chemist.

### Bloody Butcher

'But the British media were not interested in any of that. To them, Maradona's expulsion from the tournament proved he was *"Dirty-cheat Diego"* (the idea is that if you say it fast it sounds like *"Dirty, cheatin' dago"*), and they dragged out every has-been British footballer to kick him when he was down. Gary Lineker said it was a case of '*good*

# 'They have not invented a drug that can make you play like Maradona.'

*riddance'*, and Terry Butcher announced that Maradona should never have been allowed to play in the World Cup in the first place, because his previous drug conviction (for taking cocaine) meant he was setting a terrible example to young fans. Unlike Mr Butcher, who set them such a fine example by revelling in the jolly *'Up-to-our-knees-in-Fenian-blood'* culture of Rangers fans when he played in Glasgow.

## High point
'The Argie-bashing bulldogs of the British press have been waiting for revenge ever since [the 1986 World Cup], and they sunk their teeth into Maradona with relish. Maradona has been playing on drugs for most of his career. He has had to pump himself full of the pain-killer cortisone, to enable him to play on with the countless injuries inflicted by the Butchers wherever he played. There was never any outcry about that because cortisone is legal. Indeed the rich men who held his contracts insisted he take the drugs, because their bank balances needed him on the pitch, regardless of the damage which cortisone can do to the body in later life.'

# Sitting or Standing?

*'I was never convinced, regarding the smaller clubs in particular, that the removal of all-standing was necessary and I was pleased when this was relaxed following representations by MPs, fans and clubs. While safety must always be the ultimate criterion, there is no reason to ignore technological improvements made since Taylor reported, which might allow for safe standing.'*
**Tony Blair, before the 1997 General Election**

The argument rages throughout football. Should supporters be allowed to stand and watch in safe surroundings without (hopefully) the familiar piddle of the person behind relieving themselves before half-time? Proponents of the *'Safe Standing in Football'* campaign argue that it is possible to have just that – safe standing. They say:

*'We are not talking about a return to terraces of old or the dangerous fences that penned fans in. We are looking for a feasibility study to be carried out into modern safe standing areas using the latest technology. If the result of this feasibility study is positive, under current legislation it would still not be possible even to carry out a trial of the technology. Therefore we would like to transfer the power to impose an "all-seater only" restriction from the Secretary of State to the local (safety) authorities, the clubs and the supporters themselves – the people most directly affected by such decisions.'*

- The thrust of the safe standing campaign is that clubs in the lower divisions can't afford to rebuild their grounds under the directives of the Taylor Report written after the deaths of 96 Liverpool supporters at Hillsborough. *'Simply banning*

For those fans that may not remember the days of a enjoying a meat pie whilst a puddle of piss appeared around your feet, the prospect of fans being allowed to stand may appear alarming.

*standing is not addressing the issue realistically. Offering the option of safe standing areas for those who wish to use them is the best solution from a safety viewpoint.'*

- For those fans who may not remember the days of a enjoying a meat pic whilst a puddle of piss appeared around your feet, the prospect of fans being allowed to stand may appear alarming.

- So the choice is simple. Do we provide safe areas for those who wish to stand – a move that will increase the size of gates, revenue and opportunity to watch your team – or do we accept that watching football will increasingly become more like a Friday night at the local cinema where the soft drinks are flat and we are instructed to turn off all mobile phones?

# Wall Bangers

## Argentina's post-match victory celebrations

Glenn Hoddle was doing the last of his World Cup press conferences. Argentina had knocked England out on penalties in the best game of the tournament. Hoddle recalls that he had to go out and face the world media after an interview with Ray Stubbs for the BBC. *'FIFA wanted me in the mixed-zone press conference as quickly as possible. It was never going to be easy, but was made 10 times worse by the fact that Daniel Passarella was still in there talking as I walked in. So back to the dressing room I went. David Davies told the FIFA officials to let us know when they were really ready. After a few minutes, they called us in a second time. When we returned, there were five Argentinian players up on the podium talking to the press. David blew his top at the FIFA officials while I stood and talked to the English press in a small area off to the side. Some of the questions were very to the point. They were bound to be – about David Beckham, about practising penalties, etc. Other questions, probably more than I'd expected, were sympathetic. Eventually I went to the podium and talked briefly to the foreign press.'*

### Team coach

The players had already made their way to the team coach as Hoddle packed the last of his things and joined them. He recalls, *'I arrived by the side of our team coach where the players, staff and families had gathered. Just at that moment I saw another coach drawing away. I thought it was full of Argentinian fans because they were singing the same song that the fans had been singing before the game, and swinging their shirts around their heads in the same way. They were at the window goading our players. I thought to myself, "That's all we need." I didn't realize until a few minutes later that it wasn't a coach full of Argentinian fans… it was the Argentinian players' coach. I was*

# '...it wasn't a coach full of Argentinian fans... it was the Argentinian players' coach. I was outraged.'

*outraged. It was insensitive and unprofessional. Our players would never have done anything like that in a million years. It was a sporting event and we had tried to approach it as such. What they did was disgusting.'*

## Winning habit

Four years later and David Bookham was the team captain. There was talk of revenge for the red card he'd been given in the match at St Etienne, but for him and the players who were there that night in France there was something more important to redress. As Owen, Campbell, Ferdinand and Beckham left the pitch, 1-0 winners, they were going to show the South Americans how to behave when you win.

# Something's Missing

## Bobby Moore gets arrested

It started as a bit of a joke, one of those stupid scenes played out in cornershops all over England. A couple of young scamps sneak out of the store and the owner rushes out, demanding you empty your pockets, convinced there's a handful of fruit pastels stuffed in your blazer pocket.

Bobby Moore and Bobby Charlton on the other hand, were World Cup winners, ambassadors for Britain and in a Bogota jewellery store, and neither of them were amused. England were in Colombia preparing for the 1970 World Cup finals and the two Bobby's had spent the afternoon doing a spot of shopping. Moore and Charlton had been shown round the store, treated with respect, but on leaving, Moore had been accused of whipping a bracelet into his pocket and promptly bundled off to the police station. What's odd is that a bracelet was never found and Charlton was never questioned. Moore was allowed to travel with the team to Ecuador but promptly arrested when Alf Ramsey decided to return to Bogota en route to the World Cup finals in Mexico. Now the only thing the England captain was ever likely to steal was the ball from under your feet and a wave of public opinion broke out across Colombia in his favour with stories coming out about similar mishaps occurring to visiting teams from Brazil. The charges against Moore were eventually dropped and the case dismissed but the question still remains. Was this a plot designed to rock the foundations of the world champions?

## Matter of opinion

Prime Minister Harold Wilson was pressuring diplomats to do all they could to get Moore cleared of the allegation, according to recent documents disclosed under the 30-year-rule. Such was the arm-twisting instigated in London that Colombia's security service chief was even persuaded to visit the judge in the case to warn him of the ramifications if Moore were to be held any longer.

# What's odd is that a bracelet was never found and Charlton was never questioned.

Learning of what could have turned out to be a sporting catastrophe – if not a full-scale international incident – British embassy officials took the drastic measure of cabling the Foreign Secretary while he was at a NATO planning meeting.

*'We ensured that the magistrate concerned was privately made aware of the awkward implications of the case for Colombia because of the strong interest of British and world opinion,'* the diplomat wrote.

### Moore like it

The Colombians agreed to *'stretch'* the law so that Moore could stay at the home of a local football official rather than in jail.

Officials cabled the Bogota embassy and warned: *'No subject is more calculated to arouse public interest here.*

*'You must go on doing everything you can to help sort out what I trust was a misunderstanding, and to secure that he is allowed to proceed to Mexico as speedily as possible.*

*If Mr Moore's case is not settled in the course of today, the Prime Minister would like urgent advice on whether he should himself send a personal message to the President of Colombia, particularly having regard to the growing evidence of delay caused by administrative inefficiency,'* an official wrote.

# International Grudges

'Kill these red Catalans,
kill these Catalan dogs!'

**Real Madrid vs Barcelona**

# Barra Bonkers

## Boca Juniors vs River Plate

Argentina's best-known author, Jorge Luis Borges, once said, *'Football is a calamity'* – he made the statement in 1978, when Argentina was playing host to the World Cup. For many people, the same is true over 20 years later. Just ask any self-respecting supporter of Boca Juniors or River Plate – the greatest rivals in world football and neighbours in Argentina's political melting pot, Buenos Aires. Their rivalry is legendary, not just in Argentina but across Latin America. For a Boca supporter, the worst calamity is a River Plate fan, and vice versa.

For River fans, the reality is completely different. *'They can't even do sums. We are the real champions,'* says Javier Bartoli, a consultant and an expert on international affairs. *'Mind you,'* he adds, *'I don't agree that you can't have friends from the other team. Personally, I do. Those kind of comments are for monkeys! That's fanaticism, that's not football.'*

The rivalry between Argentina's Boca Juniors and River Plate stretches far beyond the boundaries of Latin America. Both clubs were formed in the Boca neighbourhood of Buenos Aires in the south of the city. But in 1938, River Plate moved to a more affluent part of the city. From then on, River fans were immortalized as *'los millonarios'* (the millionaires), a team for Argentina's upper-crust. In stark contrast, Boca Juniors, with their humble roots, are seen as the *'people's team'*. When the club was formed in 1905, the majority of people living in Boca were Italian immigrants who had come to Argentina to escape from a life of poverty. River fans describe Boca supporters as *'Bosteros'*, roughly translated as *'horse dung'* or *'pigs'*, while Boca fans started calling their rivals *'Gallinas'*, or *'chickens'*, in the 1960s because they *'couldn't take the pressure and were afraid of everything'*. River failed to win Argentina's championship for 18 years during this period.

# In 1994, a bus-load of River fans was ambushed and two people were shot dead.

## Famous players

In June 1968, 74 home fans were killed at River's El Monumental stadium when Boca fans caused panic by lobbing burning paper in the stands. In 1994 a bus-load of River fans was ambushed several miles from the ground and two people were shot dead. In 1962 former River head coach Renato Cesarini walked on to the field towards Boca fans carrying a gun and, with his players standing behind him, shouted, *'Come on River Plate!'* Diego Maradona played for Boca before signing to Barcelona for a then world record fee of £3m while Gabriel Batistuta has played for both teams.

## Pigs and chickens

GET YOUR HORSE DUNG OR SCAREDY CHICKEN FLAGS!

Argentina's hooligans are known as *'barra bravas'* (tough gangs). River's barras, *'Los borrachos del tablon'* ('The drunks from the board', the board being wooden boards used in creating the stands) have succeeded the Boca hooligans, *'La Doce'* ('The Twelve', so-called because the fans believe they are the team's 12th player) as the country's most feared gang. Of the 168 bitterly contested derbies, Boca (the pigs) have won an impressive 62 games, while River (the chickens) are just behind on 56.

# High Spirits

## Spartak Moscow vs Dynamo Moscow

Five teams have traditionally dominated football in Moscow. Dynamo was the club of the KGB, CSKA of the army, Torpedo of the Zil car plant, while to this day Lokomotiv Moscow is still funded by the railways ministry. Spartak alone was independent, unconnected to any strand of Soviet society. The fans liked to call theirs *'The Club of the People'* and supporting it was a small act of defiance to the Communist leadership. Spartak has always had an intense rivalry with CSKA but the enmity is probably greatest with Dynamo.

The first football hooligans appeared in Moscow in 1972, supporting the former USSR. They were mainly Spartak Moscow supporters, still the strongest in Russia, but by the end of the 1970s, almost all Moscow clubs had firms. To combat this, the Communist government tried to crack down on football support of any kind, prohibiting travel to away games several times. Things got better during Gorbachev's *'perestroika'* and the 1988-89 season is considered to be the most trouble-free in the history of Soviet fanatics. During this period all the premier league clubs (and several from the lower leagues) had large followings, and the most important event for a football fan was an away game. The longest trip, Moscow-Dushanbe, was over 1,800 miles (3,000km) and took three days by train. Moscow clubs usually brought about 200 to 400 supporters.

# The longest trip, Moscow-Dushanbe, was over 1,800 miles and took three days by train. Moscow clubs usually brought about 200 to 400 supporters.

### It's only a game...

In the late 1930s, at the peak of the Soviet purges, a Spartak team starring Nikolai Starostin (who founded the club in 1935) won three league titles. This irritated Lavrenti Beria, Stalin's sadistic police chief and president of Dynamo, and in 1942, Starostin was woken by a torch beam shining in his eyes and two pistols pointed at his head. He was interrogated for two years, charged dubiously with plotting to kill Stalin and sentenced to 10 years in Siberia.

### Well-dressed yobs

When the Spartak firm, *'Flint's Crew'*, began the revival of Russian football fanaticism in the mid-1990s, its members developed along English lines. Soon, other firms began to do the same. As a result, by the end of 2000, almost all hardcore, respectable Russian firms were represented by fit and stylish young men called casuals. Russian casuals not only embraced English examples of hooligan dress, but also chose to fly the Union Jack flag inside the stadium.

The most popular brands for casuals were Umbro and Lonsdale, but as in England, young people, often children, pretended to be tough *'hools'* by adopting these brands. The hardcore firms have moved on to Lacoste, Fred Perry, Ben Sherman and traditional sportswear such as Kappa, New Balance, Nike and so on. At the start of the 2002 World Cup, rival supporters exchanged their club colours for the Russian flag and rioted on the streets of Moscow after Japan beat them 1-0 in the opening group.

# Tomb Raiders

## Al Ahly vs Zamalek

There's a few old codgers knocking about the ruins of Egypt's relics who'll tell you there's nothing more frightening than the sight of an ancient stroller wrapped in toilet roll staggering towards you like he's had one pint too many. But the rivalry in Cairo between Al Ahly, the oldest and most popular club in the Arab world, and Zamalek might just make you change your mind.

The enmity that drives this outbreak is fired by a frustrated form of nationalism, an historical hatred based on one's empathy with either pre- and post-Egyptian colonial days. A time when pipe-smokers decided what a chap should get up to in his spare time and when the locals did as instructed or faced the firing squad. Not what you'd imagine to be ideal conditions for disaffected youth with emotional axes to grind.

Al Ahly was founded in 1907 when Egypt was fighting for independence from Great Britain. It was the first Egyptian-only club at which the members' interests in football outweighed their taste for snooker, cards and, in more recent times, squash. The original idea came from Edrees Rageb Pasha, Omar Sultan Pasha, Ismaeel Serry, Abdul El Khalek Tharwat, Omar Lotfi and Ameen Sammy. They came together with an idea to establish a club where high school students could spend their spare time. This perhaps helps to explain Al Ahly's popularity over Zamalek, a club that was originally for foreigners only.

Regardless of other loyalties, every Egyptian supports Al Ahly or Zamalek. Neither team takes defeat well. The 1966 derby was so violent the clubs were banned from playing each other for a year. In 1971, the fixture failed to finish after Zamalek scored a disputed penalty to take a 2-1 lead. Al Ahly's fans headed for the referee and an hour-long pitch battle raged. Nearly 300 people, including 90 policemen, were hospitalized. The season was cancelled and football banned indefinitely!

# Regardless of other loyalties, every Egyptian supports Al Ahly or Zamalek. Neither team takes defeat well.

### Troublemakers and walkouts

Al Ahly's 3-1 victory over Zamalek in July 1997 secured them another title. After their team's second goal, three Zamalek fans inflicted such severe head and body wounds on an Al Ahly-supporting neighbour that he died. Elsewhere, another Zamalek fan stabbed his Al Ahly friend to death with a kitchen knife.

In 1999, the two teams were playing once again. Both had been warned about their conduct by the Egyptian FA and it was hoped that the game would go smoothly. After four minutes the unthinkable happened. Ayman Abd El-Aziz tackled Ibrahim Hassan, who was receiving a pass, from behind. Marc Bato (the referee) immediately took out the red card, unaware of what he had just started. The Zamalek players objected to his decision and surrounded him, while on the sidelines the coach was heard to shout, *'I will not play!'* Farouk Gaafar took his team from the playing field, leaving the referee no choice but call the match 2-0 for Al-Ahly. About five minutes later, the Zamalek team returned only to leave again after saluting their fans. The team were fined and had nine points deducted, but the arguments raged on.

# Greek Tragedy

## Panathinaikos vs Olympiakos

Athens is a sprawling maze of car fumes, coffee bars and cigarette butts. If you've visited the place in your youth you'll be familiar with the grubbier part of town, Piraeus, where the signs on street posts promise cheap travel and an opportunity to enjoy the sun-baked Greek islands. It is here that the blue-collar workers sweat over their labours among the smell of fresh fish and the sound of rock music belting from the bars that play host to an unlikely collection of bikers and heavy metal-lovers.

To the north, the city expands. Marble-floored hotels, restaurants rather than tavernas and fashion boutiques indicate that you are entering posher territory. Many of Greece's hard-working islanders return after the summer to enjoy the cooler temperatures in the capital. The rich prefer to support Panathinaikos, who for years packed 76,000 fans into the Olympic stadium to fight and throw seats about the place. Known as *'vazeli'* (Vaseline), implying that the club is corrupt but nothing ever sticks, over a period of 14 years Pana have had to replace more than the stadium's total seating capacity.

### Flare-ups
At the 1998 derby, after a controversial last-minute penalty handed Olympiakos the game, a police motorbike rider was killed when he was hit by home-made firebombs thrown by fans outside the ground. Coaches and cars were stoned and hundreds of seats were hurled about the stadium.

### Troublemakers
This from local Greek internet reports:
*'Panathinaikos and Olympiakos worried about derby violence.*
On 3 November, Greek club rivals Panathinaikos and Olympiakos were ready to put

# Over a period of 14 years, Pana have had to replace more than the stadium's total seating capacity.

certain *'supporter anti-clash'* measures in place prior to their derby that will take place for the sixth round of the Greek championship at the Apostolos Nikolaidis stadium.

For the first time, police forces will put in effect the new *'club supporter movement'* law which states that police forces must accompany club supporters to and from the stadiums. The organized Olympiakos supporters will get on the Sepolia train sta-
tion in two waves under the
supervision of police forces.'

### One week later...

*'Panathinaikos stadium damage reaches 14 million drachmas.*

The Apostolos Nikolaidis stadium looked like a *'martian'* surface after Sunday's sixth round Greek championship game between Panathinaikos and Olympiakos. Supporters from both clubs before, during, and after the game went at each other by throwing objects, fire crackers

and chairs! The supporters didn't seem to care who the recipient would be when throwing all of the above objects. Proof is that during the game (20th minute) the Panathinaikos supporters threw an object on the pitch in order to hit Olympiakos player Peter Ofori Quaye but instead they hit Panathinaikos player, Leonidas Vokolos, on his head.'

# Beach Battles

## Fluminense vs Flamengo

Brazil's ultimate derby takes place under the baking sun up the road from the most famous beach in the world. Rio's intense rivalry between Flamengo and Fluminense is inbred. *'Fla-Flu began 40 minutes before nothing,'* says Brazilian journalist Nelson Rodrigues. We think this means the Rio derby predates everything, even the Big Bang. Back in 1911, a dispute over players' boots at Fluminense saw the players walk out. The club had been riven with financial bickering and the players who left set up their own side, Flamengo, in a poor part of town. Since then, the toffs have always favoured Flu while the working man still comes down on the side of Fla. It explains the massive support base for Flamengo.

In 1912, the first classically named Fla-Flu derby kicked off. Fluminense beat Flamengo 3-2. The match was a tempestuous bundle of violence and misplaced tackles. The intensity of the play was so high that many ladies in the crowd fainted. The spectator boxes laid on by local luminaries were filled with beautiful women and decorated with huge displays of flowers. Rowdy gents celebrated each goal by tossing their straw hats onto the pitch, while the ladies flapped their fans and collapsed.

More than 177,000 people crammed into the Maracana to watch the Fla-Flu in 1969, a global attendance record. However, today, Brazilian football has lost all credibility. As Flamengo's power base increases, so Fluminense's wanes. Relegated from the top division, controversially reinstated and then relegated twice more, they were recently *'reinstated'* to the top flight with the help of powerful political connections.

## Divine inspiration

In 1953, Flamengo couldn't win a thing. The most popular club in Brazil, their fans were dying of hunger but still they craved success for the team. A Catholic priest, Father Goes,

# The following year, Flamengo finally lost the championship. The players stopped going to mass and never said the rosary again.

stuck his neck out and offered a guarantee of victory as long as the players attended his mass before each game and said the rosary.

Flamengo won the cup three years in a row. Their rivals protested, arguing that Flamengo were using outlawed *'weapons'*. Father Goes claimed that all he was doing was showing his charges the way of the Lord. The players continued saying their rosaries, but something was clearly amiss, because the following year, Flamengo finally lost the championship. The players stopped going to mass and never said the rosary again. Meanwhile, a Father Romualdo started attending every Fluminense training session. Sure enough, the team started to win, and in training, the players would kiss the priest's cassock each time they scored a goal.

### Illegal football

The increase in crime, street violence and wife beatings whenever Flamengo lose is such that an eminent Brazilian jurist once suggested the creation of a law to ensure that Flamengo won every game.

# San Sironara

## AC Milan vs Inter Milan

There's nothing like a good old family row to get the adrenalin flowing. In Milan, they've been at it for more than 90 years, since a rebel faction broke away from the Milan Cricket and Football Club (later AC Milan) to form *'Internazionale'*. Although most fans still live in the same streets, work in the same places and travel on the same metro, there are plenty of insults and jokes against each other.

Unlike some other Italian derbies, the Milan fixture is more a domestic tug-of-love, a matter of prestige rather than a civil war, lacking the added edge of a political, social or religious divide. It has a lot to do with money. Inter are traditionally considered a conservative, right-wing club, drawing their support from the more prosperous strata of Milan society. Yet their president Massimo Moratti, a millionaire from his family's oil business, is on the left in politics and was even considered as a candidate for mayor of Milan by an alliance of centre-left parties.

AC Milan were once identified as the team of the city's working class, supported by large numbers of trade unionists and leftists, yet their modern success owes much to the finances of media magnate and occasional leader of the country, Silvio Berlusconi.

**What a sight!**

More a battle of style over substance. People come to marvel at the splendour of the stadium, the colour of the flags and the size of the rotten fruit fans use to pelt opponents at the corner kicks.

*'Approaching the San Siro at night takes your breathe away, with all its incredible lights and towers,'* says Inter fan, Giuseppe. *'Standing outside you get a feeling of being minute, a little unimportant thing, not able to take in anything else going on around you because your supporter's heart has just found its home, its sense of life.*

# The Milan fixture is more a domestic tug-of-love, a matter of prestige rather than a civil war.

*You can imagine what the ambience of the old Roman games must have felt like.'*

Once inside the stadium your senses are simply bombarded with the light, the noise and the colour of the fans. Flares continually illuminate the crowd. Smoke and noise fill the air. The *'Ultras'*, as always, are situated behind the goals, AC Milan fanatics in the *'fossa dei leoni'* (lion's cave) decked in red and black, Inter's *'irriducibili'* (indomitables) in their blue and black.

### Relegated

Inter fans taunt the Milanista because, unlike their rivals, Inter have never been relegated. The chant of *'Serie B'* hurled at the red and black support, refers to the 1979 season when Milan were dropped down a division after a match-fixing scandal and two years later were relegated again purely due to football factors.

# African Drums

## Kaizer Chiefs vs Orlando Pirates

As with many countries around the world, South Africa has one showpiece club match each season that brings the nation to a near standstill – the traditional derby game between the Kaizer Chiefs and Orlando Pirates. This is a rivalry that captures the imagination of the country and divides people into two distinct rival camps.

Both sides have their roots in Soweto, the sprawling township on the edge of Johannesburg from where much of South Africa's soccer tradition stems. Both share a history set against the background of apartheid, during which there was little opportunity for black footballers in a racist South African sports set-up, and both have long been a refuge for the fantasies of millions.

Pirates were formed in 1939 and have always been regarded as *'the people's team'*. The club was formed to keep youngsters from Orlando out of trouble by providing them with some organized activity. Kaizer Chiefs formed about 30 years later, composed of leading members of Pirates who broke away from the club. Pirates' most popular player, Kaizer Motaung, who had been playing in the US for the Atlanta Chiefs, formed his own invitation team to play friendly matches around the country in the off-season. The matches were called *'stake games'*, as organizers could put down prize money for the winner. Pirates objected to this team but Motaung persisted and eventually broke away with several officials and teammates.

### Unity in grief

In 2001, both clubs had to pull together after a stadium disaster at a derby fixture at Ellis Park resulted in the deaths of over 40 fans (see *'African grudges'*). With both clubs contributing to the effort to ensure there would never be a repeat, the greatest rivalry in South African football temporarily took a breather as soccer fans united.

# Both clubs share a history set against the background of apartheid, during which there was little opportunity for black footballers in a racist South African sports set-up.

Most stadiums in Africa are now too old, built in the 1960s to celebrate independence. To the factors of a crumbling infrastructure and irritable police procedure you can add the fact that there are rarely any checks on spectators as they enter the venues. Moreover, consider that alcohol is readily available inside the stadiums. Then throw into the mix some serious African social issues. *'Soccer is a reflection of our society,'* commented the *Ivoir Soir* newspaper. *'There are social crises in African countries and people go to the stadiums to unwind. Unfortunately, others go to develop their instincts for violence. Fighting starts easily.'*

## Founders

The late Gilbert Sekgabi, Clarence Mlokoti, China Ngema, and the late Ewert *'The Lip'* Nene, played huge roles in the formation and growth of the Chiefs. In 1976, Nene was stabbed to death.

# Spitting Blood

## Holland vs Germany

The Dutch supporters despise the Germans and the feeling is mutual. The Germans usually win, but there have been exceptions. Back in 1988, when the Orange brigade beat the Germans 2-1 on their home patch in the European Championships, over nine million people Dutchmen poured onto the streets to sing *'O wat zijn die Duisters stil'* – a Dutch interpretation of *'Can you hear the Germans sing?'*

Then, in Italia 1990, we witnessed one of the most explosive scenes in ever a World Cup. Quite what Frank Rijkaard and Rudi Voller said to each other during the game we don't know. But in a match where tackles flew in like a butcher's knife on a chopping board, the sending off of Rijkaard and Voller, after 20 minutes of what had hitherto been a tremendous contest, was an unfortunate example of what can happen when a ref takes it upon himself to calm things down.

The ref was about to award the Dutch a free-kick against Rudi Voller when Rijkaard decided to exact revenge on the German player himself. Voller lashed out in retaliation and the ref decided that the German had to go. The cameras were on close-up and we could see words being exchanged, with a familiar sarcastic look of self-importance beaming all over the curly-haired German player's face.

Some of us might have been wishing we could wipe that smile off Voller's visage. The Dutch player was thinking along exactly the same lines, and duly obliged by spitting twice into the face of the gob-smacked centre-forward.

## Flare-ups

After the teams met in the Euro 92 finals, fans pelted each other with stones and bottles and 500 citizens from the nation of windmills and home-made cigarettes stormed the

# The cameras were on close-up and we could see words being exchanged, with a familiar sarcastic look of self-importance beaming all over the curly-haired German player's face.

border and demolished the German town of Gronau in celebration. Since 1910, the two nations have played each other 34 times: Germany has won 13 of the matches, Holland nine and there have been 12 draws.

## The devil's hand

On the eve of the 1992 European Championships, legendary Dutch free-kick specialist Ronald Koeman announced, *'The devil himself has brought us together.'* And they don't come much more troublesome than him.

# Policing Trouble

**In modern football theatres the approach taken by police forces overseas has become starkly reactive compared with the forward-thinking measures taken out by their British counterparts.**

In Italy, the police presence at certain games can be intimidating in the extreme, with water cannon, tear gas and automatic weapons often in evidence. Laws introduced following the fatal stabbing of a Genoa fan in 1994 also imposed further restrictions on the movement of football fans and controls on their behaviour in the stadiums. The new law states that the chief constable of the province in which the sporting events take place can forbid entry to people who have been reported to the police or convicted of taking part in violent incidents during sporting events. The chief constable can also ban people who have encouraged violence by displaying symbols, posters or banners. He can force known troublemakers to report to the police during the days and hours in which the sporting events are taking place. Any person who flouts the law can be punished with a minimum jail sentence of three months and a maximum of 18 months.

- While the British and the Italian authorities favour the increased use of custodial sentencing, progressive thinking states that tackling football violence at its roots is the most effective remedy. Despite the clear limitations of the fan coaching schemes being developed in the European mainland, they do provide a basis for a more satisfactory treatment of the problem. German football clubs have also

# Sociologists argue that football clubs themselves should help to correct the disruptive and violent behaviour of a small minority of their fans.

been much more willing to support and assist such schemes than their English and Scottish counterparts.

- While some British clubs have introduced schemes to enable closer contact between fans and club officials, the large majority have washed their hands of their responsibility for the behaviour of their fans.

- While football hooliganism appears to be on the decline inside British stadiums, the problems that remain are unlikely to be eradicated simply through additional controls on the movement of fans or curbs on the availability of alcohol.

- Sociologists argue that football clubs themselves should help. This might best be achieved through the increased establishment of local fans' forums, through which supporters and club directors would have a much stronger channel of communication. Allied to the fan coaching schemes, the forums might succeed in changing supporter behaviour on the presumption that they are less likely to damage the reputation of a club in which they have an interest.

# Gob-Smacked

## Schumacher clobbers Battiston

Harald Schumacher was a man who, despite his curly locks and handlebar moustache, was pretty useful between the sticks. He was also cursed by an inability both to keep his mouth shut in the press and his hands to himself in a 50-50 situation.

When France added Euro 2000 to the world crown they won on home soil two years before, they established themselves as one of the great sides. All of which is a dramatic turnaround in fortunes for a national team that had, until 1998, always been considered underachievers on the world stage.

There are many who believe that the French team of the 1980s, led by the peerless Michel Platini, was the best side never to win the World Cup. They were certainly one of the unluckiest, losing out at the semi-final stage to far less talented German sides in both 1982 and 1986.

Few teams outside of Brazil have enjoyed the kind of popularity and widespread sympathy given to the French team that lost in Seville in 1982. Michel Hidalgo's side had made a stuttering start to the World Cup finals in Spain with a 3-1 defeat to England. But from that moment on, France swept through the tournament and looked on course for a final showdown with Italy in Madrid.

With a midfield that could boast Platini, Jean Tigana and Alain Giresse playing behind a strike-force of Dominique Rocheteau and Didier Six, it was no surprise that France prospered. But the dramatic events that took place at the Estadio Sanchez Pizjuan became, until 1998, the defining moment in France's World Cup history.

The lasting image of the match came in the 65th minute when, with the score at 1-1, French defender Patrick Battiston was put clean through. Germany's keeper, Harald Schumacher, came charging off his line and made no attempt to play the ball, crashing into Battiston with a leading arm. The Frenchman was carried off and required oxygen in

# The Frenchman was carried off and required oxygen in the dressing room before heading to hospital.

MERDE! ZE PAIN!

the dressing room before heading to hospital. That Schumacher did not receive so much as a yellow card remains one of the great World Cup mysteries. But even worse for France, he became the hero of the penalty shootout!

### Comeback

After losing in his second final in 1986, Schumacher wanted to come back in 1990 and win the World Cup at his third attempt. Then, in 1987, he wrote a book in which he claimed that 90 percent of the players in the German Bundesliga did drugs. Schumacher was never picked for the German squad again, and escaped to Turkey to play league soccer there instead.

### Fake

Commentating on the 2002 World Cup, Schumacher couldn't believe it when Rivaldo sank to the ground holding his head after a Turkish player booted the ball at his stomach. *'That is something that I cannot understand. A star as big as Rivaldo does not need to cause a red card with a theatre simulation,'* said Schumacher, himself the winner of numerous fair play awards. Not.

# Argy Bargy

## England and Argentina

World Cup encounters between these two have rarely ended without
rancour. Even the England victory in 2002 was devilled with claims
from Argentina's bench that Michael Owen dived to win a penalty.
In 1966, Geoff Hurst scored the winner at Wembley but it was the
infamous sending off of Rattin that sparked a serious of career-
threatening challenges so cynical that even the calm Bobby Charlton
had his hair ruffled.

According to Charlton, the Argentinians coaxed, spat and spoiled for a fight during and
after the game, with Rattin guilty of trying to tell the German referee, Kreitlein, how to
run things.

Rattin lost his patience with Kreitlein, seemingly angered by the fact his teammates were
being booked for kicking seven shades of the proverbial out of the opposition. Eventually
the man in black had had enough and sent him off. He later admitted he had no idea what
the player was saying but the *'look was enough'*.

Alf Ramsey ran out on to the field immediately after the final whistle – not in celebration,
but to prevent his players from swapping shirts with the Argentinians, with the comment,
*'We don't swap shirts with animals.'* Ramsay even had to lock the England team in their
dressing room when protagonists from South America banged on the door asking the
likes of Ball and Wilson to step outside. The irony was that Rattin's first booking was for a
harmless challenge on Charlton.

In 1986 we got the Hand of God, a feat of devilry so wicked, the scorn of a nation was
heaped onto one man and his actions. Some have excused the cheating devil's actions by
virtue of the wonder goal he scored later – a goal so magnificent that even the harshest
critic had to bend under this petition of football genius.

# Alf Ramsey ran out on to the field immediately after the final whistle – not in celebration, but to prevent his players from swapping shirts with the Argentinians.

### Hand of God 1986

Bobby Robson feared the Tunisian ref wasn't up to it. England had to play Argentina in the heat of Mexico City and even though Ali Bennaceur had a reputation as one of Africa's finest, he was rumoured to be a man with a pro-Argentinian bias. Hmmm.

Five minutes into the second half Maradona launched an attack, beating a couple of players before losing the ball in a failed pass to Valdano. In the confusion, Steve Hodge managed to hook the ball over his head towards Peter Shilton in goal.

Maradona, sensing an opportunity, heaved his portly frame into Shilton's path and clashed with a melange of fist and body. At the point of impact, Maradona had one arm in the air, as if he was holding on to a tantalizing thread of invincibility, a winch on which he could hoist his suspended ego. The ball ricocheted into the net and immediately Shilton, normally so impassive when the ball beat him to the goal line, raced towards our Tunisian friend, holding his arm as though he was in need of some urgent wasp bite medication. The ref was having none of it. England were stung.

# Fair Verona?

## Hellas Verona vs Chievo Verona

The working-class Verona suburb of Chievo, filled with pigeons, water rats and stray dogs, is the smallest community to field a side in Italy's top-flight football, Serie A. It's not a spot you'd find in any tourist guide.

While Hellas Verona is the city's big club, winning the league in 1985, Chievo has had the greater success in recent seasons. According to author Tim Parks, a frustrated Hellas fan, they used to be called Paluani Chievo. Paluani is the name of a company that makes panettoni, the fourth largest in Italy. It's based in Chievo and owned by the Campedelli family, which also owns the team. Alas, the company name and easy publicity had to go when the team hit the big time in 1986 and climbed into the dubiously professional world of Serie C2. Now Paluani is just stitched on the team's shirts, which used to be pale blue and white, but then rather disturbingly became dark blue and yellow, Verona colours.

*'First they invade our stadium, then they steal our strip. And at one point they very nearly took us over altogether. In 1991, Luigi Campedelli bought a small share in Hellas Verona. The plan was to buy out the bigger club and merge the teams. After all, this is a family of Veronese industrialists. They have close contacts with the local paper, the local banks. It didn't work. There are limits to what divine law will permit. In any event, that was around the same time that Chievo changed its name to Chievo Verona. Campedelli wanted the team **'to be more easily associated with the whole city'**. If you can't beat them, become them, seems to be the game.'*

For years Hellas fans mocked their neighbours: ***'The day there is a Verona derby in Serie A will be the day donkeys fly.'*** When Chievo were promoted in 2001 they adopted the donkey as the club mascot.

The first derby took place in November 2001. Verona's website carried a plea from a fan saying, ***'Win for us Hellas, and these miserable peasants will magically disappear.'***

# Hellas fans have a hard-earned reputation for violence, right-wing views and racism.

Verona's mayor played the Italian national anthem to show that the two teams were united. But as soon as it started hundreds of Hellas fans gave fascist salutes and when the music stopped there was a rousing chant of *'vaffanculo!'* (go fuck yourself!) to which some members of the Chievo crowd responded *'madre e puttana, scopa con tutti'* (your mother is a whore and fucks everyone). Italian insults are generally variations on the recurrent themes of sex, family, defecation and religion.

## Right-wing
Hellas fans have a hard-earned reputation for violence, right-wing views and racism. In 2001, Verona, who had struggled all season, were linked with a move for the highly rated Mboma, the African Player of the Year. The deal fell through. *'You need to draw your own conclusions,'* the Verona president, Giambattista Pastorello, said. *'If you have fans that do these things you need to have patience.'* The club later insisted that of course Pastorello did not mean to say racists could veto signings.

## Troublemakers
Hellas have a hooligan website but Chievo – now supported by 20,000 regulars, although the area they come from is much smaller – are the nation's favourites, everybody's second team. Except for those fans of Hellas, of course.

# Oranges and Lemons

## Real Betis vs Sevilla

Seville's two teams are divided by class and driven by mutual hatred. Sevilla is the older of the two, formed in 1905, while Betis came along four years later in 1909 after a revolt when a Sevilla director refused to hire a local factory worker. Since that time, Betis has favoured Seville's working class and Sevilla the posh knobs. The first meeting was on New Year's Day, 1916. The game ended 2-2 and violent battles littered the streets of Seville for two days.

Sevilla will be remembered for giving Maradona a chance to recover from his various health and judicial problems following the 1990 World Cup. Once the Mafia and his cocaine addiction had caught up with him, he fled Italy and it wasn't until the 1992-93 season that the by now bloated fatman was given a chance in Spain and scored four goals for Sevilla. The fact that he failed to make an impression over the 25 games he had played and, more importantly, failed to score against Real Betis, meant that Maradona was given his cards at the end of the season.

In 1999, the Betis president was sent death threats after he was accused of 'incentivizing' Sevilla's opponents with bundles of cash in a crucial championship match. Sevilla got their own back the following year, deliberating allowing Oviedo to beat them in the last game of the season, which ensured Betis suffered the humiliation of relegation. Losing 3-0 at half-time, Sevilla replaced their best player, the team keeper, Frode Olsen, to send their neighbours down. When the Betis manager Francisco Antunez joined Sevilla in the late 1940s, Radio Moscow reported, *'Sevilla, the capitalists, have trampled upon their noble proletarian neighbours Betis, abusing the power handed them by the fascist Francoist regime.'*

# Sevilla will be remembered for giving Maradona a chance to recover from his various health and judicial problems.

### Fruity

Every game is heavily policed and players bear the brunt of fan frustration with rotten oranges being a particular favourite among the fruit throwers. In a recent derby, a 10-man Sevilla held on for dear life and then almost claimed victory against their bitter rivals after a second booking saw Sevilla's Gorordo Torrado sent off for jumping into the guts of an opponent. The ref and the Real Betis players were then pelted with debris for the rest of the game, which ended 0-0.

### Denilson

Beticos, hardcore Betis fans, keep themselves busy. When the £22m Betis and Brazilian midfield signing Denilson was reported to have spent a night out on the tiles in the run-up to a key match with Sevilla, his car was attacked and the man himself was jostled by members of the Beticos. Seville is a pleasant place to visit. But check your diaries for date of the Seville derby, because the wide boulevards and courtyard bars become a no-go zone for the evening.

# Turkish Delights

## Galatasaray vs Fenerbahce

In 1994, six of the eight European teams who arrived to play at Galatasaray's Ali Sami Yen stadium lodged complaints with UEFA about the treatment they had received from the fans and the police. It therefore stands to reason that the visit of Fenerbahce every season invariably ends in widespread violence in the stands and throughout the city. Gala is the best-known team outside Turkey and is based in the European part of Istanbul. Fener is the more popular within the country – they claim to have 25 million supporters, the core of which comes from the Kadikoy district of Istanbul, on the Asian side of the Bosphorus. Rivalry is so fierce that away fans are rarely seen at matches in the other part of the city. Gala fans are famous for describing their stadium as *'Hell'*, and both Leeds and Manchester United fans can testify to the aptness of the nickname. On one occasion, Dean Saunders, one-time Galatasaray player, was travelling on the team bus before the derby and he recalls seeing a man walk a sheep into the middle of the road. *'He stopped and cut the sheep's throat,'* he recalled, adding, *'They are very passionate about their football. It means a lot to them.'*

# Gala fans are famous for describing their stadium as *'Hell'*, and both Leeds and Manchester United fans can testify to the aptness of the nickname.

## Flag

In the Turkish Cup Final of 1996, a match decided in the 116th minute of the second leg by a Dean Saunders goal for Gala, manager Graeme Souness grabbed a massive red and yellow Gala flag and legged it out to the middle of the pitch before spearing the pole into the centre circle. A riot ensued. Souness ran for the tunnel while the crowd chanted, *'You can go and fuck your mother with the cup.'* The presentation ceremony was conducted behind a wall of police riot shields as Fener fans chucked flares, fireworks and missiles at the players and dignitaries. Three people were wounded in knife attacks, police dogs were let loose into the crowd and both team coaches were smashed to bits.

## Horror movie

Where do you want to start? Up to 30,000 cram into the Ali Sami Yen Stadium with flares, banners and a capacity to create huge levels of noise. No actual songs to sing, just outright abuse at all visiting teams' fans and players. Since the visit of English club sides in the Champions League, members of notorious Turkish *'ultra'* groups have taken to wandering the streets in the hours leading up to kick-off, sporting face masks and studio props last seen on the set of *Scream* and *I Know What You Did Last Summer*. Local youngsters seem to be hell-bent on creating an atmosphere of intimidation and fear and apart from the Chelsea fans who visited the country a few years back and said they couldn't see what all the fuss was about, they seem to have succeeded. Same sentiments at Fener.

# Scotch Wrath

## Celtic vs Rangers

When it comes to sectarian squabbles, nothing on this earth can rival the intensity of hatred that exists between these two teams; Rangers Protestants vs Celtic Catholics. One lot singing *'The Sash'* and similarly inclined ditties while the opposition trot out renditions of *'The Boys of the Old Brigade'* and other eulogies to Irish Republicanism.

While Celtic have always accepted Protestants in the players' ranks, Rangers went mental in 1989 when Graeme Souness signed former Celtic forward and CATHOLIC, Mo Johnston. After scoring 55 goals in 99 games for Celtic, Mo was a hot commodity, but no goal burned hotter in the Rangers supporters' minds than a particular goal that Mo scored against them – after scoring, he crossed himself, infuriating the Rangers faithful. *Scotland on Sunday* labelled Johnston the Salman Rushdie of Scottish football, for managing to offend two sets of fundamentalists at the same time. This seems a bit harsh. At the time, Johnston was playing with Nantes in France. However, Celtic were in negotiations to bring him back and he even agreed to appear, at Celtic's urging, at a live press conference announcing to the world that he was coming home. The catch was that Celtic had not signed Johnston yet. Then Rangers stepped in and offered him an obscene amount of money to play for them, something that Celtic could not deliver. The rest, as they say, is history. Johnston signed for Rangers, infuriating Celtic and Rangers fans alike. Rangers fans were seen on TV burning their season tickets and scarves in bitter protest at the signing of a Catholic and former Celtic player. Celtic fans felt betrayed by their prodigal son and labelled him the greatest soccer Judas in history.

Attempts have been made to ban the Old Firm fixture. In the 1930s, Glasgow's chief constable thought it might help reduce the city crime rate if the match was called off . More recently, booze bans, early morning kick-offs and a greater degree of Catholic and Protestant cross-marriage have helped to reduce the crowd trouble, but players still dive

*Scotland on Sunday* labelled Johnston the Salman Rushdie of Scottish football, for managing to offend two sets of fundamentalists at the same time.

into tackles like they've been instructed to break a few bones and referee Hugh Dallas can testify to coin-throwing in more games than he'd care to mention. According to former Rangers legend Ally McCoist, *'The saddest sound in the world is sitting in the losing dressing room after an Old Firm game listening to the other team singing.'*

### Stadium disaster

On 2 January 1971, 66 fans were crushed to death and 145 were injured as they left Ibrox at the end of the game. In 1975 there were two attempted murders, two cleaver attacks, one axe attack, nine stabbings and over 35 common assaults.

Gazza famously mimicked the playing of the flute in front of a furious Celtic support in his first derby match. The Orange flute signified Loyalist supremacy and the fact that his teammates had egged him on to do it didn't stop several death threats coming his way.

# Spanish Thrillers

## Barcelona vs Real Madrid

To reduce this match to a mere battle between rivals would be to miss what a Barca-Real Madrid match is all about. According to Spanish writer Jose Vicente Hernaez in the Madrid-based sports daily, *Marca*, *'It's the match par excellence, it's the match of the year and of the century... who is going to win? It's anyone's guess, it's a mystery. Don't believe anyone who says he knows. There is the pride of 22 players out on the pitch, of the 10 on the sub's bench, of the directors of the club, of the whole stadium, of the millions who are watching it on TV, and of another million who can't bear to watch it even on TV because they can't handle so much tension.'* It is the only fixture that draws more than 100,000 fans twice a year. As Bobby Robson once said, *'Throw into that equation all the history, the politicking and the media attention, and you're looking at a powder keg.'*

Much of Catalonian history is mixed up in this match. Barcelona, as the focus of Catalonia's aspirations as a regional state, bears the brunt of centralizing tendencies handed down from the capital, Madrid. The formation of the club at the turn of the 20th century by a group of Swiss and English gents gave the Mediterranean city a sense of unity and focus. Whenever Madrid tried to dictate terms and impose its authority, the people of the region were drawn to the club, giving the crowd a sense of collective self-confidence. Barcelona's identity has been forged by persecution.

In the 1920s, Barcelona was banned from playing for six months after the fans greeted the Spanish national anthem with whistles, and during the Spanish Civil War, club president Josep Sunyol was executed by General Franco's troops on a mountain road outside Madrid.

As Bobby Robson once said, *'Throw into that equation all the history, the politicking and the media attention, and you're looking at a powder keg.'*

For Barcelona fans, Real Madrid was not just backed by Franco, it *was* Franco, while for many Real Madrid fans, FC Barcelona was – and always will be – separatist scum.

### Franco

During the 1943 semi-finals of the Spanish Championship, renamed the Generalissimo's Cup in Franco's honour, the matches were marred by biased refereeing, violent tackles, crowd violence and arrests. After the first leg, which Barcelona won, the Director of State Security visited the players and informed them, *'Do not forget that some of you are only playing because of the generosity of the regime that has forgiven you for your lack of patriotism.'* Three members of the team had fled Spain during the Civil War and his comments were interpreted as a warning not to attempt to win the match. The score finished 11-1 to Real Madrid and Barcelona's team masseur was arrested for protesting, as a military man standing next to the dugout shouted, *'Kill these red Catalans, kill these Catalan dogs!'*

### Website

The *'Boixos Nois'* website hosts most of the Barca hooligan fringe. Morphed photos of Madrid players provide daily amusement while Real Madrid look to the *'Orgullo Vikingo'* site for regular pictorial essays of their most recent *'conquests'*. Like many hooligan offerings online you get photos, forums and the chance to pick out a tasteful tattoo and waste countless hours linking from one woeful website offering to another.

# Football Specials

**West Ham's ICF (Inter City Firm) made the name of the high speed trains of the seventies synonymous with football violence. But ironically it was the clapped-out train carriages that shuttled the greater number of troublemakers during this time. The West Ham hooligans decided to travel first class, dress smartly and get to away games quicker by using the Inter City service. Regular punters relied on the tried and trusted *'football specials'* to move around.**

The English already had a long history of football violence going back to the early days of the professional sport in England in the 19th century. Then, referees were often the targets for attack. But football fights between rival gangs using weapons – including bottles and knives – were not uncommon in the 1920s and 1930s in England and Scotland.

- During a football match in Birmingham in 1920, it was reported that *'bottles were flying around like hailstones'* on the terraces and that men in the crowd used half-pint stout bottles instead of clubs to fight with. Taking this mentality onto the filthy, slow, packed railway carriages was going to be a disaster. The popularity of the *'away day'* meant that by the 1970s, the public demand for an efficient, cheap, national travel network to support the mass exodus of football fans around the country meant the government was forced to lay on the special train services.

Trains were selected for their robust capacity to withstand hordes of drinking, singing football fans. And just to be on the safe side, a couple of coppers would be dispatched to go along for the ride.

- Trains were selected for their robust capacity to withstand hordes of drinking, singing football fans. And just to be on the safe side, a couple of coppers would be dispatched to go along for the ride. It was pure madness. Trains would become targets for rival gangs lobbing concrete slabs over bridges and, of course, it was easy to march your firm down to the station to greet the away support because everything was running on a timetable. But the fans seemed to love it. They could get about the country on-the-cheap whilst the camaraderie of the *'all lads in it together'* mentality fostered on board each carriage meant it was easy for troublemakers to garner support and stir up trouble. By the time a train arrived at its destination the mob would be drunk, baying and ready for a scrap.

# Who is Luis?

## Luis Figo and Barca fans

How coveted is Luis Figo? Real Madrid, a club that at the time was reportedly more than $150m in debt, shelled out $67m to pry the Portuguese midfielder from hated rivals, Barcelona. Team official Florentino Perez was made president of the organization after pulling off the most costly transfer in history. In the build-up to the election for Real's president, Florentino Perez signed a pre-contract with Figo's agent, Jose Veiga, agreeing that Figo would become a Real player if Florentino were chosen as president. Florentino avowed, *'If I become president and Figo does not come to Madrid, I will pay the salaries for the forthcoming season for all the other players.'* In addition, and just to make sure he had everybody on his side, he promised he would refund money to the club's season ticket holders if he failed to nab Figo.

But this isn't the first time Figo has spread his love among loyal club supporters. Several years ago, Figo reportedly signed contracts with two Italian teams at the same time. He ended up playing for neither. In 1998, he reportedly signed a secret contract with Milan before the agreement was broken. Figo denied all reports of a deal with Real Madrid before signing with the team, breaking the hearts of Catalan fans, who accused him of being everything from a sell-out to a traitor to a criminal.

# Figo denied all reports of a deal with Real Madrid before signing with the team, breaking the hearts of Catalan fans.

## Anti-Figo

At the website www.antifigo.com, Barcelona supporters compare Figo to Judas. You can order Figo pizzas from a display that features the large head of the Portuguese star and a bag of dollars indicating that he's sold out. To access every link you have to click on large suitcases filled with dollars and in a Top 10 of insults the famous Number 7 gets compared to a vampire. Figo may not have been the only player to have switched clubs – the great Dane Michael Laudrup and the Argentinian genius Alfredo Di Stéfano are perhaps the most highly rated side-switchers. But Laudrup and the Argentinian were seen as hired hands, mercenaries prepared to go where the money took them, whereas Figo was Barcelona's captain, the best player in the world and loved by his Catalan fans above all others.

## Moving on

Figo has spent the last few seasons at Real Madrid and the experience seems to have got the better of him. His form has dipped and there's now a permanent frown line across his forehead that suggests the pressure could be getting to the man. In 2002, a Spanish newspaper revealed that Figo had kept up his club membership at Barcelona, something that has fuelled anger among the Madrid supporters and sparked rumours that the former captain might be coming home. The only major signing going the other way has been Luis Enrique who spent two seasons with Real Madrid before making the switch to Barcelona. Often compared to Roy Keane, Enrique has a glare that keeps him out of trouble and allows him to enjoy Las Ramblas with the minimum of fuss.

# Firenze Brigade

## Baggio and Fiorentina fans

Roberto Baggio was born on 18 February 1967, to Matilde and Fiorindo Baggio, in the small Italian town of Caldogno, north of the city of Vicenza. He had a number of brothers and sisters: Gianna, Walter, Carla, Giorgio, Anna Maria, Nadia and Eddy. As a child he spent most of his time riding his motorcycle or playing football. His father often took him to a park field where he stayed until late evening. When he saw his father coming to get him, he would run away because he didn't want to go home.

In his first year at Fiorentina, he played five games in the Italian Cup, but failed to score. The next season, 1986-87, Baggio played his first Serie A match against Sampdoria, but had to wait until May 1987 for his first goal, against Napoli; the same year saw the first appearance on the pitch of that world-famous ponytail. In 1988, Baggio converted to Buddhism, joining the Soka Gakkai sect. The following year he started to really get noticed. He played in 30 Serie A matches, amassing 15 goals, and 10 Italian Cup matches in which he racked up an amazing nine goals. After such a great year, he was called up in November 1988 for his first international match in Rome against Holland.

The 1989-90 season was another success for Baggio: he made 32 appearances for Fiorentina in Serie A and scored 17 goals. Baggio led his team into European Cup action for the first time, and made a total of 12 appearances in the UEFA Cup, scoring only one goal. Fiorentina lost in the final against Juventus. Baggio played in two Italian Cup matches, again scoring a single goal. That's the background.

## Flare-ups

At the end of the season, Fiorentina sold Roberto to rivals Juventus for a then world-record transfer fee of $17m. Fiorentina fans went berserk, rampaging through the streets and *'sacking'* shops and official buildings like a marauding legion of squaddies on a big

# Fiorentina fans went berserk, rampaging through the streets and *'sacking'* shops and official buildings.

night out. Their beloved *'little prince'* had been sold to the hated *'old lady'* of Italian football. The people felt betrayed and the riots in the streets of Florence lasted for more than two days. The city of Florence was struggling with its finances and the Baggio sale was confirmation that Fiorentina could never make the step up to the Italian elite. For the people of the city it encapsulated how they felt about more than just football. They had become nothing more than a tourist stopover.

## Ultras

Fiorentina has numerous *'ultras'* who these days regularly trash the trains that trundle in from the north via Bologna but back then, security had never seen anything on this scale. To think that women and children joined in the mayhem was unthinkable but the sale of Roberto Baggio says more about Florence and its place in Italian culture than the simple sale of a talented footballer.

# Old Enemies

## England vs Scotland

You could say there's a bit of history between these two sides, but there's more to this than a dozen re-runs of *Braveheart* could ever do justice to. England vs Scotland matches have represented all that is good and all that is bad about football since the fixture began in 1872. Hampden Park and Wembley have played host to many splendid battles between the two nations, but a bitter rivalry and a thinly veiled antagonism bordering on hatred has often led to scenes that ultimately saw the annual fixture abandoned in 1989.

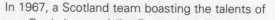

In 1967, a Scotland team boasting the talents of Denis Law and Jim Baxter beat England's World Cup winners 3-2 at Wembley, allowing the Scottish media to hail the team as the best in the world for a day.

Resounding English victories in 1955 and 1961 – 7-2 and 9-3 respectively – brought Scottish goalkeepers an unwanted reputation as second-rate, a tag which has been difficult to shake off. But the Scots got their revenge in 1976 when a Kenny Dalglish shot squirmed between the legs of England goalkeeper Ray Clemence as Scotland sealed a 2-1 win.

Whether one remembers these matches for the passion that they ignite, the football they produce, or

# England vs Scotland matches have represented all that is good and all that is bad about football since the fixture began in 1872.

the bitter rivalries they prolong, they are always games that provoke debate.
The fixture was blighted by crowd trouble long before the advent of *'hooligans'*. Scottish fans travelled en masse to London and earned a reputation for a fondness for booze. Inevitably, in the days when drinking at football matches was as common as a half-time pie and Bovril, emotions ran high and often spilled over onto the streets.

**Jovial (not)**

The most remarkable scenes were those at Wembley in 1977. A 2-1 victory for Scotland was reason enough for thousands of Scots fans to invade the pitch following the final whistle. Helpless members of Her Majesty's finest watched as dozens of the Tartan Army perched on the goalposts, sending them crashing to the ground as overweight Plod pointed their fingers somewhat helplessly, saying, *'Gert orf!'*

This marked the beginning of a period in which the behaviour of many supporters' became increasingly *'exuberant'*, with every fixture bringing fresh fears of running battles between the two sets of fans. A ban on alcohol in football grounds did little to quell the violence and, in 1989, despite a great deal of protest, the football authorities decided to discontinue the annual fixture.

# England and the Poles

## Clowns and donkeys beat England

Football punditry on television was in its infancy and ahead of England's game against Poland, that shy, quiet introvert Brian Clough christened their keeper Jan Tomaszewski a *'clown'*. Cloughie's side-kick, Peter Taylor, compounded the felony by labelling the entire Polish team *'donkeys'*. Perhaps Messrs Clough and Taylor should have heeded the fact that Poland were the reigning Olympic Champions, usually a fair barometer of standing in world football.

The games took place in 1973. In Poland, the home side won 2-0. Not only was it their first victory over England, it was also the first time England had lost a World Cup qualifier. For the Wembley return, the home side simply needed to win. Any other result would see the visitors qualify for the finals and England go out.

For those not around at the time, the game was so one-sided that Peter Shilton could have sold burgers from his goal line. The Polish goal was under siege as England created

chance after chance, hit the woodwork, missed sitters and generally made a superstar out of the keeper, who grew in stature and confidence as the evening of one-way traffic wore on. But the game ended in a 1-1 draw, enough to send the Poles through.

### Clowns and Donkeys

With *'Murphy's Law'* ruling, the Poles broke, Norman Hunter got the ball but instead of thumping it on to the North Circular he attempted to control it. BIG MISTAKE. The ball squirmed away and Gregorz

# England's penalty equalizer hardly mattered. The *'clown'* and his *'donkeys'* had the last laugh and were heading for the West German finals.

Lato was through. He squared the ball and Jan Domarski scored as Shilton took what seemed like three days to drop his muscular frame earthwards. England's penalty equalizer hardly mattered. The *'clown'* and his *'donkeys'* had the last laugh and were heading for the West German finals. Jan Tomaszewski went on to make history by being the first goalkeeper to save two penalties in a World Cup when he shut out attempts from Sweden's Tapper and West Germany's Hoeness during the 1974 World Cup. Today he is often seen as a commentator on TV and a soccer journalist in newspapers.

## Studio tension

Skip a decade. Cloughie is working as a panelist for ITV and begins to discuss England's options for the final game in the first round against Poland in 1986. So far, the English have lost to Portugal and drawn with Morocco, so if they are to progress, they need to win. The tension in the studio is palpable. *'We've got to get players forward,'* says Mick Channon, another panelist, *'we've got to get bodies in the box.'* Cloughie looks at him in pity, shaking his head, saying, *'believe me, we are trying, you'd be amazed how hard they are trying!'*

Channon keeps talking over Clough, while at the same time Clough tries to agree with him, as a youthful Brian Moore looks on helplessly. *'The Irish are doing it,'* says Channon, *'the French are doing it, the West Germans are doing it. We don't.'* All the while the camera stays on Clough, who is looking at his crotch as if he might have misplaced an ejector seat button for either himself or the rambling nutter across the table. Clough takes a deep breath and fiddles with his left ear. He fixes Channon with a stare and says, *'And even educated bees do it.'*

# Rome Burns

## Lazio and racism

SS Lazio was founded on 9 January 1900, by a group of young men –
mostly students with little money but with great passion for sports.
They played their first football in 1902.

Forty minutes to kick-off in a game typical of any recent meeting between Lazio and
Parma and the boys of the Curva Nord are waiting. It is an atrocious night, rain sluicing
down the Stadio Olimpico's roof, saturating the pitch and front 18 rows of the stand. This
is where Lazio's *'irriducibili'* (indomitables) gather. Front-page headlines wonder whether
Roma can be prevented from winning the *'scudetto'* (championship). Tucked inside are
the other stories: a match stopped because of a riot in the stands; probes into players'
fake passports; stars pleading innocence after testing positive for banned substances;
referees accused of taking bribes...

Twelve minutes to kick-off and it is down to business. Paolo, a chunky man in boots and
black bomber jacket, goes first, stomping to the front to cheers. Another follows and
another until more than 200 stand in the downpour. Their chants are picked up by the rest
of the Curva. *'Parma vaffanculo'* becomes a roar. Fists are raised. Marco's eyes gleam.
The Parma contingent, a patch of maybe 300 visitors on the opposite Curva Sud, are
forgotten as the irriducibili's rage widens. *'Tutto e tutti vaffanculo!'* Everyone and
everything is being invited to go fuck itself.

Red flares fizz overhead. The rain hardens and thunder rolls in theatrical timing as the
players jog into the arena. A forest of right arms stretches upward in a fascist salute. A
giant screen flashes the players' names and faces. The Curva Nord inhales as one and
erupts at the first black face. ***'Booh-booh-booh-booh.'*** In staccato, it sounds like
thousands of monkeys. Parma are fielding four black players. A feast for the *irriducibili*.
Lazio has been a featherbed of racism and right-wing factions since its inception, but
recently it seems the factions have become more obvious.

# Red flares fizz overhead... a forest of right arms stretches upward in a fascist salute.

### Racism

There have been attacks on players by their own supporters, a trend that has included besieged dressing rooms, assaults on players' relatives and a firebomb attack on a team bus. When the club was fined after fans barracked black defender Bruno N'Gotty, Zoff – the most capped player in Italian history and a former national team coach – couldn't have been less concerned. *'I don't know whether you could really call that racism,'* he said. *'It's more a question of people making fun.'* When Dutch defender Aron Winter signed for Lazio in 1992, graffiti appeared welcoming the *'nigger Jew'* to the club.

### Troublemakers

The hackneyed symbols include Celtic crosses and swastikas as well as banners, some 40 yards long. *'Auschwitz is your town, the ovens your houses'*, *'Honour to the Tiger Arkan'*. Death camps. Serb war criminals. Anything goes.

# Two World Wars...

## England vs Germany

I suppose we could go back as far as that game in 1936 when the England players were told they must line up to shake hands with the little man with the tash and give him a salute now fashionable among some of our less savoury national team supporters. But Gary Lineker summed it up better when he said, *'Football is a game played by 22 players. And then Germany win.'* While England have beaten Germany twice in recent years, the memory of defeats by penalty shoot-out continues to haunt those who believed England had a chance at Italia 90 and Euro 96.

Back in the 1970 World Cup quarter-final, England were defending champions. In Leon, the game would be remembered for the goalkeeper who didn't play and the respective coaches' tactics. Would it be overdoing it to suggest that England would have won had Gordon Banks not drunk a Mexican beer? Was it a dodgy bottle of lager that brought down the curtain on England's World Cup reign? Oh the irony! Despite Banks's absence, the England players were toying with the West Germans in the first half. Such was the defending champions' early dominance. Then the game changed. Chelsea's Peter Bonetti had never let England down before, but as the Germans found fresh heart, the England reserve goalkeeper proceeded to have a nightmare. First, Franz

# Gary Lineker summed it up when he said, *'Football is a game played by 22 players. And then Germany win.'*

Beckenbauer's limp effort somehow squeezed under *'The Cat'* and into the net. Then Ramsey took off Bobby Charlton and Martin Peters, apparently so they could be rested for the semis, and brought on Manchester City's Colin Bell and Leeds' Norman Hunter. Extra-time, and the Germans were never going to blow it. Gerd Müller blasted them into the semi-finals. Germany had beaten England for the first time just two years earlier after 67 years of trying. For the next 30 years, the pendulum swung decisively towards the Germans. While it has become normal to blame the Chelsea keeper, the fact is that England's manager simply got his tactics wrong and wasn't big enough to admit it.

**Blame**

Ramsey wouldn't be the last England manager to wash his hands of all blame but at least his successors in the 1990s gave the nation hope with some exciting football that led to two semi-final battles with our brothers from across the Rhine. Bobby Robson would claim that his side could have beaten Argentina in 1990 had they got past the Germans, but was gracious in defeat. Terry Venables had no bad feelings either at Wembley in 1996. Knowing how to lose has been described as the hardest discipline in sport but perhaps it should be added that working out how to beat the Germans is proving to be just as tricky.

# Drum Excuses

## African football

To say that African football is ridden with grudges, enmity and bad attitudes would be to do such words a disservice. With over 200 people killed while watching derbies, cup games and internationals in less than 12 months, the prospect of an African nation hosting the 2010 World Cup continues to be a controversial one.

In 2001, a match between Hearts of Oak and Asante Kotoko in a Ghanaian stadium in Accra turned into African football's biggest tragedy, with 123 deaths and 93 injuries following a crowd stampede and excessive retaliation from the police. The mayhem came as a result of poor organization, inefficient security and incompetent administration. There was also indiscriminate use of teargas, which police readily fired into the crowd.

The Accra tragedy came after Asante Kotoko supporters began ripping up seats and chucking them on to the athletics track surrounding the pitch. They were furious, unable to comprehend how their team had somehow managed to throw away a 1-0 lead and lose their unbeaten record to defending champions Hearts, of Oak. Hearts scored the winning goal in the last minute.

With several escape exits already closed, the police fired teargas into the baying mob, causing many in the crowd, including young women and children, to panic and run for cover. Carnage ensued as people were trampled to death.

## Stadium crush

In July 2000, 12 people were killed in a World Cup qualifier between Zimbabwe and South Africa, and in Lubumbashi in the Democratic Republic of Congo on 29 April, 10 people died in crowd violence. There was a stadium crush during a match in Johannesburg in April when an estimated 75,000 sought to gain access to the 60,000-

# Objects were pelted at the celebrating players, with police quickly reacting by firing teargas directly into the stadium.

capacity stadium to watch a top-of-the-table clash between the country's two most popular clubs, Kaizer Chiefs and Orlando Pirates. 43 people died.

**Teargas**

Teargas is a popular tool among the African police forces and with impatient supporters quick to show their frustration with their team's football, poor facilities, non-existent stewarding and a humour-sapping heat, police believe that hitting back hard is the only option when the violence kicks off in the stands.

At the 2001 African Champions league final, won by Hearts of Oak, police fired teargas into the upper tiers of the 50,000-capacity stadium after Hearts supporters threw objects at one of the linesmen. A stray canister landed in the VIP box, forcing former Ghanaian vice-president John Atta-Mills and the leadership of CAF to flee for safety.

The 10 deaths in Lubumbashi at the end of April 2000 resulted from another stampede caused by teargas. The tragedy in Zimbabwe in July 2001 came after the home team went 2-0 down in their World Cup qualifier against neighbours South Africa. Objects were pelted at the celebrating South African players, with police quickly reacting by firing teargas directly into the stadium. As the spectators rushed towards the exits, police continued firing teargas. An inquest later found the police action to blame for the 13 deaths, but there have been no prosecutions of suspended police officers.

# Football vs Soccer

**Is it football in your household or soccer? Are you European or American? Maybe you support more than one team and get to watch as many games as you can on television. Perhaps the sound of television football theme tunes makes the hair stand up on the back of your neck. Perhaps you get fed up with the interminable adverts on commercial television and prefer to watch the BBC.**

- Do you scrutinize the match reports at the weekend and disagree with everything the reporter is saying? Or do you skip the vacuous match reports and head straight for the sections with articles written by ageing columnists?

- Do you know what it is like to watch a pathetic, inept performance and spend four hours talking about it on the way home? Do you wonder how some footballers can look at themselves and say, *'Yes, I gave it my best today?'*

- Is the dashboard of your car littered with hastily scrawled directions to the ground and match day ticket stubs? Do you find the idea that there are people who abhor the notion that some fans of the beautiful game are sad individuals who never seem to get out much, odd? Is the money players get these days something that bothers you or none of your business?

- Would you remember the last time someone passed a ball to you and you scored? If so, pause for a moment, replay it in your head and smile, a big goofy Ronaldo smile, and think about how you can make that moment happen again.

# Is the dashboard of your car littered with hastily scrawled directions to the ground and match day ticket stubs?

- How would you decide between attending a wedding celebration and the chance to go to an away-leg decider with three of your mates in a hire car?

- If your child decided to pick up the ball and run with it during sports day would you fish out the directory for local rugby-playing grammar schools? Or would you take him, or her, to one side for a strong lecture?

- Do you wonder about the fuss people make about the days before satellite television injected huge sums of cash into the game and created a vacuum between clubs at the top and everyone else? Do you believe that if a club can't run itself within the confines of standard business practice it should suffer the consequences and go to the wall? Do you know what that might mean to the local community? Do you care?

- Have a look at how you've responded to the questions posed in this piece and pause before you answer. Are you football, or are you soccer?

# Leeds vs Galatasaray

## 20 April 2000

The terrors of Turkey pitched up in Leeds on 19 April, on the eve of an historic match that had already become a national cause in Turkey. Passions were stirred by the UEFA decision to ban Turkish supporters from travelling to Britain to watch the return game of this UEFA Cup semi-final.

Two weeks before, two Leeds United supporters had been stabbed to death in Istanbul, a day before the first encounter between Galatasaray and Leeds. Understandably there was grief and anger in Britain, and several violent incidents broke out against Turks living in Blighty. In this atmosphere, Leeds United officials feared they could not guarantee the security of Turkish visitors during the match and asked UEFA to prevent them from coming. UEFA asked Galatasaray to return 1,750 tickets that had already been sent to them. Not surprisingly, Galatasaray supporters deemed the decision unfair, claiming that their club could not be held responsible for the deaths of the Leeds supporters. They were furious. On the same day, a Turkish court charged four people with the murder of the two British fans, who were stabbed several times. Fourteen other men faced charges of assault. One of the suspects admitted buying a knife when he heard that drunken British fans were insulting passers-by. And somewhere amongst all this a game of football was due to take place.

### Politics

The issue took a political dimension when a number of prominent Turks voiced their dissatisfaction with the handling of the issue. First, Fatih Terim, Galatasaray's technical director, had a go at the Turkish authorities for not contacting their British counterparts immediately to lobby on Galatasaray's behalf. Terim later complained that, although he had notified the Turkish embassy of his arrival, he had not been protected and escorted

# The fear was that while UEFA could prevent fans from Turkey gaining access to the stadium, they were unlikely to stop Galatasaray fans living in Europe from travelling to Britain.

when he visited Britain briefly to watch Leeds United play against Arsenal. Opposition leaders in Turkey were quick to back Fatih Terim.

The fear was that while UEFA could prevent fans from Turkey gaining access to the stadium, they were unlikely to stop Galatasaray fans living in Europe from travelling to Britain. Turks living in England were expected to be in Leeds en masse to defy the ban.

## Flowers

In Leeds, security was tightened. The Turkish government took the additional measure of sending 11 bodyguards to protect the players. There was even a suggestion that the Galatasaray players should wear flak jackets until the game started.

In an attempt to reduce tension prior to Galatasaray's arrival, Leeds United officials removed tons of flowers deposited in front of the stadium in tribute to the two dead supporters. Officials from both clubs appealed for calm. In the end, the drama was more in the build-up than the event itself. The game passed off peacefully and Leeds failed to win. Home supporters felt that it was almost impossible for Leeds to win given the issues. Galatasaray had muscled their way into the next round and their reputation for intimidation continues to do them no favours.

# Barca bust up

## Bernd Schuster and Terry Venables

Who can forget the flowing locks of the German playmaker, Bernd Schuster? He was a footballer with the strength and trickery to rival Maradona as the greatest player in the world, were it not for his ability to self-destruct and impose a Trappist Monk-tight grip on his real emotions.

Schuster had come out of the 1984 European Championships a star and his relationship with Barcelona manager Terry Venables went well in their first season together at the Nou Camp. The team, the coach and the playmaker had won the Spanish league title in 1985 and Schuster not only considered himself a star, he expected to be treated like one. Venables regarded him highly and he was impressed by the way the German stayed behind after training, knocking balls into the top left corner of the goal – curling the ball into the goal from the corner flag, the 'Schuster special'.

And yet, things were beginning to change.

Schuster was strutting his stuff off the pitch as well as on it. Players, staff and even Venables struggled to cope with the player's outlandish wife, a German model called Gabi. She would march into the dressing room when the players were coming out of the showers, taking the time to let everybody get a good look at her before she sashayed her way into the manager's office to have a moan about something or other. Understandably this was making everyone tense, not least the hapless Schuster.

### Faith

Increasingly Schuster complained that the team were losing faith with him. In the aftermath of a European Cup Winners' Cup match against Metz, Schuster argued with Venables that the reason he was failing to deliver was because the Scottish international, Steve Archibald, was unable to give him the support he needed upfront. Venables wouldn't have a bad word said against his tenacious forward, a man he had bought from

# Schuster not only considered himself a star, he expected to be treated like one.

Tottenham to replace Maradona of all people. He claimed Schuster was damaging team spirit and told the German to take a look at his own workload.

## Walkout

This proved to be a mere prelude to the main event. During the 1986 European Cup final in Seville, all eyes were on the playmaker, seeing if he could take Barcelona to the peak of European football against the unfancied Steaua Bucharest. With the east Europeans' manning a solid defence, Schuster appeared to lose interest in the effort to break down the opposition and before normal time had ended, Venables astounded the fans by pulling his playmaker off.

Schuster couldn't believe it either. He was furious and walked off the pitch and straight out of the stadium in disgust. Bucharest held on for penalties and in one of the dreariest finals ever seen, the underdogs won 3-1 and Venables was looking at an unlikely future at the Spanish club.

Schuster was eventually dismissed and spent most of the following season mounting a legal action against the club on the grounds of unfair dismissal. Within a year Venables had gone too.

Tax inspections, conducted at the club during the legal wrangles, brought to light some alarming facts. The club had given Schuster two contracts although only one had been fully declared to the authorities. It then transpired many other Barca players had received similar deals. As the club stumbled from crisis to crisis, Venables went back to England working his charms on Tottenham and the Catalan giants waited for their salvation. In the form of Johan Cruyff.

# Barca and Cruyff

## Managerial hot seat

For most of the Johan Cruyff era, Barcelona fans lived with the expectation of victory. There was a collective will to succeed. When Cruyff suffered a heart attack, brought on by his legendary appetite for smoking, he agreed to have local medical staff take care of him, something that endeared the Dutchman to the hearts of Barcelona's rabid support. His son Jordi was already a Barca player and there was something heart-warming about the sight of the Cruyff family rallying round their father. An anti-smoking poster was drawn up with the words, *'In my life I've had two vices: smoking and playing football. Football has given me everything in life. Smoking nearly took it all away from me.'* From that moment, Cruyff replaced his chain-smoking with chain-sucking; lollipops – the Chupa Chup – became his trademark. Winning the Spanish Championship was the sole objective in 1991. With the league in the bag, no-one seemed to mind that Barca then lost to Manchester United in the European Cup Winners' Cup in Rotterdam.

The following season the league and the European Cup became the objective and both were achieved. Barca were now in possession of a dream team; Guardiola, Basques, Bakero, Goikoetxea, Koeman, Laudrup and Stoichkov. Two more championships inspired by the Brazilian striker Romario, and Barca were on top of the world.

## Waste

Three years later and Cruyff was gone. Barcelona had been beaten in Athens in the Champions League final 4-0 by AC Milan and the club President Nunez no longer felt he could put up with Cruyff. Jordi Cruyff's performances for the club hadn't done his father any favours and when Cruyff presented the club chairman with a wishlist of players that

# When vice-president Joan Gaspart came to visit Cruyff in the team dressing room, Cruyff cried out, *'You're Judas!'*

included Ryan Giggs and the Liverpool pair, Steve McManaman and Robbie Fowler, the President accused him of wanting to waste money. The dream team were getting old and Cruyff realised too late that Nunez was doing business behind his back. Bobby Robson had been lined up as a replacement manager and when the news came, it was delivered by the media.

### Regrets
On 18 May 1996 the morning papers ran stories that Robson was coming. Cruyff was taking charge of the team for the second to last game of the season and when vice-president Joan Gaspart came to visit Cruyff in the team dressing room Cruyff cried out, *'You're Judas!'* to which Gaspart replied, *'You no longer belong here.'* One of the club's most celebrated and successful players and managers had been dumped. Nunez claims not to have any regrets. *'Cruyff's contract was coming to an end, the fact that one week before that contract expired he was told his services were no longer needed seems to be quite normal in the world of sport.'* As for Cruyff, he remains bitter about the whole business. The power struggle between himself and Nunez threatened to split the great club in two and in the end he remained the same as so many non-Catalans before him – just a hired hand. The players were divided, but the supporters weren't and continue to call for Cruyff's return.